£8.90 /x2

NUMBER 569

THE ENGLISH EXPERIENCE

ITS RECORD IN EARLY PRINTED BOOKS
PUBLISHED IN FACSIMILE

A NEWE BOKE
OF PRESIDENTES
IN MANER OF A REGISTER

LONDON, 1543

DA CAPO PRESS
THEATRVM ORBIS TERRARVM LTD.
AMSTERDAM 1973 NEW YORK

The publishers acknowledge their gratitude to
the Syndics of Cambridge University Library
for their permission to reproduce the
Library's copy, Shelfmark: Syn.7.54.44 and
to the Trustees of the British Museum for
their permission to reproduce the
sections A and F, and the pages: R2v, R3r,
S3v, V1, Z2r, Z3, Ff1v, Ff2r, Ff3v, Ff4r
and Gg1v from the Library's copy,
Shelfmark: C.112.b.3.

S.T.C.No. 3327

Collation: a^4, $A\text{-}Z^4$, $Aa\text{-}Gg^4$

Published in 1973 by

Theatrum Orbis Terrarum Ltd.,
O.Z. Voorburgwal 85, Amsterdam

&

Da Capo Press Inc.
- a subsidiary of Plenum Publishing Corporation -
277 West 17th Street, New York N.Y. 1011

Printed in the Netherlands
ISBN 90 221 0569 5

Library of Congress Catalog Card Number:
73-6100

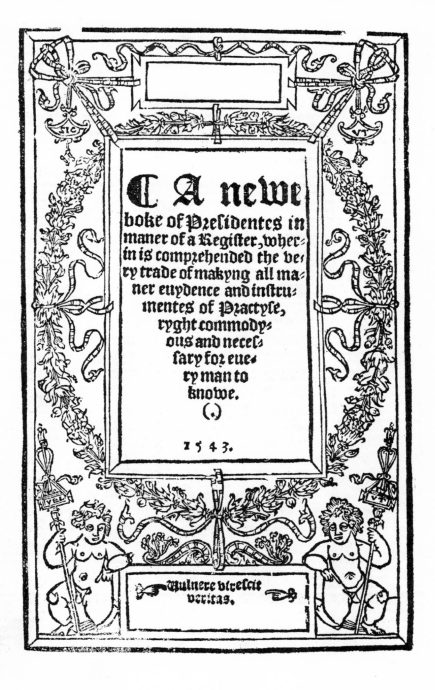

¶ A newe
boke of Presidentes in
maner of a Register, wherin is compzehended the very trade of makyng all maner euydence and instru-
mentes of Practyse,
ryght commody-
ous and neces-
sary foz eue-
ry man to
knowe.
(.)

1543.

Vulnere virescit
veritas.

¶A preface to the reader, by Thomas Phayer.

Onsydzyng the great vtilitie and as
suraüce vnto parties, when their euy
dence and wzytynges of recozde, are
wel and substancyally cõpounded, foz
by suche euidence (as by the moost p-
fecte waye of credyte) are matters in
the lawe cotinuallye decysed, truthe is made open &
falsshed detected, ryght aduaunced and wzonge sup-
przessed, matters of dout are put out of questyon, and
by suche euydence is iustyce and equitie to euery mã
yelded, sute and contention auoyded, vnitie and con-
cozde induced, vertuous and polityke ozdze obserued
fynallye loue & amytie encreaseth, wyth all kynde of
goodnesse in quyet, which is the chefe parte of felici-
tie oz happynesse in this life, as sayth ẏ Philosopher
in the .x. of Ethikes. And contrarywyse, how greate
incõmodities and daüger done aryse dayly betwene
man and man, by the negligence oz rather ignoraüce
of some which other przesumynge vpon theyz owne
wyttes, oz els by occasion foz lacke of good przesiden
tes, oz better learned counsell, make mens euydence
oftentymes so sclendze, that it were as good to be vt
terlye wythout them, comtymes so difficile, double &
obscure, that there may be founde as many doubtes
as sentences (a very great occasion of wzanglyng &
stryfe) yea and that is wozse, many tymes so false &
erronious, that nothing lesse appeareth then ẏ truth
of those thynges that the wzytyng was deuysed foz,
J suppose foz lacke of the cõmon & vsuall trade of ẏ
makyng of euidence, and the termes therof, whyche

a.s.

as they be moost auncient, so withoute doubte are
they surest, and of most baylable effecte, and a great
daunger is it for any not exactly learned in ye lawes
to altre or vary from the same. For these and manye
other consyderations it shalbe very good, not onlye
to all them that are desyrous to haue theyr affayres
and necessarye wrytynges, earnestlye, and pleada-
blye recorded, but also to suche as professe the knowledge of the same facultie, and are not fully grounded
or experte therein, to peruse ouer this lytle treatyse,
wherin they shal fynde many notable & goodly presi
dentes of practyse of all sortes, fourmes & fashyons,
aswell for the assuraunce of landes, both free and co
pye holde, as for all maner bargaynes, couenauntes
and other matters belongyng to the lawe, as aduou
sons of benefices and other promotions, psentatiõs
and thynges perteynyng to the same, Indentures,
dedes, feoffementes, dowers, ioyntures, bondes, releases, quytaunces, warrauntes, exchaunges, charters patentes of offyces, fees, and annuities, letters
safeconduyte, bylles of cõplayntes, tytles, plees and
answers, transuptes and letters of testimonie, with
dyuers other instrumentes and necessarye wrytynges, dayly practysed and had in vse among ye people
And in this study can no man cõplayne for losyng of
hys tyme, for he shalbe well & vertuouslye occupyed.
Yea euery good person that can wryte and reade and
entendeth to haue any thyng to do amonge the common weale, must of very nede, for his owne aduan-
tage, apply his mynde somwhat vnto this kynde of
learnynge, specyally yf he do consydre how greate a
faute it is to be rude & ignoraunt in so pleasaunte, so

a.ij.   easy

eafye & fo cõmodious a ftudy as this is. For yf other
bokes whiche are made eyther for delyte & pleafure
of the eares, as are rymes, ieftes, and fuche other, or
for the memorial of thynges that are gone and paft,
as ftoryes, chronicles and lyke, are had in eftimation
(as they be in dede no leffe worthy:) how moch more
then ought this to be regarded, yea and dilygently
ftudyed, that fheweth the makyng of thofe thinges,
wherupon dependeth the welth and lyuyng of men,
without which thinges there can no tytle lawfullye
be claymed, no landes nor houfes purchafed, no right
recouered agaynft falfe vfurpers, no fufficient tefti=
monye of the actes of our aunceftours, fynallye no
man can be fure of hys owne lyuelod without helpe
of euidence, which as a trufty anker, holdeth ý right
of euery mans poffeffions fafely and furely agaynft
all troublous and ftormy tempeftes of iniuryes, not
of men only but of tyme alfo the confumer of all, of
which euydence (whofoeuer fhall loke vpon this ly=
tle treatyfe) fhal fynde it I truft, reafonably furnyf=
fhed aboue other bookes that haue heretofore ben v=
fed, as it fhall appeare to euery iuft reader. And ther=
fore is it cõpounded both in Englifh and in Latyne,
to ý intent it may be the eafelyer taken and percey=
ued of them that are but meanely learned in the La
tyne tonge, and alfo for fuche as wyll applye theyr
chyldren to the readynge and vnderftandyng of cõ=
mon euydences and wrytynges. Wherin I befeche
God that they maye procede both to theyr owne cõ=
modytie, and profyte of theyr poore neyghbours.
AMEN.

The Table.

❧ The contentes of this booke.

a.iij.   ¶A lease

The Table.

An

The Table.

a.iiij.   A letter

The Table.

FINIS.

A RIGHT FRU-
TEFVL BOKE OF EXEM=
PLARS OR COPIES OF SVNDRY
sortes of instrumentes or wrytynges.

Ⓡ : Ⓔ

¶An aduouson of a parsonage oʒ bicarage
graunted by the kynge.

Ꝛ Er omnibus ad quos.ꝛc.Salutem.
Sciatis cp nos erſpeciali gratia no=
ſtra certacꝫ ſciētia, dedimus ꝗ cōceſ=
ſimus,ac per pʒeſentes damus et cō=
cedimus dilectis ſeruientibꝰ noſtris
I. B.ct.C.D.militibus pʒimā ,pri=
mamcꝫ aduocationē,donationē,collationem, pʒeſen
tationē, liberamcꝫ diſpoſittonē eccleſte parochialis
(oʒ if be of a bicarage)bicarie perpetue eccleſie de Ꞥ
in comitatu nēo Ꞃanc.Cantuarieñ.dioceſis ꝗ noſtri
patronatꝰ pleno iure eriſteñ. bel in iure corone no=
ſtre bel ratione ducatus nēi Lancaſtrie,bel er cōceſ=
ſione.I.B.hac bice tantū.ꝛc.Habend. et tenend.pʒe
dictam pʒimā ,primamcꝫ aduocationē,donationem,
collationē, pſentationem, liberamcꝫ diſpoſittonem,
pʒefatis.I.B.et.C.D. coniunctim bel diuiſim, aut
eoꝛ aſſignatis ꝗ eoꝛ cuilibʒ pʒo bnica et ,prima ba=
catione eiuſdem dūtarat. Ita cp bene licebit eiſdem
I.B.et.C.D.cōiūctim bel diuiſim aut eoꝛ aſſigna=
tis,ſeu coʒum cuilibʒ authoʒitate pſentis doni et cō=
ceſſionis noſtre bnū aliquē idoneum birū ad dictam
eccleſiam Dioceſano eiuſdem,aut alteri iudici in ea
parte cōpetenti, pʒeſentare cū pʒimo et pʒorime pʒe=
fatā ecclīam(bt pʒefertur)per moʒtē,reſignationem,

ſiue ratione
temporaliū
epiſcopatus
N.in mani-
bus nīis iā
eriſten.

I.i.   pʒiua=

pziuationẽ,cessionẽ,seu quacũ𝔮 alia rationẽ vacare
contigerit.Ac oĩa alia et singula, que circa pzemissa
necessaria fuerint seu quomodolib𝔷 oppoztuna per=
agere et implere,tam plene,libere,ac integre, 𝔮 nos
ipsi pageremus,si pñs cõcessio nostra pzefatis.A.B
et.C.D.facta non fuisset.In cuius rei.𝔯c.

❡An aduouson of a Deanry, Pzouostshyp,oz
mastershyp of a college,by the kynge.

Ex omnibus ad quos.𝔯c.Salutẽ. Sciatis 𝔮
nos ex gĩa nostra speciali,certa sciẽtia,et mero
motu nĩo dedimus et concessimus ac tenoze pñtium
damus et concedimus dilectis subditis nĩis.A.B.𝔯
C.D.armigeris pzimã ac pzoximã aduocationẽ.𝔯c.
Decanatus,Pzepositu𝔯e,magisterij,siue pzefecture
collegij nĩt de.N.in cõm.nĩo.M.𝔯c.Hẽnd,vt supza.

❡An aduouson of a benefice graunted by a
Baron,knyght oz Esquyer.𝔯c.

Omnibus Chzisti fidelibus ad quos pñs scriptũ
peruenerit.A.P.dominus.P.aut.A.B. miles,
vel armiger, verus et indubitatus patronus recto=
siue uicariæ rie ecclíe parochíal.de N.Ebozacẽ. diocesis salutem
&c.prout in dño sempiternã. Noueritis me pzefatũ I. dedisse
casus exigit concessisse et hoc pñti scripto meo confirmasse dilec.
mihi Czistophozo P.et Edmundo L.generosis con=
tunctim et eozũ alteri per se diuisim,executozibus et
assignatis suis pzimã 𝔯 pzoximã aduocatione dona
cõem,noiatione, pzesentacõem liberã𝔮𝔷 dispositione
pdicte rectozie ecclíe poch.de N. Volens et hoc pñti
scripto meo concedẽs, 𝔮 bene liceat et licebit dictis
Chzistophozo et Edmundo coniũctim et eozũ alteri
per

per se diuisim execut.et assign suis ad pdict eccliam
quandocūcꝫ quomodocūcꝫ et qualitercūcꝫ ꝑ moztē,
resignatione,ꝓiuacōem,cessionē ꝑmutacōem,dimis
sionē,siue quocūcꝫ alio mō pzimo et ꝓxime bacare
cōtigerit,bnū aliquē bitū honestū ⁊ literatū ꝑsitare,
ceteracꝫ oīa que ad patroni munus seu officiū spec=
tant ꝑsicere pzo huiusmodi pzima pzoximacꝫ baca=
tione tantum,adeo plene et integre sicuti egomet ea
in parte facerē,si hoc ꝑsis scriptū meū factū minime
fuisset. Jn cui⁹ rei testimoniū huic pūti scripto meo
sigillū meū ad arma adposui. Dat secūdo die Julij
Anno dūi millimo quingētesimo quadzagesimo pzi
mo.Et anno regni dūi nūi H.octaui dei gīa Anglie.
ꝛc.trigesimo tertio.

℄The kynges letters to a Deane and chapter
    foz an aduouson.

TRustie and welbyloued we grete you wel.Foz=
    asmuche as we muche tendze the conuenient
pzeferment of our welbeloued seruaunt A.B.to the
entent he may be the moze encouraged and also the
better hable to pzosequute ⁊ finally to accomplyshe
the effecte and purpose of hys learnyng: We haue
thought it mete by these oure letters to desyze and
pzaye you,that foz our sake,ye wol immediatly bpō
the syghte hereof bnder your chapter seale,conferre
and gyue the nexte auoydance of the pzebende of C. *or of the*
oz of the nexte pzebende in that our churche whyche *ꝑsonage*
shalbe in your gyfte and disposition to suche perso= *of N ꝛc.*
nes as our sayde seruaunt shal name to his bse and
behoufe.wherin ye shal administre bnto bs a right
acceptable pleasure, to be herafter remēbzed in any
                        A.ij.   your

pour lauful ſutes when occaſió ſhal therunto ſerue, accozdyngly.Ɏeuen vnder our Signet.ꝛc.

To an Arch biſhop ye ſhall write mooſt reue= rend father &c.

℧To a byſhop foʒ a lyke thynge, by the kyng. Ɍyght reuerend father in god right truſty and ryght welbeloued we grete you wel.where as we be very deſyʒouſe foʒ the honeſt qualities which we vnderſtãd to be in our welbeloued chaplayne Ꝕ. B.to ſe hym furnyſhed wyth conuenient lyuynges accoʒdyngly: We haue thought good to deſyʒe and pʒay you,that the rather foʒ our ſake, and at the cõ= templacion of theſe our letters, ye woll foʒthewyth vnder your ſufficiente wʒytynge enſealed gyue and graũt to his behouſe the nexte aduouſon of the pʒe= bende oʒ parſonage of N. Wherin ye ſhall deſerue our ryght harty thankes.ꝛc.

℧An aduouſon of a pʒebend in the kynges col= lege in Oʒfoʒde.

Ɍex omnib’ ano quos.ꝛc. Sciatis nos de gra nͣa ſpeciali, ac ex certa ſcientia , meroꝗ motu noſtro, dediſſe cõceſſiſſe et cõfirmaſſe,ac pͣti ſcripto noſtro dare concedere ꞇ confirmare diͤctis nobis T. H. et N.M.pʒimaín et pʒoxímã aduocationem cano nicat⁹ et pʒebende in collegio noſtro Oxoñ,Uulga= riter nũcupato kynge Henry the eyghtes college ac plenam et integrã collattionem huiuſmodi canoni= catus et pͬbende ꝓ pʒima et pʒoxíma vacattone eiuſ= dem tantũ. Ita ꝗ bñ licebit eiſdem T. H. et N.M. ac eoʒũ vtriꝗ cõtũctim ꞇ diuiſim execut.ꞇ aſſig.ſuis ac coʒ vtriſꝗ canonicatũ ꞇ pͬbendã ꝓdict.ſic(vt pʒe= míttiͭ) pʒimo et pʒoxíne vacant, vni alicui perſone idonee

idonee vere et actualiter intuitu charitatis conferre
Necnon literas collattonis ad hoc sufficientes et in
iure validas facere sigillare et tradere, Decanoꝛ
et Canonicis dicti collegij nostri pꝛoꝩmōt persone
receptione, admissione, et installatione rescribere, ce=
teraꝗ omnia circa pꝰmissa necessaria facere et exequi
pꝛoꝩmōt pꝛima (vt pꝛemittitur) ac ꝑprima vacatione
tantū, adeo plene ac integre sicut nosꝑī faceremus
et exequeremur, si pꝰns hec nostra concessio facta ne=
quaꝗ fuisset. In cuius rei.ꝛc.

℟ The fourme of a pꝛesentaciō to a personage,
   by the kynge.

REx Reuerendissimo in Chꝛisto patri ꝗ dūo do=
mino E. permissione diuina Eboꝛ. Archiepo
Anglie pꝛimati et metropolitano, eiusue in absentia
vicario suo in reb⁹ ecclesiasticis generali, Salutē. *seu ad vica=*
Ad eccłiam pochialem de N. vꝛe dioceseos modo ꝑ *riā ꝑpetuā.*
moꝛtem vltimi incūbentis ibidem vacaū, ꝗ ad nēam
donationem pleno iure spectantem, Dilʒum Capel= *melius Sa=*
lanū nūm I.B.clericū intuitu charitatis vobis pꝰ= *cellanum.*
tamus, Mandantes vti dictū I.Capellanū nūm ad
pꝛefatā eccłiam admittere, eumꝗ rectoꝛem eiusdem
instituere cū suis iurib⁹ ꝗ ptineū vntuersis, ceteraꝗ
expedire et peragere que vꝛo in hac parte incumbūt
officio muneriꝗ pastoꝛali, velitis cum fauoꝛe. In
cuius rei.ꝛc.

But if the churche be voyde by resignation then
ye shall saye.
Modo per liberam et spontaneā resignationem I.
B.vltimi incumbentis eiusdem vacaū.ꝛc.

If by attepnder then thus.

A.iij. Per

per attincturam A.B. vltimi incumbentis ibidem
qui de alta proditione nuper attinctus fuit vacan.
Et sic de consimilibus.

Nota.

Also ye shall vnderstande, that the kynges maie=
stie hath as ÿ case requireth sundry titles to present
for somtyme he presenteth by his prerogatiue royal
and than ye shall say.

Et ad nostram donationem ratione prerogatiue
nostre regie spectantem. &c.

Sumtyme by reason that the temporalties of a
byshopriche be in hys handes, and then ye shal say.
Ratione temporaltiu epat⁹ N.in manib⁹ nris existen.

Sumtyme his grace presenteteth by the graunt
of an aduouson of another man, & then ye shall say,
ratione concessionis A.B. qua idem A.primã et pri=
mam aduocationem eiusdem nobis largitus est. &c.

And if the Manour wherunto the aduouson is
appendant be parcell of the Douchy of Lancastre:
then ye shall say.

Et ad nraz donationem ratione Ducatus nri Lan=
castrie spectantem. &c. Et sic de reliquis.

❧The fourme of a presentacion where an arch=
  deacon or other ecclesiasticall person hath iu=
  risdiction ordinary.

REx. &c. Venerabili viro dno Willmo K. Archi=
  diacono Richmond, eiusue in absentia vicario
in spiritualib⁹ generali, Salutem. Ad vicariam de
Lancastre vre iurisdictionis modo p mortem vltimi
incumbentis ibidem vacantem, atqz ad nram dona=
tionẽ pleno iure spectañ, dilectum capellanum t.ẽ
A.B. cĺicum vobis psitamus, requirentes quaten⁹
                                            presa=

pꝛefatum A. ad vicariam pꝛedictã admittere,ipͫcꝫ
vicarium in eadem instituere, cum oibus suis iurt=
bus ⁊ pertineñ vniuersis, Ceteracꝫ oia ⁊ singula fa
cere et exequi, que bͬo in hac pte incumbunt officio
pastoꝛali,velitis cum fauoꝛe. In cuius rei.⁊c.

¶ The fourme of a pꝛesentation in the marches
of Caleis voyde by attepnder.

R Ex Reuerendissimo in Xpo patri dño Thome
diuina pmissione Cantuarieñ Archiepo ac to=
tius Anglie pꝛimati,eiusue vicario in spiritualibus
generali, salutem. Ad rectoꝛiam de B. in merchijs
nostris Calis.dioc. Moꝛoneñ, modo p attincturam
W. P. vltimi ibidem incumbentis vacañ,et ad no=
stram donationem pleno iure spectañ,dꝛcum capel=
lanum nostrum w.W.clꝛicum vobis pfentamꝰ, ro=
gantes vti pfatum w.ad rectoꝛiam pꝛedcãm admit
tere, atcꝗ eum rectoꝛem eiusdem ecclesie instituere,
cum oibus suis iuribus et fructibus ab attinctura
dicti P.vniuersis, ceteracꝗ oia et singula peragere,
que ad vestrum munus epale pertinere videbuntur
velitis cum fauoꝛe.In cuius rei.⁊c.

¶ The fourme of a pꝛesentation made by a
knyght oꝛ gentleman.

R Euerendo in Chͬo patri.⁊c.Richardus B.mi=
les verus et indubitatus patronus rectoꝛie ec
clesie parochialis de N. Salutem in dño sempiter=
nam. Ad eccſiam de N.pꝛedictã vestre dioc.modo p
moꝛtem C.D.vltimi incumbentis ibidem vacãtem
et ad meam pſentationem pleno iure spectañ. dꝛcm
mihi in Chꝛisto Jacobum P.clꝛicum vestre paterni=

uel armi-
ger gene-
rosus &c.

tati

tati pſento, humiliter rogans quatenus pfatum J.
ad dictã eccłiam admittere, ipſumꝗ in rectozem eiuſ
dem eccłie inſtitui et induci facere cum ſuis iuribus
et ptinentijs vniuerſis, ceteracꝗ pagere et adimple=
re, que veſtro in hac parte incumbunt officio paſtoza
lt dignemini cum fauoze. Jn cuius rei teſtimonium
ſigillum meum appoſui. Dat. ꝛc.

    ¶ A pzeſentation to a perſonage oz vicarage by
    a maiſter of an hoſpitall and hys bzethzen, oz
    by a Dean and chapter oz ſuch other.

Euerendo in Xpo patri, et dño dño N. pmiſſio=
ne diuina Couentrieñ et Lichfild. epo, etuſue
vicario in ſpiritualibus generali, veſter humilis et
deuot⁹ frater R. T. Magiſter Hoſpitalis N. et eiuſ=
dem confratres, ſiue Decanus Collegij de N. et ca=
pitulum eiuſdem. ꝛc. Lincolñ dioc, omnimodã reue=
reñ tanto patri debitam. Ad ppetuã vicariam eccłie
pochiał de N. veſtre. dioceſ. iam p moztem C. D. vl=
timi vicarij eiuſdem vacantem, ad nſamcꝗ pzeſenta=
tionem pleno iure ſpectantem, dilectũ nobis in Xpo
Johannem B. ſacre theologie pzofeſſozem paternita
ti ueſtre pſentamus, humiliter ſupplicantes, vt pze=
fatum Joãnem ad dictã vicariã admittere, ipſumcꝗ
in eadẽ canonice inſtituere, ceteracꝗ pagere, que hac
in parte veſtro paſtozali incumbunt officio dignem
ni cum fauoze. Jn cuius rei teſtiñ ſigillũ noſtrum
commune pzeſentibus eſt appenſum, Dat. ꝛc.

    A pzeſention ſede vacante.

Euerẽdiſſimo in Xpo patri et domino, domino
Thome permiſſione diuina Cantuarienſi Ar=
chiepo, tottus Anglie pzimati ꝗ metropolitano, eiuſ
ue vicario in eccleſiaſticis generali, Lincolñ dioceſ
ſede

ſede vacante.Ad rectoriam eccłie parochiał.⁊c.

In other fourme of a pꝛeſentation ſede vacáte.

HEnricus octauus dei gratia Anglie ⁊ Francie
Rex,fidei defenſoꝛ, Domin⁹ Hibernie,et in ter
ta ſub Xpo ſupꝛemū caput Anglicane eccłie, Ac ver⁹
et indubitatus patron⁹ Rectoꝛie ſiue eccłie pochiał
de N in Comitatu noſtro Somerſet Bathen ⁊ wel
leñ dioceſ.ipſa ſede Batheñ ⁊ Welleñ iam vacante,
Reuerendiſſimo in Xpo patri T.Cantuarienſi Ar=
chiepo totius Anglie pꝛimati eiuſue in abſeutia vi=
cario dicte ſedis in ſpiritualibꝛ generali Salutem .
Ad dictam Rectoriā ſiue eccłiā pochiał de W.modo
vacauté p moꝛtem.⁊c.

　　❡Letters miſſiue to a byſhop foꝛ the Collarion
　　　of a benefice,by the kynge.

RYght Reuerende father in God, ryght truſty
and ryght welbeloued we grete you well. And
where as we be credibly enfoꝛmed,that ẏ benefice of
N.is nowe voyde and in pour gyfte ⁊ collation : we
muche tenderyng the pꝛeferment of our welbeloued
chaplayne I.B.deſyꝛe ⁊ pꝛay you,that foꝛ our ſake,
and at contemplacion of our letters, ye woll gyue ⁊
conferre the ſayde benefice to our ſayde chaplayne.
Whereby ye ſhall adminiſter vnto vs very thank=
full pleaſure and gratuitte,which we ſhall not fayle
to remembꝛe,when occaſiō ſhalbe offred to the ſame
accoꝛdyngly.Yeuen.⁊c.

　　❡The fourme of a lettre from one frende to an
　　　other foꝛ lyke purpoſe.

IN my right harty maner I cōmend me vnto yott
Foꝛaſmuche as I vnderſtande, that the benefice
of N. which ſuche a perſon nowe enioyeth(oꝛ which
　　　　　　　　B.i.　　　is nowe

is nowe voyde)is of your gyfte & patronage:These
shalbe instantly to desyre and pray you,that ye woll
vouchsafe,to graunt me the nexte aduouson therof,
for to bestowe vpon suche one, as I shall therunto
present, or (if the benefice be alredy voyde ye may write)
that ye woll do so muche, as for my sake to presente
A.B.to the same who is my very louing frende and
suche a persone as bothe for hys learnyng and out=
warde conuersation and lyuyng is very mete for the
same. whyche doyng ye shall minister vnto me ac=
ceptable pleasure,and gyue me cause to requyte the
same with thankes accordyng.And of your resolute
mynde herin.I praye you that I may be aduertised
by the brynger herof. Thus fare you hartely well.
From London.&c.

I presentation to a Chauntery by the kynge.

REx Reuerendo in Xpo patri Edmundo Londoni=
ensi epo,eiusue vicario in spiritualibz generali
salutem.Ad Cantariã beate Marie virginis in ec=
clesia parochiali sci Olani Londoniensis vestre di=
oces.iam vacãtẽ et ad nostrã donationem spectãtem,
Dilectũ nobis in Xpo J.H.Clericum uobis presen=
tamus, rogantes quatenus ipsum J.ad cantariam
predictam admittatis & instituatis in eadem. In cu
ius rei &c.

☞   Lyke fourme of psentacion is of a Chapell whe=
ther it be of the kynges patronage or of a subiectes,
mutatis mutandis.

I presentation to a prebende by the kynge.

REx &c.Reuerendo in Christo patri W.Meneuesi
epo,eiusuc in absentia vicario suo in spiritua=
libus generali, aut alij cuicunq potestatem suffici=
entem

entem ea in parte habēti, Salutem. Ad canonicatū
in eccłia Collegiata de N. vře dioc.et prebendam de
C.in eadem per liberam resignationem A.B. vltimi
incumbentis et possessoris eorundem iam vacañ , et
ad nřam donationem ratione prerogatiue nře regie *Vel ple-*
hac vice spectañ.dilectū nobis in Christo Joānē T. *no iure*
in artibus magistrū clericū vobis pñtam⁹ intuitu *&c.*
charitatis, Uolentes et requirētes quatenus pfatū
Joānem ad dict.Canonicatū et prebendā admittere
ipmcz Canonicū et prebendariū eorundē ac in eisdē
cum suis iurib⁹ et ptineñ vniuersis rite et legitime
instituere ceteracz facere et peragere,que vřo hac in
re officio pastorali incūbūt,velitis. In cuius rei.ɫc.

¶ Notes to be diligently obserued.

YE shall note that in a pñtation by thys worde ☞
ecclesiam parochialem is intended alwayes a
parsonage.Howbeit nowe adayes many be wont to
wryte ad rectoriam ecclie parochialis de N.But if
the presentacion be to a vicarage : then ye may not
say ad ecclesiam,but ad vicariam. And ye shall vnderstande that the presentmēt to a vicarage apperteyneth of cōmon right to the parsone,for the vicare
is in effecte but the parsons deputie. Howebeit the *The pa-*
parson with the assent of hys patrone and ordinary *tronage*
may graūt away the patronage of the vicarage frō *of a vi-*
him and his successours to another man and to hys *carage.*
heyres or successours for euer.

Furthermore ye shall vnderstande,that somtime
one man hath the nomination to a benefice, and an *Nomi-*
other the presētacion, in whych case he that hath the *nation.*
presentacion can presente none other person to the
ordinary,but suche as the other man shall name by
B.ij. his

hys sufficient wrytyng vnder seale.

☞ Also the kynge shall ioyne with no man in presēt=
ment, but shall haue the hole presentment alone in
al cases. And if the kyng be intitled by reason of the
custodie of hys warde: then ye shall say, et ad nostrã
donationē ratiōe custodiæ terræ et heredis quon
dam Comitis de A. defūcti, qui de nobis tenuit in
capite, et in manu nr̄a existentis, spectañ. &c. And
yf the kynge be intitled by reason of the tempozal=
ties and possessions of an archbishopziche oz bishop
riche beyng in time of vacation in his handes: then
ye shall say in the presentacion. Et quæ ad nostram
spectat donationē ratione episcopatus Cantuariēñ
iam vacantis et in manu nr̄a existeñ. oz ratione vaca
tionis sedis Cantuariēsis et temporaliũ eiusdē iam
de iure et facto vacañ, et i manib⁹ nr̄is existētis &c.

a diuisiō   Finally concernynge chauntries, free chapelles,
and przebendes, ye shall obserue ꝫ knowe, that some
Presen= be presentatiue, and some donatiue. Przesentatiue be
tatiues. of suche nature, that ye can not cōferre them but by
waye of przesentacion to the Ozdinary, the fourme
wherof is set fozth befoze. But chauntreies, free cha
Donati= pelles and przebendes donatiues be of that nature
ues. that ye nede not to przesente the person to whom ye
woll conferre the same, to the Ozdinary, but it suffi=
ceth to gyue the same by your charter of graunt vn
der your seale, the fourme wherof ensueth herafter.

☞ But take hede ye present not your clerke to the Oz=
dinary vnto that which is donatiue by your lettres
patentes, foz yf ye do the nature of it is chaunged,
and ye can nomoze make collation of it, but ye must
nedes

nedes nowe þſent pour clerke to the oɔdinary which
if ye do not within.vj.monethes,the oɔdinary maye
take auantage of the laps.

¶ The gyfte of a free chapel,by the kynge.

REx omnibus ad quos.ꝛc.ſalutem.Sciatis.ꝛc.
dediſſe et côceſſiſſe.ꝛc.liberam capellam ſancti
S.apud L.in coṁ noſtro Lincol Habenᵭ et tenenᵭ
dcãm liberã capellã þfato A. B. durãte vita ipi⁹ cũ
oĩb⁹ ſuis iurib⁹ et ꝑtineñ vniuerſis. In cui⁹ rei.ꝛc.

¶ An other fourme of a collation by an eſquier
oɔ other cômon perſon.

VNiuerſis Chɔiſti fidelibus ad quos pñtes li=
tere puenerint, Joânes N. armiger dominus
manerij de B.Cantucieñ dioc.ſalutem et ſyncerã in
dño charitatem. Cum capella libera de R.dicte dio=
ceſ. iam vacare,et ad meam donationem pleno iure
ſpectare dignoſcitur:Noueritis me pɔedictã capellã
cũ omĩbȝ ſuis iuribuȝ, et pertineñ vniuerſis, dilecto
mihi in Xpo Ricardo C.clerico viro tam pɔobo ꝙ li=
terato donaſſe et côceſſiſſe,ac tenoɔe þſentiũ ipſũ Ri=
chartũ in coɔpoɔalê poſſeſſionê dicte capelle cũ perti=
neñ me inducere. In cui⁹ rei ꝛc.ſigillũ meũ þſentibȝ
appoſui.Daᵵ in Manerio meo de B.þdicto ꝛc.

¶ A patent donatyue of a pɔebende,voyde by
the pɔomotion of the laſt incumbent.

REx Oṁnibȝ ad quos ꝛc.ſaluᵵ. Sciatis nos ex
gɾa nɾa ſpeciali ac intuitu charitatis dediſſe ⁊
côceſſiſſe,ac p þſentes dare et concedere dilecto ſcho=
lari noſtro J. L. canonicatũ in eccɭia nɾa cathedɔali
Saɽ,⁊ pbendã de H.in eadem.modo p pmotionem
dilecti nobis in Xpo R.C.dudũ ac vltimi incũbêtis
eoɽũdê ad ᵵpatũ N.vacanᵵ,⁊ ad nɾam donationê ra

Miles generoſus, &c.

Siue per noiationem.

B.iij.   tione

Sine ple
no iure
&c.

tione ac iure prerogatiue nre regie spectan. Habend
et tenend Canonicatu et prebendam predict.prefato
Joani ad terminu vite ipsius Joanis vna cu oibus
et omnimodis iuribus preeminencijs et ptinen vni=
uersis. In cuius rei.

¶The gyfte of a prebend in the kynges college
in Orforde.

Henric9 octauus.&c. Dilectis nobis Joani D.
Decano Collegij nri Oron vulgariter nucu=
pati kynge Henry the eyghtes College, ac eiusdem
collegij canonicis salute. Sciatis nos er mero mo=
tu nro,atq; er gra nra spiali,dedisse cocessisse ac pre
senti scripto nro cofirmasse,dilecto capellano nro J.
B.sacre theologie professori canonicatu siue preben=

Vel p re
signatio
nem,fo=
risfactu=
ram.&c,

dam in collegio nro predicto, modo per morte J.H.
vltimi incubentis ibidem vacantem, atq; ad dona=
tionem nram pleno iure attinen. Habend et tenend
pfato J.B.canonicatu siue prebeda pdick cum suis
iuribus et pertinen vniuersis vnacu hospitio qd ide
J.H.ratione dicti canonicatus siue pbende nup pos
sidebat. Uobis igit coniuctim et diuisim comittim9
et stricte mandamus,quatenus pfatu J.B.ad dictu
canonicatu siue prebenda statim,his literis nris in=
spectis admittatis,necno eudem in reale et corpora=
lem possessione dicti canonicatus siue prebende iuri
umq; et pertinen suorum vniuersor inducatis,put
decet.In cuius rei.&c.

¶A prebend in Windesour.

Rer.&c.Sciatis p nos er gra nra spiali.&c. de=
dimus et cocessimus,ac tenore pntiu damus et

aut in ar
tib9 ma
gistro&c

concedimus dilecto Sacellano nro J.B.sacre theo=
logie bacchalaurio(or pf he be a Doctour)professori
cauo

canonicatuȝ ſiue p̃ebenoã infra eccłiam nr̃am col=
legiatã ſiue liberã capellã nr̃am regiã ſcti Geoꝛgij
infra caſtrũ nr̃m oe Woinoeſour mooo p.ꝛc.vacañ,
atꝗ ao nr̃am oonationẽ pleno iure ſpectañ.Ḣẽno et
teneno canonicatũ ſiue pꝛebẽoã p̃oicḟ pꝛefato Ⱥ.B.
ourante vita eius naturali cum oĩbus ſuis iuribus
et ꝑtinẽ vniuerſis.Ĵn cuius rei.ꝛc.

¶ Ⱥ warrant foꝛ a felawſhip in the kynges hall
    in Cambꝛige.

Henry.ꝛc. To oure truſtye ano welbiloueo the
mapſter of our College calleo the kynges hall
within our vniuerſitie of Cambꝛige, ano in his ab=
ſence to hys lieutenante oꝛ oeputie there, gretynge.
Foꝛaſmuche as we be crediblp enfourmeo, that our
welbeloueo ſubiecte Ⱥ.B. ſcholar of our ſayoe vni=
uerſitie is greatly oeſperouſe ano mynoeo to conty=
newe at ſchole foꝛ his foꝛther increaſe in vertue ano
learnyng : we late pou wete that conſioerynge hys
vertuouſe intent ano purpoſe, foꝛ his better exhibi=
cion in that behalfe, we haue gyuen ano graunteo,
ano by theſe pꝛeſẽtes oo gyue ano graunt vnto him
the roume of a felawe of ꝛ within our ſayoe college
yf any be nowe vopoe there, oꝛ elles the roume of a
felawe of ano within our ſayoe college whiche ſhall
fyꝛſt ano nexte fall vopoe within the ſame by oeath,
oimiſſion,ſurrenoꝛe oꝛ otherwyſe. To haue ano en=
ioye the ſayo roume with almaner ryghtes,pꝛofites
emolumẽtes ano outies therunto belongyng to the Or.xx.
ſayo Ⱥ.B.foꝛ terme of his lyfe with a benefice oꝛ be= or.xl. li.
nefices penſion oꝛ annuitie not excedyng the yearly as the
value of tenne pounoes in as ample ano large ma. caſe ſhal
ner as any hertofoꝛe hath hao oꝛ enioyeo the roume require.
                                 afoꝛe=

afozesapde, any acte, statute, ozdinaunce, oz other
thing to the contrary herof in any wyse notwithstā=
dyng.wherfoze we wol and cōmaunde you,that ac=
cozdyng to the effecte ⁊ purpozte of this our graūte,
ye do admytte the sayde A.B.vnto the sayde roume
of felawe accozdyngly. And these our letters shalbe
pour sufficient warrante and discharge in thys be=
halfe.Yeuen.⁊c.

C The fourme of the kynges letters patentes
of collation of a pzebende made causa per=
mutationis.

Enricus octauus.⁊c. Omnibus ad
quos.⁊c.salutem,Sciatis ꝙ cum A
B. rcctoz ecclesie parochialis de w.
Nozwicen dioc.et C.D.Canonicus
in ecclia Catheð sancti Pauli Lon=
don ac pzebendarius pzebende de H
in eadem ecclesia intendunt(vt asserunt) bñficia sua
ꝑdcā adinuicē pmutare : Nos ꝑbēdā ꝑdcām ad ñra꞉
donacōem spectañ racōe tēpozaliū Epatus Londoñ
in manu ñra in pñti existeñ,ꝑfato A.B.ex causa hu=
iusmodi pmutacōis dedim⁹ et cōcessimus,ac per pze
sentes damus et concedimus.Habenð et tenenð ⁊c.

C The fourme of pzesentation causa permuta=
tionis inter rectores.

Euerendo in Chzisto patri Joāni pmissione di
uina Lincoln epo,vester humilis et deuotus fi
lius A.B.miles obedientiā et honozē tanto patri de
bitam. Dilecti nobis in Chzisto magister S.T. rec
toz ecclie de w.⁊ Jacobus E.clericus rectoz ecclesie
pochialis de B.bre dioc.intēdunt(vt asserunt) bñfi=
cia sua certis et legitimis ex causis ipos ad hoc mo=
uenti=

uētibus adinuicem permutare, egoꝗ permutationi
hmōi fiende meū pɀebens assensū pariter et cōsensū,
pfatū Jacobū E. ad dcām ecclīam de W. p modū et
ex causa pmutacōis pͦdicte bacātē, et ad meā psͤtaᵃ
cōem spectaū, bͤe paternitati reuerēde psͤto intuitu
charitatis, humiliter supplicans, quaten⁹ ipͭm Jaco
bū ad dcām ecclīam pochiaͦl de W. ex causa pmutati
onis pͦdicte admittere et institucre in eadē, ceteraꝗ
oīa et singula que bͤo in hac pte pastoɀali officio in
cūbere dinoscūtur eidē Jacobo facere et pagere dignemini cū fauoɀe. Jn cui⁹ rei ꝛc.

An other fourme of the same.

REuerendo in Chͤo patri willͤmo pmissione diuina Herefoɀdeñ epͦo ꝛc. bͤi humiles et deuoti
in Chͤo filij J.S.et J.A. armigeri omnimoꝺ reue-
rentias tanto patre dignas. Cū honesti biri M.T.
ecclīe pochiaͦl de A.Noɀwiceñ dioc.et C.D.ecclīe po
chialis de B. bͤe dioc. rectoɀes intendāt (bt asserūt)
beneficia sua pͦdcā certis de causis beris quidē et legitimis ipͦos mouētib⁹ (dū tñ quoɀ interest cōsēsus
et authoɀitas interuenerint in hac parte)adinuicē ca
nonice pmutare:Nos igitur pmutattōe hmōi facie-
end,nͤtm pbentes assensū pariter et cōsensū, pɀefatū
M.T.ad dcām ecclīam de B.pͦdcē bͤe dioc.nͤtiꝗ pa
tronatus,paternitati bͤe reuerende,ex causa pꭒnuta
cōis hmōi et nō alͤt nec alio modo, psͤtam⁹ p psͤtes,
humiliter supplicātes et deuote quatenus supɀadcͭm
M.T.ad dcām ecclīam de B.admittere,ipsuꭑꝗ rec-
toɀē ex causa hmōi pmutacōis canonice instituere in
eadē,cū suis iuribᷓ et ptineñ bniuersis, ceteraꝗ pa
gere, que bͤo in hac parte incūbunt officio pastoɀali, dignemini cū fauoɀe. Jn cui⁹ rei testimoniū sigil-
　　　　　　　　　C.i.　　　　la nͤta

la nr̄a pñtibz duximus append. Dat. &c.

¶The fourme of a warrant for a Congie delicr.

Harissime Consanguinee &c. Sup-
plicauerunt nobis humiliter Decan⁹ et capitulū Ecclie nr̄e Cathedral
de N. Ut cū sedes epalis infra ecclī
nr̄az Cathedral predcām p morte na-
turalē pie memorie I.B. vltimi Epī

Vel per translati onē A.B ad epa- rum w.

eiusdē. sit pastoris solatio destituta, aliū in loci illi⁹
epm et pastorem eligendi facultatē licēciāmqz nr̄am
graciose cōredere dignaremur. Nos igitur eoz sup-
plicationibz fauorabiliter inclinati, facultatem atqz
licenciam nr̄am huiusmodi duximus concedendam.
Quocirca. vobis mādam⁹ qp sub priuato sigillo nr̄o
in custodia vr̄a existen literas &c. Mandantes et vt
sub magno sigillo nostro in eius custodia existen literas nr̄as patefi fieri faciat in hac parte debitas et
in tali casu cōsuetas. Et he lr̄e nr̄e &c.

And ye shal vnderstande that herupon the chauncelour of Englande shall graunt vnto them the kingſ
letters patentes of licence to procede to theyr electió.
¶The fourme wherof appeareth in the register. With
which lr̄es patétes of licence vnder the great Seale
shalbe sent a lr̄e missiue conteynyng the name of the
persone to be elected, which maye be made after this
sorte.

¶The fourme of the lr̄e missiue to the Deane
and Chapter.

By the kynge.

TRusty and welbiloued we grete you well, And
being now the bishoprich of Hereford voyd by
the traslation of the ryght reuerende father in God,
our

our ryght trusty and ryght welbiloued Consaillour
the late byschop of the same, vnto the byschopryche of
London: We haupnge respecte to the honest quali=
ties vertue ⁊ lernpnge of our trusty and welbiloued
Chaplayn Maister Doctour N. oure Almner, haue
named and appopnted hpm to the same bischopriche.
Wherfoze we woll and commaunde you, that fozth=
with vpon the receipt hereof, ye pzocede to the electi=
on of him accozdynge to the tenour and purpozte of
our lawes and statutes in that behalfe made ⁊ pzo=
uided, and the same so elected to certify accozdingly.
And these our lres shalbe pour sufficient warraut ⁊
discharge in ẏ be halfe. Yeue vnder our Signet ⁊c.

    ⸿ A warraunt foz a Royall assent.

Harissime et ⁊c. Uacante nuper sede epali infra
ecclam nram Cathedzalem de N. per mozte bo
ne memozie J. B. vltimi epi ibidem, Decanus et ca=
pitulum eiusdé, facultate a nobis pzius per ipsos a=
lium eligédi in ipsoz epm et pastoze petita pariter et
obtéta, venerabil et egregiu viru C. D. in suu pasto=
rem elegerut et noiauerut. Cui nos electioni et viro
sic electo, humilibz eoz interuenientibz suppplicati=
onibz, regium nrm adhibemus assensu pariter et fa=
uozem. eundemcz electu apud vos comendatu habe=
mus. Quocirca vobis mandamus ⁊c.

Aut per translatí oné, &c.

And vpon thps warraunt the lozde Chauncelour of
Englande shal do make the kinges letters patentes
of hps Royal assente direcced to the Metropolitane
to confirme and consecrate the lozde elected, oz pf ye
wol, the wozds of the patent may be set fozth at légth
in the warraunt that the kyng shal signe, in thps oz
like fourme folowing.

               C. ij.   ⸿ The

⸿ The patent of a Royall assent with a significauit to the Metropolitane.

R Ex ꝛc. Reuerēdissimo in Chꝛo patri ꝛc. salutē. Cū vacaū nup ecclia nīa cathed sancti Andꝛee Wellen per moꝛtem bone memoꝛie dūi J. C. eiusdē

vel, sub-decanus & presi-dens, ab sēte De-cano.

ecclie dudū epi, Decan⁹, et Capitulū ecclie nīe ꝑdcē, pꝛius licentia a nobis ꝑ eos aliū eligēdi in eoꝛ eꝑm et pastoꝛem petita pariter et obtenta, venerabilē vi-rū A. B. in ipsoꝛ eꝑm ac pastoꝛem canonice elegerūt et noiaucrūt, sicuti per eoꝛ līas, quas vobis mitti-mus pꝛesētibꝫ inclusas, plentius liquet: Vobis signi-ficamus, ꝙ dcē quidem electioni et persone sic electe, humilibꝫ eoꝛ mediantibꝫ supplicationibꝫ, nīm regiū adhibuimus fauoꝛem pariter et assensū, Et eundem electum apud vos recōmendatum hēmus. Quocir-ea vobis mādamus, ꝙ cetera oīa, que per vos ad cō-firmacōem et consecracōem eiusdem in dicto Eꝑatu fieri cōsueuerunt scdm leges et statuta regni nīi An-glie hac parte edita et pꝛouisa, cum fauoꝛe et diligē-tia facere velitis. Jn cuius rei ꝛc.

☞ Jf ye lyst to know further after what maner ꝑ Arch-bishops and bishops be at thys day chosen, nomina-ted, pꝛesented, inuested and consecrated to the digni-tie and office of an Archebishop oꝛ byshop, ye muste reade ꝑ foꝛsaid statute therof made in the .xxv. peare of our moost dꝛad soueraygne loꝛde kyng Henry the eyght.

⸿ The fourme of a Significauit to the Metro politane of the pꝛouince vpon a newe foundati-on of a byshopꝛiche.

R Ex reuerēdissimo. ꝛc. Cū nos nouā sedem eꝑa-lē infra eccliam nīaꝫ Cathedꝛaľ sci P. Westm̄ nuper

nup fúdauerimus ⁊ erexerimus, ac dil'cm Confilia=
rium nm̄ T.T.ad epatū illū noīauerimus et p̃efe=
cerimus, ip̃mcʒ iñ ep̃m loci illus et paſtoʒem oʒdina=
uerimus et conſtituerimus: hoc vobis tenoʒe p̃ntiū
duximus ſignificādū,Rogātes ac iñ fide et dileccōe,
quibʒ nobis tenemini firmiter vobis mādātes, qua=
tenus pʒefatū T.T.in Ep̃m Weſtm̄ conſecrare, ip=
ſūcʒ,pʒout moʒis eſt, ep̃alibʒ inſignijs inueſtire,cete
racʒ peragere,que veſtro iñ hac parte incūbunt offi=
cio,velitis diligenter cū effcū.In cuius rei.⁊c.

    ¶A warraunt foʒ the reſtitution of the poſſeſſi=
ons of the byſhopʒiche.

Ryght truſty.⁊c.we grete you wel.Wheras the
Dean and Chapter of our Cathedʒall churche
of ſaynte A.in Welles vpon the late vacation of the
byſhopʒyche there, by reaſon of oure licence to them
grāuted haue elected and choſen our welbeloued iñ
God A.B.to be byſhop and paſtour there, to whiche
election ⁊ perſon ſo elected,we haue giuen our Roy=
all aſſent, who hath done homage ⁊ fealtie vnto vs
and hath compowned ⁊ agreed wyth vs foʒ the poſ=
ſeſſions of the ſaide byſhopʒiche:We woll and com=
maunde you.⁊c.cōmaundynge him by the ſame that
he make out ſuch ⁊ as many our wʒittes vnder our
great ſeale, as ſhalbe neceſſary and requiſite foʒ the
reſtitution of the poſſeſſions of the ſame to the ſayd
Biſhop accoʒdyngly.And theſe our letters.⁊c.
And vpō thys warrāt, the partie ſhall haue a wʒitte
foʒ the reſtitution of all poſſeſſions aſwell ſpirituall
as tēpoʒal only out of the kinges handes accoʒding
to the ſtatute therof made,anno xxb.H.octaui.

                 C.iij.   The

¶ The fourme of a Charter of fee simple, wyth a lettre of Atturney.

SCIANT pñtes ꝛ futuri, ꝙ ego W. H. gentylmã cõsanguineus et heres R. H. videlicet filius J. H. armigeri defuncti fratris dict R. dedi, conces= si et hac pñti charta mea cõfirmaui W. C. armigero et J. S. clico Ma= neriũ meũ de T. cũ omibʒ suis membris et pertiñ, ac omia terras et tenãta mea, redditus, reuersiones, et seruicia pʒata, pascuas, pasturas, boscos, et subbos= cos cũ suis ptiñ. in T. in Com B. HABEND. et tenendũ predictũ maneriũ cũ omibʒ suis membris et pertiñ, ac etiã omia pdicta terras ꝛ tenemẽta, red= ditus, reuersiones, et seruic. cũ suis ptiñ pʒefato W. C. et J. S. heredibʒ ꝛ assignatis suis imperpetuũ de capitalibus dominis feodi illius per seruic. inde de= bita et de iure consueta. Et ego vero pdictus W. H. et hered mei predictũ maneriũ cũ omibus suis mem= bʒis et ptiñ pʒefatis W. C. ꝛ S. heredibus et assigñ suis, cõtra õnes gentes warantizabim⁹ et imperpe= tuũ defẽdem⁹ per pñtes. ET VLTERIVS sciant me prefatum W. fecisse, oʒdinasse, cõstituisse, et in lo= co meo posuisse dilectos michi in Chʒisto R. F. ꝛ W. S. meos veros et legittimos atturnatos cõiunctim et diuisim ad possessionem capiendã ꝑ me et in noíe meo, de et in pʒedict manerio, terris tenemẽtis, red= dit reuers. et seruic. cũ omibʒ suis pertiñ et post hu= iusmodi possessionẽ sic inde captam et habitam, de= inde pʒo me, et noíc meo plenam et pacificam posses= sionem et seisinã pʒefat W. ꝛ J. vel eoʒ in hac pte atturnat deliberand, secundũ tenoʒem, vim, foʒmam
et

et effectum huius pñtis charte mei sup hoc confecte,
ratũ et gratũ habentẽ et habituƷ totum et quicquid
predicti aturnař mei noïe meo fecerint. vel alter eoƷ
fecerit in premissis. IN CVIVS REI testimoniũ
huic presenti charte mee sigillum meũ apposui. Dat
apud T.predicř, ãno Regni Regis H.Octaui xxxiij.
his testibus A.B.C.S.řc.

    ¶ A Charter of fee simple to the husbande and
wyfe ioyntly infeffed.

SCIANT presentes et futuri, ꝙ ego R.B.de S.
  dedi, concessi, et hac pñti charta mea confirmaui
I. T. de eadem et E. vxoꝛ sue totũ illud mesuagiũ
meum ꝙ ego habeo in dicř villa de S. et sexaginta
acres terre arabilis in cãpis dicte ville, ꝙ quidem
mesuagiũ situatũ est inter tenemẽtũ R.B. ex pte au=
strali, et tenemẽtũ I.B.ex pte Boꝛiali, et abuttat sup
stratam regiam versus occidentem, et predicte sexa=
ginta acre terre iacent in campo oꝛientali dicte ville
queƷ viginti acre terre iacẽt simul in quodam fur=
longo vocař L. et alie viginti acre terre iacẽt ex par=
te australi eiusdem campi similiter inter terras do=
minicales, et abuttãt versus austrũ sup pꝛatũ vocař
B. et alie viginti acre iacẽt diuisim in dicto campo,
queƷ qui꜕ iacent inter terram I.B.ex parte boꝛia=
li et terram E.D. ex parte australi et extẽdunt se ad
quãdam riuulum aque vocař C.ex pte oꝛiẽtali dicti
campi: et quin꜕ acre iacent inter terrã S.H. ex pte
boꝛiali et terrã I.K. ex pte australi, et extendunt se
super semitam de L.predicř versus occidentẽ et alia
vij.acre iacẽt ex opposito territorij dcẽ ville inter ter
ras L.M.ex pte boꝛiali et australi et extẽdũt se vs꜕
ad Croftũ H.D, versus occidentẽ,   HABEND·
                                               et

et tenēdū pdict mesuagium et seraginta acras ter¤
re arabilis cū oiꝫ suis pertiñ,pꝛefatis ℭ. et Ꝁ .he¤
redibus et assigñ suis imperpetuū ,de capitalibꝫ do¤
minis feodi illius per seruicia inde debita et de iure
cōsueta.Et ego pꝛedict R .B.ꝫ heredes mei pꝛedictū
mesuagiū et seraginta acras terre arabilis cū oibus
pertiñ pꝛefatis Ꝁ. ℭ.ꝫ E. heredibus et assigñ suis
contra omnes gentes warantizabim⁹ et imperpetu¤
um defēdem⁹ per pñtes.Jn cuius rei testi.ꝟt supra.

℩ ℭhe fourme of a wydowes gyfte in her wy=
dowhode.

SCIANT presentes ꝛc. ꝙ ego Alicia w. relicta
cuiusdā R.W.de N.in pura bidiuitate mea ꝫ le
gitima potestate,dedi,concessi,et hac pñti chatta ꝛc.
ꝟt supra.

℩ ℭhe fourme of a charter of fee ferme made
by the chief loꝛde.

SCIANT ꝛc.ꝙ ego J.S.dñs de D.dedi,conces=
si.ꝛc.w.E.bnū mesuagium cum gardino, ꝫ bi
ginti acras terre arabilis in billa et in cāpis de D.
ꝙ quidem mesuagiū boc.ℭ.et pꝛedicte biginti acre
terre iacent simul iūcte dicto gardino er parte boꝛi¤
ali dicti gardini.HABENDVM et tenendum pꝛe¤
dictū mesuagiū cum gardino,et pꝛedictas biginti a¤
cras terre arabilis cum pertiñ pꝛefato w.heredibus
et assigñ suis imperpetuū de me et heredibus meis
Reddendo inde annuatim michi et heredibus meis
rrs. sterlyng. ad festa sci Michis archangeli,et Jn¤
nūciattonis beate Marie birginis, per equales poꝛ=
ciones et fac.sectā Curie mee de D.pꝛedict quociens
dictam curiam teneri contigerit ꝑ oñibus alijs se¤
cularibus seruicijs,eractis et dñis.ET EGO bero
pꝛe=

pꝛedictꝰ J.S.et hered mei pꝛedictū mesuagium cum
gardino,pꝛedictꝰ viginti acras terre arabilis cū suis
pertiñ pꝛefato W. hered et assigñ suis cōtra omnes
gētes warantizabimus imperpetuū et defendemꝰ p
pñtes. Jn cuiꝰ rei testimoniū huic pꝛesenti carte mee
sigillū armoꝛ meoꝛ apposui.Dat̄.ꝛc.his testibꝫ ꝛc.

℘The fourme of a purchase of landes in fe sim=
ple of the kynge,to be holden in Capite.

Rex omibꝫ ad quos.ꝛc.salutē Sciatis ꝙ nos ꝑ
sūma ducentarū duaꝛ libꝛarū decem ð et vniꝰ
obuli legalis monete Anglie ad manꝰ Thesaurarij
Reuētionū Augmentationū Coꝛone nostre ad vsum
nostrum per dilectum nobis H.W. de R. in com̄ ño
Ñ. generosū soluꝭ de gracia nostra speciali ac ex cer
ta scientia et mero motu nostris, dedimus et cōcessi=
mus, ac per pñtes damus et concedimus eidē H.W.
totum Scitum et capitale mesuagium Manerij nñi
de R.in R.in Com̄ nostro Ñ.nup Monasterio de C.
in eodem Com̄ ño Ñ. modo dissoluto dudū spectañ
et ꝑtineñ ac ꝑcell possessionū inde existeñ , ac omnes
terras dominicales Manerij pꝛedicti.Necnon omĩa
mesuagia domos oꝛrea edificia oꝛtos pomeria gar=
dina curtilagia terras, pꝛata, pascuas, pasturas,a=
quas,piscarias,coĩas,iura,cōmoditates, et heredita
menta nostra quecunꝗ , cum suis ꝑtineñ vniuersis
in R.in Com̄ pꝛdicto, ac alibi, vbicūꝗ in eodē Com̄ ,
dicto capitꝭ mesuagio Manerij pꝛedicti quoquomo
do spectañ vel pertineñ, aut cum eodē capitꝭ mesua
gio dimissa, vsitata, seu occupata existeñ, ac nup ĩ
tenura H.T.armigeri et modo in tenura seu occupa
tione dc̄i H. W. cum dicto capitꝭ mesuagio existeñ,
ac etiam omnes et omnimoð boscos de in et sup dic=

D.i.　　　tis

vel The
saurarij
Camere
nostre.

tis terris et ceteris p̃emiſſis creſcen et eriſteñ.DA͞
MVS etiam ac per p͂ntes ꝓ conſideracione p̃dict͞
concedimus.p̃fato H. W.aduocationem,donatio͞
nem,liberam diſpoſitionem, et ius p͂onatus recto͞
rie et eccl̃e parochialis de A.in d͞co com̃ n͞ro M.HA͞
BEND.tenend̃ et gaudend̃ totum p̃dictũ ſcitum
et capitale meſuagiũ manerij p̃dicti,ac p͂dicta ter͞
ras,p̃ata,paſturas,aduocationem, et cetera omnia
et ſingula p̃miſſa ſuperius exp̃ſſa et ſpecificata
cũ ſuis pertiñ vniuerſis p͂fato H. W. hered̃ et aſſig͞
natis ſuis imperpetuũ TENEND. de nobis here͞
dibus et ſucceſſoꝛibus noſtris in capite per ſeruiciũ
vicesime partis vnius feodi militis ac reddendo in͞
de annuatim nobis heredibus et ſucceſſoꝛibus noſ͞
tris viginti vnum ſolidos et quatuoꝛ denarios ad
Curiã noſtrã Augmētationũ reueñ Coꝛone n͞re ad
feſtũ ſci Michaelis Archangeli ſigulis ãnis ſoluc͞d̃
pꝛo oĩbʒ reddit̃ibus,ſeruicijs, et demaund̃ quibus͞
cũꝗʒ pꝛoinde nobis, heredibus, vel ſucceſſoꝛibʒ noſ͞
tris quoquomodo reddend̃,ſoluc͞d̃,vel facicnd̃. ET
VLTERIVS volumus, et p p͂ntes concedimus,
p̃fato H.W.heredibus et aſſignatis ſuis, ꝙ nos,
heredes, et ſucceſſoꝛes noſtri imperpetuũ annuatim
et de tempoꝛe in tempus exonerabimus,acquietabi͞
mus et indemnes conſeruabimus eũdem H. W. he͞
redes,et aſſigñ ſuos verſus nos,hered̃ et ſucceſſoꝛeꝫ
n͞ros et verſus quaſcũꝗʒ alias perſonas de oĩbus et
omiod̃ redditibus,feod̃ ãnuitatibus,penſionibus,et
denarioꝛ ſũmis quibuſcũꝗʒ de p̃miſſis ſeu de ali͞
quo p̃miſſoꝛ exeuñ ſeu ſoluend̃ vel ſuperinde one͞
rat̃ ſeu onerand̃,ꝓterꝗ de redditu et ſeruicio ſuperi͞
us p p͂ntes reſeruat̃, VOLENTES eni et firmiter
iniun͞

iniungendo pꝛecipientes tam Cancellario et cõsilio
dicte Curie noſtre Augmẽtationũ Reuẽtionum Co=
rone noſtre ꝑ tẽpoꝛe exiſteñ.ꝙ omibꝝ Receptoꝛibus,
Auditoꝛibꝝ, et alijs officiarijs et miniſtris nꞇis qui=
buſcũꝗ.ꝙ ipſi et eoꝛ quiſꝗ ſuper ſolã demõſtratio=
ñe haꝝ lꞇaꝝ noſtraꝝ pateñ vel ſup irrotꞇamento ea=
rũdẽ abſꝗ aliquo alio bꞃi ſeu waráto a nobis heredꞟ
vel ſucceſſoꝛib⁹ noſtris quoquomodo impetráꝺ ſeu
pꝛoſequenꝺ ſuper ſolucõe dicti annui redditus.ꝝꝛiꞟ.
ſoliꝺ et quatuoꝛ denarioꝛ plenã,integrã,debitamcꝗ
allocacõem,defalcacõem, deductiõe, et exoneratio=
nem manifeſtam de omib⁹ et omimoꝺ hmõi redditi=
bus,feoꝺ, ãnuitatibꝝ, penſionibꝝ,et denarioꝛ ſũmis
de pꝛmiſſis ſeu de aliqua inde pcella(vt pꝛefertur)ex=
euñ ſeu ſoluẽꝺ pꝛfato H.ꝥ.heredꞟ,et aſſignꞟ ſuis faci=
ent et fieri curabũt. Et he lꞇe noſtre pateñ erunt an=
nuatim et de tẽpore in tẽpus tam dicto Cancellario
et Conſilio nꞇo,ꝙ omibꝝ Receptoꝛibꝝ,Auditoꝛib⁹, et
alijs officiarijs,et miniſtris nꞇis,ſufficiens warran=
tũ et exoneratio in hac parte. ET INSVPER de
amplioꝛi gꞃa noſtra damus et per pꝛñſentes concedi=
mus pꝛfato H.ꝥ.omia exitus,redditus,reuentiones
et ꝓficua omniũ et ſinguloꝛũ pꝛmiſſoꝛũ ſuperius ex=
pꝛeſſoꝛũ et ſpecificatoꝛũ cũ pertineñ.a feſto Sꞇi Mi=
chis Archãgeli vltimo pꝛterito hucuſꝗ,puenieñ ſiue
creſceñ. HABEND.eidẽ H.ex dono noſtro abſꝗ
compoto ſeu aliquo alio pꝛoinde nobis heredib⁹ vel
ſucceſſoꝛibꝝ nꞇis quoquomodo reddenꝺ,ſoluenꝺ,vel
facienꝺ. ET VLTERIVS de vberioꝛi gꞃa nꞇa Note
volumus et per pꝛñtes concedimus pꝛefato H.ꝥ.ꝙ this
habeat ꝗ habebit has literas nꞇas pateñ ſub magno clauſe.
Sigillo nꞇo Anglie debiꞇ modo facꞇ et ſigillaꞇ abſꝗ

                    D.ij.   abſꝗ

fine feu feodo magno vel paruo ,pinde nobis in ha=
napio noftro feu alibi ad vfū noftrū quoquomō red
dend,foluend , vel faciend. EO QVOD expreffa
mencio.&c.Jn cuius rei.&c.

℮The fourme of a patent for a benefice or lan=
des giuen by the kyng in pure almes

Ex omibȝ ad quos.&c. falutē. Sciatis, qd̄ nos
de grā noftra fpeciali ac ex certa fcientia et me=
ro motu nr̄is,dedimus et cōceffimus, ac p pn̄tes da=
mus et cōcedim9 dilcis nobis in Chrifto Decano et
canonicis libere Capelle noftre Regie fancti Geor=
gij infra caftrū noftrū de Windfour aduocationem
& patronatū bicarie ecclefie de N.in com H.Habend
et tenend aduocationem & patronatū bicarie ecclefie
pdcē cū omibȝ fuis ptineñ et appēdēc.pfato Decano
& canonicis & fucceffozibȝ fuis imppetuū in purā & p
petuā eleinofinā abfcȝ aliquo impedimento,impeti=
cōe,pturbacōe,moleftatione,inquietacōe,feu graua=
mine nr̄o feu hered noftroȝ, Jufticiarioȝ,Efcaetoȝ,
bic.Cozonaꝝ,aut alioȝ balliuoȝū feu miniftroȝū no=
ftroȝū vel hered noftroȝū quoȝūcuncȝ,abfcȝ appozto
firma , cōpoto vel raciocinio,aut alio proficuo quo=
cūcȝ nobis vel hered nr̄is inde reddēd,foluēd feu fa=
ciēd,Statuꝷ de terris et tenemētis ad manū moztu=
am nō ponēd edito, aut aliquo ftatuto de poffeffioni
b9 alienigeñ facꝷ,edito,fiue prouifo,in cōtratiū non
obftanti. Aut eo qd̄ expreffa mētio de bero baloze ā
nuo aut de certitudine premifforum feu alicuius eo=
rundē,aut de alijs donis, fiue cōceffionibus prefato
Decano et canonicis vel pdeceffozibȝ fuis p nos vel
pgenitozes noftros ante hec tempoza facꝷ in pfētib9
minime facꝷ exiftit.Aut aliquo alio ftatuto, actu,oz=
dina=

dinacōe ſiue pꝛouiſ. ediꝉ, facꝉ, vel ,puiſ. aut aliqua
alia re, cauſa, vel materia quacunꜣ in contrarium
non obſtanꞇ IN CVIVS rei teſtimonium ꝛc.

⫶Ca Charter of fee ſimple wyth a condition.
SCIANT Pñtcs, ꝛc. ꝗ ego J.w.de O.dedi, cō=
ceſſi, et hac pñti charta mea indētata cōfirmaui
S.w.de eadē oia illa terras et teñta, redditus, ſer=
uiꞇ. prata, paſcuas, paſtuꝛ, cū boſcis, ſepibꝫ foſſatis ꝗ
ſuis ptiñ que habeo in villa et in cāpis de H. in com̄
Oꝛoñ, HABEND. et tenenð oia pꝛedicꞇ terras et
teñta, reddiꞇ⁹, ſeruitia, prata, paſcuas et paſturas, cū
boſtis, ſepibus, foſſis, et foſſatis, et ſuis pertiñ pꝛefa
to S.w. hereð et aſſigñ ſuis imperpetuum, de capi=
talibus Dñis feodi illius p ſeruitia inde debita, et
de iure conſueta ſub foꝛma et cōdicione ſubſequētì,
videlicet ꝗ ſi ego pꝛedicꞇ J. ſoluam, ſeu ſolui faciā
heredes vel executores met ſoluāt, aut ſolui faciant
pꝛefato S. w.aut eius certo atturnato, heredibus
vel executoꝛibus ſuis ad feſtum Paſche pꝛoxime fu=
turum in parochiali eccƚia oīm Sanctoꝛum Oꝛoñ
viginti libꝛas ſterƚ. quod extunc pñs charta inden=
tata, ac ſeiſina inde deliberata caſſe ſint et vane, nul=
liuſꝗ baloꝛis, ac tunc bene licebit mihi pꝛefato J.
hereð et aſſignatis meis in oia illa terras et teñta,
reddiꞇ ſeruicia, prata, paſcuas, paſturas, cū ceteris
pꝛenōatis et ſuis pertiñ reintrare, reſeſire, et ea reha
bere, et tenere, vt in ſtatu meo priſtino : ac pꝛefatum
S.w.heredes et aſſigñ ſuos inde totaliter expellere
pꝛeſenti charta indentata, ac ſeiſina inde liberata vl
lo mō non obſtāte.Et ſi defectus fiat in ſolucōe pꝛe=
dicꞇ viginti libꝛaꝛ contra foꝛmam pꝛedictā, extunc
pñs hec charta mea indentata, et ſeiſina, inde libe=
Diij. rata.

rata suum robur obtineant et effectum , ⁊ tunc bene
liceat pꝛefat S. W. heredibʒ et assign suis ea reha=
bere et pacifice gaudere imperpetuũ IN CVIVS
rei testimonium vni parti huius charte indẽtate pe=
nes me remanen pꝛefatus S. W. sigillum suũ ap=
posuit.Alteri vero parti huius charte indentate pe=
nes pꝛefat S.w.remanenꝭ ego pꝛedictus I. w. si=
gillum meum apposui,his testib⁹ ⁊c.Daꝭ ⁊c.

⸿ An other fourme of a dede of fee simple with
condicõn to refeffe the moꝛgageour.

OMNIBVS Chꝛistifidelibus ad quos pꝛesens
scriptum indentatum peruenerit, I.R.de Oꝛ=
oñ salutem.⁊c.Cum C.W.de eadem dederit,conces=
serit et per chartam suam feoffamenti gerẽꝭ daꝭ vl=
timo die Decembꝛis ante datum pñtiũ vltimo pꝛe=
terito michi pꝛefato I. confirmauerit oĩa illa terras
et teñta sua, reuersiones pꝛata pascuas,et pasturas
cum boscis,sepibʒ,fossis,et fossatis , et suis ꝑtiñ que
habuit in villa,et in cãpis de H.in coñ Oꝛoñ. HA=
BEND.et tenenꝺ mihi hered et assign meis imper=
petuum,put in eadem charta sua mihi inde cõfecta,
plenius contineꝭ.Noueritis me pꝛefatũ I.dimisisse
concessisse et hoc pñti scripto meo indentato,confir=
masse pꝺicto C. oĩa illa pꝺicta terras et teñta , red=
ditus,seruic.pꝛata,pascuas,et pasturas,cum boscis,
sepibus,fossis,et fossatis,et suis ꝑtiñ. HABEND.
sibi heredibus et assign suis imppetuum, sub foꝛma
et cõdicõe,sequẽtibʒ, videlicet ꝗ si pꝛedicꝭ⁹ C.soluat
seu solui faciat heredes et executoꝛes sui soluãt, aut
solui faciãt mihi ꝑfato I. attoꝛnato vel executoꝛib⁹
meis in parochiali eccꝛia omniũ Sanctoꝛũ in Oꝛoñ
xx.libꝛas sterling.ad festũ Pasche pꝛoxime futurũ,ꝗ
extũc pñs carta indẽtata , et seisina inde liberata su=
um

um robur obtiniant et effectum . Et ſi defect⁹ fiat in
ſolucõe pdicᵗ biginti libʒaᵗum cõtra foʒmã pʒedictã
ertunc pñs charta indentata et ſeiſina inde liberata
caſſe ſint et bane,ac p nullis habeantur,ꞅ tunc bene
leceat mihi pfato I. heredibʒ et aſſigñ meis in omĩa
pdicta terras,et tenemẽta,redditus,reuerſiones,ſer=
uitia ,pʒata,paſcua,et paſturas,cum ceteris pnomi=
natis et ſuis ptñ reintrare,rehabere,et ea reſeſire,et
retinere, bt in ſtatu meo pʒiſtino.ac pfatum C.here=
des et aſſignatos ſuos inde totaliter erpellere, pſen=
ti charta indẽtata aut ſeiſina inde liberata bllo mo=
do non obſtante. IN CVIVS rei teſtimonium.ꞅc.
bni pti huius indẽture.ꞅc.

But yf there be many dayes of payment then ye may pro
cede after thys fourme folowing

Si pʒedictus C.ſoluat aut ſolui faciat, heredes ſeu ᴐ
erecutoʒes ſui ſoluãt·, aut ſolui faciãt mihi pfato I.
attoʒnato ſeu erecutoʒibus meis in parochiali eccliã
omĩum Sãctoʒum Oroñ biginti libʒas ſterling.in
foʒma ſubſcripta, bidelicet ad feſtum Paſche pʒori=
me futurũ poſt datum pſentium.rrꝫ.ad feſtum Na=
tiuitatis ſci Iohĩs Baptiſte,tũc prime ſequẽtis.rrꝫ
ꞅ ſic de feſto in feſtum , de anno in annum, bnũ poſt
alium continue ſequẽᵗ, ad quodlibet feſtoʒum pdic=
toʒum biginti ſolidos,quouſcꝫ pdicte.rr.libʒe plena
rie pſoluãtur; ertũc pñs charta indẽtata.ꞅc.bt ſupra.
Et ſi defectus fiat in aliqua ſolucõe pdictaʒũ bigin= **Note**
ti libʒaʒum in parte bel in toto,cõtra foʒmã pdictam **thys**
ertunc.ꞅc.bt in charta predicta.Pʒouiſo ſẽp cp ſi pdic= **clauſe.**
tus C.bel aliqnis alius noĩe ſuo allegauerit aliquã
acquietantiam ſeu ſolutionem dcẽ pecunie alibi foʒe
factᵗ cp in eccleſia omnium Sanctoʒũ pʒedicta cõtra
me

The boke of fundry

me pfatum J.ꝙ extunc idem C.bult,et concedit per
pñtes ,ꝙ hmōi acquietañ in foluc.foꝛinfeca nullius
fit baloꝛis . I N C V I V S rei ꝛc.

℃The fourme of a gyfte of a Manour wyth
thaduoufon appendant therunto by the kynge
to a man and to hys heyꝛes males.

REX ꝛc.Oibꝫ ad quos ꝛc.Sal. Sciatis ꝙ nos
ex gfa ñra fpiali et in confideratione veri et fidelis feruitij ꝗd diktus feruiēs uf J.B.nobis pꝛeſti
tit et durante vita fua pꝛeſtare intēdit,dedim⁹ et cō-
ceſſimus,ac tenore pñtium,damus et cōcedim⁹ pꝛefato J. Manerium nf̄m de B.cum fuis membꝛis et
pertiñ in Com nf̄o S.necnon rectoꝛiā de B. in eodē
com S.ac aduocationem eccfie de B.pꝛedict̄ vnacū
oibꝫ et fingulis fuis glebis,decimis,oblacōibꝫ,moꝛ-
tuar̄,poꝛtionibꝫ,penfionibus et alijs pficuis quibꝫ-
cūꝗ eidem rectoꝛie de B.aliquo modo ptiñ fiue fpectañ. Acetiam aduocationem et patronatum vicarie
de B.pꝛedict̄ cum fuis iuribꝫ et pertiñ vniuerfis nec
non oia et fingula mefuagia terras teñt̄ pꝛata paf-
cua paſtur̄ bofcos fubbofcos redditus reuerfiones
molendina feruitia feod militum ward maritag. releuia Efcaetas,coias,aquas,ſtagna baſk̄, warren-
nas,libertat̄ franchef.cuf̄, let.ac pquificōes cuf̄, ad-
uocacōem et pꝛōnatū vicarie de B. pdict̄ ac etiā oia
alia aduocaciones et pꝛōnat̄ eccfiaꝛ capellarum cā-
triarum ac alia iura et hereditament̄ quecūꝗ cū fuis pertiñ vniuerfis in B. pdict̄ ac alibi vbicūꝗ pꝛe-
dict̄ manerio rectoꝛie vicarie feu eoꝛū alicui fpectañ
fiue aliquo modo ptineñ aut que vt membꝛa vel per
cellf̄ eoꝛundem manerij rectoꝛie vicarie fiue eoꝛum a
licuius hit̄ cognit̄ fiue reputat̄ fuerūt Quod quidē
mane-

maneriū de B.necnō ℟ectoꝛia,bicaria terre teñ. et ce
tera omnia et ſingula pꝛemiſſa cū eoꝛū ꝑtineñ . inter
alia ad manus nꝛas deuenerint, ac in manibus nꝛis
tā exiſtūt ratione cuiuſdam finis inter nos , et ℟ .B.
leuaꝼ.pꝛout de recoꝛdo de termino ſancte Trinitatis,
anno regni nꝛi.xxix.plene liquet . Habenð.et tenenð.
oīa ⁊ ſigula ſupꝛadicta maneriū, meſuag.terꝼ.teñta
pꝛata,paſcuas,paſturas,boſcos,ſubboſcos,reditus
reuerſiones,molendina,ſeruitia,feoda militū,warð
maritagia, releuia,eſcaetas coias aquas,ſtagna,ba
ſta,warennas,libertates,francheſias,Curias,lctas
pquiſitiones curie,rectoꝛiā,aduocationes , et patro ⸗
nat⁹ eccꝉiarū,capellarū,cantriarū, et bicariarū ꝓdict
glebas,decimas, oblationes:obuētiōes,moꝛtuaria,
poꝛciones,penciones , ac omnia et ſingula cetera ꝓ⸗
miſſa cū ſuis mēbꝛis et ꝑtineñ bniuerſis pꝛefato ℟.B
et herredibus maſculis de coꝛpoꝛe ſuo legittime pꝛo⸗
creatis. Tenenð de nobis et heredibus nꝛis in capite
per ſeruitium quinte partis bnius feodi militis pꝛo
omni ſeruitio,exactione,et demando quocūꝗ, abſꝗ
compoto ſeu ratiocinio ſiue aliquo alio nobis heredi⸗
bus aut ſucceſſoꝛibus noſtris pꝛo eiiſdem reddendo,
bel faciendo. Et blterius ex bberioꝛi gratia nꝼa de⸗
dimus et conceſſimus,ac tenore pꝛeſentiū damus , et
concedimus pꝛefato ℟.B.omnes et ſingulos exitus,
reddit⁹,firmas,ꝓficua,⁊ emolumenta Manerij,me
ſuagioꝛū,terꝼ.teñꝼ,rectoꝼ.et ceteroꝛum , ꝑmiſſoꝛum
ſupius expꝛeſſoꝛū et ſpecificatoꝛū cum ꝑtineñ a feſto
ſancti Michaelis archāgeli bltimo pꝛeterito hucuſꝗ
ꝓuenientia et creſcentia . Habenð eidem ℟ . ex dono
nꝼo abſꝗ compoto aliquo ve alio ꝑ eiiſdem nobis he
redibus bel ſucceſſoꝛibus nꝛis quoquo modo ſoluen⸗
℮   do

do reddendo exigendo feu faciendo. Eo ꝙ expreſſa
mentio.ꝛc.In cuius rei.ꝛc.

A Charter of fee tayle tripartite.

Ciant preſentes ac futuri ꝙ ego A.B.de Or=
ſoñ.dedi, conceſſi, et hac preſenti Charta mea
tripertita indentata confirmaui C.B.filio meo
totum illud tenementum meum bnacum hozto ſeu
gardino adiacente,et ſuis pertinenciis quod habeo in
tali bico,nempe in parochia diue Marie in Oroñ pre
dicta iacens et ſituatum inter tenementum P.C. ex
parte auſtrali,et tenementum W.M.ex bozialipar=
te,cuius bnum quidem caput abuttat ſuper pomeri=
um P.C.verſus occidentem alterum bero caput eiuſ=
dem abuttat ſuper bicum predictum ozientem berſ.
Habenð et tenenð predictum tenementum cum hozto
ſeu gardino ſuiſꝗ pertinentiis prefato C.B. et here=
dibus de cozpoze eius legittime pzocreatis. Et pzo
defectu heredis de cozpoze dicti C. legittime pzocrea=
to bolo , ꝙ predictum Tenementum cum gardino,
ſuiſꝗ pertineñ D.B.filio meo natu minozi ſeu iunio
ri integre remaneat,hadenð ꝗ tenenð illi et hereð de
cozpoze ſuo legittime pzocreatis , de capitalibus do=
minis feodi. Et pzo defectu heredum de cozpoze ip=
ſius D.legittime pzocreatis , bolo quod predictum
tenementum cum gardino ſeu hozto ſuiſꝗ pertineñ
integre remaneat heredibus legittimis predicti C.
B.imperpetuum. Et ego bero pzonominatus A.B.
et heredes mei predictum tenementum cum gardino
et ſuis pertinentiis prefato C.B.heredibuſꝗ de coz=
poze ſuo legittime pzocreatis in fozma premiſſa con=
tra

tra omnes gentes warantizabimus, et imperpetu=
um defendemus.　　Iu cuius rei teſtimonium dua=
bus quidem partibus huius charte mee tripertite in=
dentate penes pꝛefatos C. et D. remanentibus ſigil=
lum meum appoſui, tertie vero parti eiuſdem charte
penes me pꝛefatum A.B. remanenti, pꝛedicti C. et D
ſigilla ſua appoſuerunt, his teſtibus. ꝛc.

　　Eodem modo de chartis quadꝛipartitis, quin=
quepartitis, et ſimilibus dicendum eſt.

⸿The fourme of a gyſte made in
franke Maryage.

SCiant tam pꝛeſentes quam futuri, me. W. H.
de w. dediſſe et conceſſiſſe, ac pñti charta mea cõ
firmaſſe Ioh. H. filio meo, et Margarete vxo=
ri eius filie vero T. N. in liberum maritagium, vnũ
meſuagium. quod habeo. ꝛc. Habend et tenend pꝛedi=
dictum. ꝛc. pꝛefatis I. et Margarete vxoꝛi ſue, et he=
redibus de eoꝛum coꝛpoꝛibus legittime pꝛocreatis
de me et heredibus meis imperpetuum. Et ego vero
pꝛenominatus W. H. et heredes mei pꝛedictum me=
ſuagium. ꝛc. pꝛefatis I. et Margarete vxoꝛi ſue, et
heredibus de eoꝛumdem coꝛpoꝛibus legittime pꝛo=
creatis contra omnes gentes warantizabimus, ac
aduerſus capitales ac pꝛincipales dominos, ceteroſq̃
vniuerſos acquietabimus et defendemus imperpe=
tuum. In cuius rei teſtimonium huic pꝛeſenti char=
te mee. ꝛc.

⸿An other fourme of a gyſte in
the ſpecyall tayle.

　　　　　　　　C.ii.　　　Dm

The boke of sondzye

Omnibus.&c.dediſſe et cõceſſiſſe ac tenoze pzeſen
tium dare et concedere A.B.totam domum.&c.
habenð,tenenð, et gaudenð dictam domũ . &c.
pzefato A.B . et heredibus maſculis de cozpoze ipſi⁹
A.inter eundem A . et dominam Elizabeth vzozem
eiuſdem A.legittime pzocreatis,et pzocreandis. Tenenð..&c.

An other fozme of a
ſpeciall tayle.

Pateat pñtibus et futuris quod ego A.B.dedi et
conceſſi ac per pzeſentes do et cõcedo chariſſi-
mo mihi in Chzifto Henrico. D . et Anne vzozi
eius Manerium illud meum.&c. Habenð,tenenð, et
fruenð. pzedictum Manerium. &c . pzefatis Henrico
D.et Anne vzozi ſue, ac heredib⁹ maſculis de cozpo-
ribus eozum inter eos legittime pzocreatis.&c.

A dede of fee ſymple made in exchaunge
of two partes,of a Maner,
and aduouſon.

Sciant pzeſentes et futuri me W . S. militem
dediſſe,conceſſiſſe,et hac pzeſéti charta mea in
dentata confirmaſſe Iohanni S . militi duas
partes manerij mei de C.in comitatu B.cum omnib⁹
natiuis meis ac mancipijs et eozum ſequela tam pzo-
creata ꝙ pcreanda vna cũ omnibus terris, fundis et
tenementis,redditibus et ſeruiciis tam liberis ꝙ ſer-
uilibus ſeu natiuis:ac cũ tribus molendinis,quozum
bnũ eſt aquaticũ,duo vero bétilia,necnõ cũ ſecta mul
ture tam liberozũ quã natiuozũ, vna cum pzatis paſ-
cuis, paſturis, viis, ſemitis , ripis, aquis , piſcinis,
ſtagnis,biuarijs,turbarijs,hoztis, pomeriis, gardi-
nis,

nis, curtilagiis, homagijs, wardis, maritagijs, com-
munijs, boſcis, ſubboſcis, warennis, moꝛis, mariſcis
releuijs, eſcaetis, curijs, ꝗ ſectis curie, cū biſu franciplegij, cūꝗ alijs ſuis iuribus ptinentiis, conſuetudi-
nibus, libertatibus, cōmoditatibus, ꝗ emolumentis
quibuſcūꝗ, eidem Manerio ſpectantibus. Dedi in-
ſuper ꝗ conceſſi pꝛefato Johanni S. aduocatiōe eccleſie de E. pꝛedicto Manerio ſpectantem, necnon re-
uerſionē tertie partis pꝛedicti manerij quā quidē ter-
tiā partēꝭicta mater mea tenet ratione ac noie dotis
ſue, cū acciderit nempe poſt deceſſum eiuſdē Alicie.
Habend. ꝗ tenend pꝛedictas duas partes manerij pꝛe
dicti cū omnibus natiuis ſeu billanis meis. ꝗc. bna cū
aduocatione dicte eccleſie, ac reuerſiōnē tertie partis
pꝛedicti Manerij, cū acciderit, pꝛenominato Johanni
heredib⁹ ꝗ aſſignatis ſuis imperpetuū, in cōmutatio-
nē ſeu excambiū plenāꝗ recompenſatiōnē pꝛo Manerio ſuo de H. M. in com Oꝛon, quod ego habeo ex
dono ꝗ feoffamento pꝛefati Johānis per excambium
pꝛedictū, de capitalibus dominis feodi illius per ſeruitia inde debita ꝗ de iure conſueta, ſub foꝛma ꝗ conditione ſequenti, videlicet, ſi pꝛedictum Maneriū de
H. cū ſuis pertinentijs, bel aliqua eiuſdē parcella im-
poſterū ac deinceps, a me, bel heredibus meis, aut a
meis aſſignatis iuſto titulo ꝗ ex antiquo tempoꝛe mo
to per legis pceſſum ꝗ iudiciū in Curia dn̄i regis red
ditū, ſeu reddendū, recuperetur, aut per ſtatutū Sta-
pule bel mercatoꝛis, recognitiōnē, bel conceſſiōnē annuitatis ante hec tempoꝛa per poſſeſſoꝛes dicti manerij de H. fact ſeu cognitum oneretur ſeu extendatur ꝗ
extunc bene liceat mihi pꝛefato W. heredibus ꝗ aſſignatis meis, pꝛedictū Maneriū de C. cū oibus na-

tiuis meis ⁊ eoꝛum sequela.⁊c.vna cū aduocatione et
reuersione pꝛedict reseisire,reintrare,⁊ ea rehabere et
retinere,vt in statu meo pꝛistino, hac pꝛesenti charta
mea indentata,ac seisina inde liberata tradita be vllo
modo nō obstáte.Et ego sane pꝛedictus W.⁊ heredes
mei pꝛedictū maneriū de C. cū oībus natiuis meis et
eoꝛū sequela.⁊c. vna cū aduocatione. ⁊c. ac reuersione
tertie partis.⁊c.cū acciderit,pꝛefato Johanni heredi=
bus ⁊ assignatis suis in foꝛma pꝛemissa, cōtra omnes
gentes warrantizabimus pꝛestabimus ⁊ imperpetuū
defendemus. Jn cuius rei testimoniū.⁊c.vni quidem
parti huius charte mee indentate penes pꝛefatū Jo=
hannē C.remanenti sigillum meū apposui,alteri be=
ro parti eiusdem charte.⁊c.

⁋An other foꝛme of an
exchaunge.

EX,oībus ad quos.⁊c. salutē. Sciatis quod nos
tam in cōtemplatiōe boni ⁊ fidelis seruitij no=
bis per dilectū famulū nostrū Joannē C.in com̄
nostro Surꝛ generosum antehac pꝛestiti ⁊ impensi,
quā in consideratione ac in plenā recompensationem
cuiusdā mesuagij cū pertinentiis bocati W.per dictū
Joannē C.nobis heredibus ⁊ successoꝛibꝰ nr̄is imper
petuū nuper dati et benditi,ac etiā in cōsideratiōe cen
tū libꝛarū legalis monete Anglie nobis ⁊ ad vsum no
strū per ipsum Joannē C.heredes,executoꝛes,bel ad=
ministratoꝛes suos solutarū ⁊ soluendarū, de gratia
nostra speciali.⁊c.dedimus ⁊ cōcessimus. ⁊c. maneriū
nostrum de N.⁊c.

⁋A Charter foꝛ terme of lyfe,of a Mesuage,
wythout impechement of wast.

Sciant

Ciant pꝛeſentes ⁊ futuri quod ego Walterus
H.de Waltā. ꝛc. Ricardo L. bnū meſuagiū cū
curtilagio adiacente ⁊ tribus acris terre,⁊ bno
crofto adiacente nimirū inter terras. ꝛc. Habend pꝛe=
dictū meſuagiū cū curtilagio.ꝛc. pꝛefato Richardo ad
terminū bite ſue de me ⁊ heredibus meis abſcꝫ impe=
titione baſti,reddend inde annuatim mihi ⁊ heredib⁹
meis bnā roſam rubeā,ſi tamē petatur,ad feſtū ſancti
Johannis Baptiſte.ꝛc.Et faciend ſectā Curie mee de
W.de menſe in menſem pꝛo oibus alijs ſeruitijs, ex=
actionib⁹ et demandis,toties quoties dicta curia mea
teneri contigerit.Et poſt deceſſum pꝛedicti Richardi,
tunc pꝛedictū meſuagiū cū curtilagio.ꝛc.mihi pꝛefato
Waltero heredibus ⁊ aſſignatis meis imperpetuū
reuertatur abſcꝫ impetitione baſti.Et ego bero pꝛefa=
tus walterus ⁊ heredes mei pꝛedictū meſuagiū cum
curtilagio.ꝛc. pꝛefato Ricardo ad terminū bite ſue p
ſeruitia ſuperius dicta ⁊ expꝛeſſa,contra omnes gen=
tes warrantizabim⁹,tuebimur, ⁊ defendemus p pꝛe=
ſentes. In cui⁹ rei teſtimoniū bni parti hui⁹ pꝛeſentis
charte mee ſigillū.ꝛc.alteri bero parti.ꝛc.

¶ A graunt foꝛ terme of lyfe of manours woyth thap=
purtinaunces to a ſpūal perſon woyth a diſpenſa=
tion of the ſtatute made.xxi.Henrici.biij.

Ex,Oib⁹ ad quos.ꝛc.ſalutē Sciatis qð nos.ꝛc.
Roberto F. clerico maneria dominia ⁊ tenemē=
ta nꞇa de M.ꝛc.Ac oīa ⁊ ſingula edificia,domos
gardina,terras,tenemēta,pꝛata,paſcuas,paſturas,
boſcos, ſubboſcos ac reddit⁹ ⁊ ſeruitia oīm ⁊ ſingulo
rū tenentiū tā liberoꝛū ꝙ natiuoꝛū ac tenentiū per co
pias Rotuloꝛum Curiarum et ceteroꝛum tenentium
cuſtuma=

custumarioꝛū ꟻ tenentiū ad terminū bite bel ad ter‡
minos annoꝛū ac omnes ꟻ singulos redditus ꟻ fir‡
mas super quibuscunꝗ dimissionibus, concessionib⁹
siue traditionibus de pꝛemissis bel eoꝛū aliquo factis
quouis modo reseruatas.Et insuper reuersiones,feo
da militū, wardas, maritagia, Curias, letas, bisus
franciplegij,et omnia ea que ad bisum francipleg.per‡
tineñ,fines,amerciamenta,exitus,pꝛoficua, warren‡
nas,aquas,piscarias,libertates,franchessas,cōmodi
tates,emolumenta,ꟻ hereditamenta nostra quecunꝗ
cū suis pertineñ,dictis Maneriis,dominijs, et tene‡
mentis de N.ꟻc. ꟻ eoꝛū cuilibet siue eoꝛū alicui per‡
tineñ siue spectañ seu percellā aut percellas eoꝛun‡
dem aut eoꝛū.alicuius existeñ aut foꝛe reputaꞇ.Et bl
terius. ꟻc. Rectoꝛiam nostram ecclesie pochialis de
N. ꟻc.

Habenꝺ ꟻ tenenꝺ omnia et singula pꝛedicta Mane
ria.ꟻc.pꝛefato Roberto et assignatis suis pꝛo termi‡
no et ad terminum bite ipsius Roberti.

Tenenꝺ de nobis heredibus ꟻ successoꝛibus no‡
stris per fidelitatem ꟻ redditū. xl. libꝛar. ꟻc. Pꝛo om‡
nibus seruitijs redditibus et demandis quibus‡
cunꝗ.ꟻc.

Ac insuper de gratia nostra pꝛedicta bolumus et
per pñtes pꝛo nobis heredibus ꟻ successoꝛibus no‡
stris licentiam facultatemꝗ specialem pꝛefato R.da‡
mus ꟻ concedim⁹,quod idem R. et assignati eius om
nia ꟻ singula pꝛedicta maneria Mesuagia terras, te‡
nementa,pꝛata,pascuas,pasturas,boscos subboscos,
redditus , reuersiones reuentiones seruitia ꟻcetera
pꝛemissa cum suis pertineñ birtute et bigoꝛe harum
literarū pateñ habere gaudere et tenere possit ꟻ ba‡
leat

leat pro termino bite ipsius. R. erga nos heredes et
successozes nostros, quodam statuto in anno bicesimo
przimo regni nostri edito spiritualibus seu ecclesiasti=
cis personis concernente atcp spectante per quod qui
dem statutu ozdinatu et stabilitu existit inter alia, qd
nulla spualis seu ecclesiastica persona secularis bel
regularis cuiuscuncp gradus existit, deinceps ad fir=
ma recipere possit-sibi bel alicui persone bel aliqui=
bus personis ad eius bsum, ex dimissione seu conces=
sione nostra aut alicuius siue aliquaru aliaru persona
rum per literas patentes, Indenturas, scripta, ber=
ba, bel quocuncp alio modo, aliqua maneria, terras,
tenementa, seu alia hereditamenta ad terminu bite,
annozu, bel ad boluntate sub pena in eodem actu ex=
przessa, non obstante. Ac quod idem Robertus z assig=
nati sui omnia z singula Maneria przedicta, fundos,
terras, tenementa ceteracp przemissa bniuersa, habere
tenere z occupare possit z baleat pro termino bite ip=
sius R. abscp aliquibus przimis fructibus pro przemis=
sis seu aliqua inde percella nobis heredibus bel suc=
cessozibus nostris pro eiisdem reddend soluend seu fa
ciend, aliquo statuto ozdinatione, siue przouisione seu
aliqua alia re, causa, bel materia quacuncp in contra=
riu huius edito seu przouiso, non obstanti. zc.

✠ Here after ensue di=
uerse fozmes and maners of leases.

¶ The fozme of a lease by indentur of a tene=
ment in London oz elles where.
                                        f   Thys

Hys indenture made the .xrvi.day of A=
pzil in the .xrriiij.yere of our soueraigne
Lozde kynge Henry the eyght betwene
W.P.Citizen & Goldsmyth of London
master of the gild oz fraternitie of saint
N.founded within the parysh church of saint.N.Ri=
chard A.& R.C.citezens & marchaut tailours of Lon
don, wardens of the sayd gild oz fraternitie on thone
parte,& R.S.of Londo esquyer on thother parte,wit
nesseth,that the sayd master & wardeyns foz the and
theyz successours wyth thassent wyl & cosent of all the
bzethern & susters of the sayd fraternitie oz gyld haue
graunted dimised & to ferme letten to the sayd R. S.
by these pzesentes all that theyz mesuage oz tenement
& gardeyn theruto adioynynge wo sellers solders & al
other appourtenauces therto bilongyng called A.B.
set & beyng in fletestrete afozsayd in p sayd paryshe of
s.N.that is to wit betwene the tenemet perteynyng
to the Deane & Canons of the kynges Chappell of
sainct Stephanes wythin the palace in Westmon=
ster nowe in the holdyng of J.C. on the este part and
a tenemet perteynyng to the sayd fraternitie now in
the tenure of T.U.on the West parte and the gardes
perteynyng to the crafte oz mystery of Goldsmythes
of Londo in the Nozth parte & the tenementes per=
teynynge to the sayd fraternitie wherin J.D. ware
chaundelour and J.F.gentleman nowe dwel on the
south parte. To haue and to holde the sayde mesuage
oz tenemet and other the pzemisses aboue lette with
thappourtenauces to the sayd R. S. hys executours
and assignes from the feast of Thanunciation of our
blessed Ladye the virgine latte past befoze the date
herof

herof vnto the ende and terme of.ｒｒｒ. yeares thē next
enſuynge and fullye to be complete,yeldynge and pa=
ynge therefoꝛe yearly durynge the ſayde terme to the
ſayde Maſtre and wardeyns and to theyꝛ ſucceſſours
oꝛ aſſygnes foure poundes of good and lawefull mo=
ney of Englande at foure termes of the yeare that is
to ſaye, at the feaſtes of the natiuitie of ſaynt John
Baptyſt, ſainte Michael tharchꝛangell, the natiuitie
ef oure loꝛde God,and thannunciation of our Ladye
the virgine by euen poꝛtions. And yf it happen the
ſayde yearly rent of foure poundes to be behynde vn=
payde in parte oꝛ in all by the ſpace of one moneth
next after anye of the ſayde feaſtes of payment at the
whyche it ought to be payde ,that than it ſhalbe lau=
full to the ſayde mayſter and wardeyns and theyꝛ
ſucceſſours into the ſayde meſuage oꝛ tenement and
other the pꝛemiſſes aboue letten wyth thappourte=
naunces and euery percell therof to entre ⁊ diſtrayne,
⁊ ꝑ diſtreſſes ſo there takē lefully to beare, lede,dꝛyue
and carye awey,and the ſame to wytholde and kepe
vntyll they of the ſayde pearlye rent and euerye per=
cell thereof wyth the areragies of the ſame, yf anye
be, vnto them be fullye contented , ſatiſfyed and
payde. And the ſayde R. S. foꝛ hym hys executours
and aſſygnes couenaunteth and graunteth to ⁊ wyth
the ſayde mayſtere and wardeyns and theyꝛ ſucceſ=
ſours by theſe pꝛeſentes that he the ſame R. S. hys
execꝛtours and aſſygnes at his ⁊ theyꝛ pꝛopꝛe coſtes
and charges the ſaid meſuage oꝛ tenement and other
the pꝛemiſſes aboue letten wyth thappourtenaunces
wyth the pauementes and wydꝛaughtes of the ſame
in and by all thynges well and ſufficientlye ſhall re=

pare, susteyne, maynteyne, skoure, and clense as of
ten as neade shall requyze, durynge the sayde terme,
And the same so repared, scoured and clensed wyth
all glasse wyndowes, yzon, dozes, lockes, and keyes
(as it is thereof and therwyth nowe fully furnisshed
and garnished) at thend of the same terme shall leaue
and yelde vp.   And it shalbe lawefull to the sayde
Master and wardeyns and theyz successours at all
tymes, durynge the sayde terme at theyz libertie
and pleasure to come and entre into the sayde mesuage oz tenemente and other the pzemisses aboue
letten wyth thappurtenaunces and euery percell ther
of, there to vewe and serche what reparations shalbe nedefull to be made and doon, and vpon suche
vewe and serche had, the sayde R. S. foz hym hys
executours and assignes couenaunteth and graunteth to and wyth the sayde mayster and wardeyns
and theyz successours by these pzesentes, that he the
same. R. hys executours and assygnes at hys and
theyz pzoper costes and charges shall, durynge the
sayde terme wythin one quarter of a yeare next after
monition and knowlege to hym oz them gyuen, by ẏ
sayde mayster and wardeyns oz theyz successours,
well and sufficientlye from tyme to tyme repare and
amend all suche defaultes and lackes of reparations
as there shall happen to be founde, and that he the
same R. hys executours and assygnes, durynge the
sayd terme, shall peacibly and quietly pmitte & suffre
the sayde T. U. and all other tenauntes of the sayde
fraternitie dwellynge there aboute, to haue, vse, and
enioye all suche lyghtes, pentesses, and other easemẽ-
tes as now be and apperteyne to theyz seuerall tenementes

mentes oz manſions without any ſtoppyng, darke-
nyng, appeyzyng, bzeakyng, hurting, oz diminiſhyng,
and wythoute lette, interruption, oz diſturbaunce of
the ſame R.his executours oz aſſignes, oz of anye o-
ther perſon oz perſones by his oz theyz commaundement oz pzocurement.

AND it ſhall not be lawfull to the ſayde Rycharde
S.his executours noz aſſignes to bargayne, graunt,
alien, lette oz ſette his leaſe, intereſt, oz terme of and
in the ſayde meſſuage and other the pzemiſſes aboue
letten, noz any parcell thereof to any perſon oz perſones, durynge the ſayde terme, but onely at wyl from
yere to yere, without the conſent & agremente of the
ſayde maſter and wardens, oz theyz ſucceſſours fyzſt
had and obteyned in wzytyng vnder the comune ſeal
of the ſayde fraternitie. AND the ſayde maſter and
wardens foz them and theyz ſucceſſours, couenaunte
and graunte to and with the ſayde R. S. his executours and aſſignes by theſe pzeſentes, that the ſame
maſter and wardeins, and theyz ſucceſſours at theyz
pzopze coſtes and charges ſhall beare and pay al maner quyte rentes yf any ſuche be, due oz to be due, and
goinge out of and foz the ſayde meſſuage oz tenemēt
and other the pzemiſſes aboue letten, duryng the ſaid
terme, and thereof ſhall acquyte, diſcharge, and ſaue
harmeles the ſayde R.S.his executours and aſſignes durynge the ſame terme by theſe pzeſentes.

AND the ſayde maſter and wardeins foz them and
theyz ſucceſſours couenaunt and graunt to and wyth
the ſayde R.S. by theſe pzeſentes, that yf the ſame
R.his executours and aſſygnes, well and truly kepe,
perfourme and fulfyll al and euery the couenauntes,

F.iij.   graun

grauntes, agrementes, articles, & paymentes aboue
reherſed which on his and theyr part are to be holdē
perfourmed, fulfylled and kept, then an obligatiō of
the date hereof, wherin the ſayde K. S. ſtandeth and
is boūden to the ſayd maſter and wardeins and their
ſucceſſours in the ſume of. xl. li. ſterlyng ſhalbe boyde
and of none effect. In wytnes wherof, to thone parte
of thys indenture remaynyng wyth the ſayd maſter
and wardeyns and theyr ſucceſſours, the ſayd. K. S.
hath put hys ſeale, and to thother pte of the ſame indenture remaynyng wͦ the ſame K. the ſayd maſter &
wardeyns haue put theyr cōmon ſeale of the ſayd fra
ternitie. Gyuen the daye and yere aboue wrytten.

⸿ A copye of a leaſe made by a perſon of a
paryſh churche, of his perſonage. &c.

This Indenture made the. xx. daye of March, in
the. &c. betwene I. C. deane of ỹ college of ſaynt
S. in ỹ coūtie of M. & pſon of ỹ pyſh churche of
G. wͦin the lordſhip of B. in N. of the one parrie. And
T. B. gentlemā of the other partie. Wytneſſeth that
the ſayd I C. pſon of the piſh aforeſayd hath dimiſed
graunted, and by theſe preſentes for hím & his ſucceſ
ſours pſons of the ſame pariſh church dimiſeth, grau
teth, & to ferme letteth vnto the ſaid T. B. all that the
forſayd pariſh church and pſonage of G. aforeſayd &
al that the mancion place of the ſayde pſonage wͦ all
houſes, barnes, ſtables, and other edifices therunto
in any maner wyſe apteynynge or belongynge, togyther wͦ al gieblandes & all other landes, tenementes,
rētes, reuercións, ſeruices, tythes, porcions, ānuities,
free Chapelles, oblacions, offrynges, frutes, obuen-
cions: emolumentes, cōmodities, profites, caſualties
and

and aduautages to the sayd pish churche ℈ psonage,
and eyther of them,or to the sayd J.C,by reasō ther=
of in any maner wyse appteynyng or belongyng ex=
cept ℈ reserued vnto ẏ sayd J.C. and his successours
psons there,duryng ℈ for such tyme onely,as ẏ same
J.C.or his successours parsons there,shalbe psonal=
ly resident and abydyng on the sayd psonage these p=
cels of the pmisses hereafter folowyng,that is to say
the hall,a great chābre ouer the same hall,ẏ butterie,
the larder,the kytchyn,with all chābres ouer ẏ same
kytchyn,butterie and larder , togyther with a stable
parcell of the premisses. TO HAUE and to holde
all the sayd parysh churche and personage and all o=
ther the pmisses wᵗ all and singuler theyr apurtenaū
ces aboue letten (except in maner and fourme before
excepted)vnto the sayde T. B. his executours , and
assignes frō the feast of the annunciation of our lady
saynt Mary next cōmyng after the date of these pre=
sēt indētures vnto thende and terme of.rr.yeres then
next and immediatly folowyng, ℈ fully frōhēceforth
to be cōplete and ended. YELDING and payinge
therfore yerely duryng the sayde terme of.rri.yeres,
vnto the sayd. J.C. and his successours psons of the
sayd church one yearelye rent of lrrr.li . of good and
lawfull money of Englande to be payed yerely at.ij.
termes in the yere,that is to say at the feastes of saint
Mighel Tharchangell, and the annunciacion of our
lady saynt Mary by euen porcions.or wᵗin.rr. dayes
next and imediatly ensuinge either of ẏ same feastes,
which sayde yerely rent of.lrrr.the sayde T.B. coue=
uaunteth and graunteth by these presentes to and wᵗ
the sayd J.C. truly to content and pay yerely vnto ẏ

A clause of
reseruation

              F.iiij.   sayde

fayd. J.C. at þ dwelling houfe of þ fayd. J.C. at faint
S. afoɀefayd at the feaſtes & dayes of paymēt afoɀefayd oɀ wꞵin þ fpace of.xx. dayes next & immediatlye
enfuinge the fame feaſtes and dayes of payment foɀ
and by all fuche tyme as the fayde J.C. fhall contynue and be perſon of the fayde churche of G. AND
the fayd J.C. and hys fucceſſours perſons of þ fayd
churche of G. couenaunteth and graunteth to and wꞵ
the fayde T.B. his executours and aſſignes by theſe
pɀefentes, that he the fayde J.C. and his fucceſſours
parſons of the fayde churche of G. at hys and theyɀ
coſtes, charges, and expéces, fhal from tyme to tyme
as often as nede fhal requyɀe, duryng the fayd terme
of, xxi.yeres, well and fufficyently mayntayn, repayɀ
make and amende afwell the Chauncell of the fayde
churche and all other thynges thereunto belongyng,
as the fayde manſion houſe, ſtables, barnes, & other
edifices, the reparaunce of thatchyng, and dawbyng
of them onely except, which thatchyng & dawbing þ

A clauſe foɀ fayde T.B. his executours and aſſignes, at theyɀ pɀo
diſmes, fub per coſtes and charges fhall repayɀe, make and amēd
ſidies and durynge the fayde terme. AND alſo the fayde J.C.
other char- foɀ hym and his fucceſſours perſons of þ fayd church
ges. of G, at theyɀ pɀopɀe coſtes, charges & expenſes, fhal
beare & pay al maner diſmes, fubſidies, graūtes, ſū-
mes of moneye, & other charges whatſoeuer they be,
afwel now graūted oɀ hereafter to be graūted, to our
foueraygne loɀd the kyng, his heyɀes and fucceſſours
as all other oɀdinarie charges to any other perſon oɀ
perſons due oɀ to be due, and nowe goinge out of the
faid paryſh church and perſonage oɀ of any other the
pɀemiſſes, oɀ wherewith the pɀemiſſes oɀ anye parte
therof

therof be oz may be charged , and that the sayd J.C.
and his successours parsons there , shall therof and
of euery parte thereof clerely acquyte,discharge,saue
and kepe harmelesse the sayd T.B. hys executours &
assignes,duryng the sayde terme,except proxces and
Sinages of the premisses befoze letten, which p said
T. foz hym, his executours and assignes promitteth
and graunteth to beare and pay during p sayd terme.
AND the sayde T.B. couenaunteth and graunteth
to and w the sayde J.C. and his successours parsons
there by these presentes, that he the same T. his executours and assignes at theyz propze costes and charges durynge the sayde terme , shall fynde an hable &
sufficient pzeest to serue and kepe the cure at N.being
a membze oz chapel of the sayd psonage to synge and
saye diuyne seruyce daylye, and there to mynistre di-
uine sacramentes and sacramentals to the parishens
there inhabityng,during the terme afozesayd.AND
also it is agreed betwene the sayde partyes , that the
same T.B.noz his executours ne assignes , shall not
sell,gyue,ne graunte, durynge the sayde terme anye
parte of the woodes belongyng to the sayd psonage
ne cutte downe any parte thereof,but onely foz the ne
cessary housebote,hedgebote,plowbote,and fyzewod
to be spent onely in,vpon,and aboute the premisses.
AND YF IT FORTUNE the sayd yerely ferm
of lrrr.li. oz any parte thereof to be behynde and not
payed by the space of syre monethes next after any of
the sayde feastes oz dayes of paymente , in whiche it
ought to be payed in maner and fourme afozesayde,
that then it shalbe lefull to the sayd J.and his successours parsons there into the sayd churche and perso-

G   nage,

nage, and into all and singuler other the premisses,
with theyr appurtenaunces aboue letten holy to reentre, and thereof the sayde T. his executours, and
assygnes vtterly to expell and put oute, and the same
to haue and repossede agayne, as in theyr former a-
state, thys Indenture or any thynge therein conteyned, to the contrarye not withstandynge.
IN WITNES whereof the partyes aforesayde
to these present Indentures interchaungeablye haue
sette to theyr seales the daye and yere aboue written.

Ye shall note, that yf any fyne or porcion of
money be payed on the behalfe of the fermer for thobteynynge of the lease, then it
were not amysse to expresse the same, in
the lease after this sorte.

This Indenture made the.&c.betwene A. B. &c.
on thone parte, and C. D.&c. on thother parte,
wytnesseth, that the sayde A. B. for a certayne
sume of money to hym by the sayde C. D. in hande cō
tented and payed, whereof the sayde A.B. knowledgeth hym self to be fully satisfied, contented and payed, and the sayde C. his heyres, executours, and assygnes, thereof to be acquyte and discharged for euer,
by these presentes, hathe dimised, graunted, and to
ferme letten.&c.

The fourme of a lease made by a Deane
and Chapter, of a parsonage appropriate.

THIS Indenture made betwene B. F.
deane of the College of M. in the coūtye
of S. and the chapter of the same college
of the one partie, and Nicolas L. of A.

iii

in the same countie of S.squyer of the other partye.
Wytnesseth,that the sayd deane and chapter w̄ hole
mynde,voyce,and assent,haue graunted,and to ferm
letten to the sayde N.his heyres and assignes, theyr
parsonage of A.aforesayde,w̄ all theyr laye fee lādes
and other the appurtenaūces to the same belongyng,
w̄in the sayd piish of A.and C.(the aduouson of p̄ vi-
carege,wardes,mariages,harietes,relieffes,wodes
and vnderwodes, to the sayde deane and chapter alwayes except and reserued) To haue and to holde al
the premisses(excepte before excepted)to the sayd N.
his heyres,executours,or assignes,from thee feast of
Chriistmas last past before the date of this indenture
to the ende and terme of.xxi.yeres then next ensuing.
YELDING and payinge yerely therfore.ix.li. of
good and lawfull moneye of Englande,by euen porcyons,that is to saye, at the feaste of the Natiuitie
of saynct John Baptyst, and Chryystmas. And the
sayde Deane and Chapter,shall paye and discharge
the sade N.his executours and assignes to the kynge
our soueraygne lorde of all maner of dymes or other
dutyes due graunted,or hereafter graunted, duryng
the sayde terme,and also the sayde Deane and Chapter shall mayntayne,sustayne,and kepe , all maner
of reparacyons necessarye for the Mansion house of
the sayde parsonage, and euery parcell thereof.
AND ALSO of the Chauncell , and of the sayde
churche of A.as moche as shal belonge to the charge
of the sayde Deane and Chapter , all tymes when
nede shall requyre duryng the sayd terme.And p̄ sayd
deane and chapter graūt by these presentes, that the

sayd N. his heyres and assignes shall haue yerely du
rynge the sayde terme, necessary fyrebote, hedgebote,
housebote, cartebote, and ploughebote, for the sayde
house, landes, and for occupyinge the sayde lande, to
be taken within theyr sayde grounde belongynge to
the sayde grounde and parsonage durynge the sayde
terme without strippe or waste. And the foresayd N.
couenaunteth and graūteth by these presentes, that he
nor none other for hym shall pay no maner of tythes
nor otherwyse to the vicare of A. for the sayde deane
and chapter other then of olde custome hath wont to
be payed, without the licence of the sayde deane and
chapter. Furthermore it is agreed by these presentes,
that yf it fortune the foresayde rent or ferme, or anye
parcell thereof to be behynde vnpayde by the space of
one hole moneth next ensuynge anye of the sayde feastes before limited, that then it shalbe lawfull to the
sayde deane and chapter, and to theyr successours and
theyr assignes in theyr parsonage and euerye parcell
thereof to entre and to distreine, and the distresses so
taken, to reteine tyll suche tyme as the foresayde rent
or ferme be fully to them satisfyed, contented & payd.
AND the sayde N. couenaunteth and agreeth, that
yf it happen the sayde rent or ferme to be behynde vn
payed, or anye parcell thereof by the space of thre monethes next ensuinge any or the sayde feastes. That
then it shalbe lawfull to the foresayde deane & chapter, and to theyr successours, into theyr sayde personage, and every parcell thereof to reentre, and to distreyne the sayde N. his heyres, executours, and assignes, & them thereof to put out & amoue, this Inden
ture in any wyse notwithstandyng. AND ALSO
the

the ſayde N.couenaunteth by theſe pꝛeſentes that the
manſtone houſe of the ſayde perſonage ſhall yearelye
durynge the ſayde terme be inhabited and houſholde
kept in it, ⁊ that the Coꝛne and grayne that groweth
yearelye in the landes of the ſayde parſonage ſhalbe
layed in the barnes and houſeyng of the ſayde parſonage. In wytnes whereof the parties afoꝛeſayde in-
terchangeablye haue putto theyꝛ ſeales the daye and
moneth and yeare aboue ſayde.

℄ The fourme of a leaſe of grayne whyche the
fermer ought to paye to hys leſſour wyth
a clauſe of defeſaunce of the hole leaſe
foꝛ lacke of payment of the rent.

Ec indentura facta inter dñm regem er v-
ra parte, ⁊ J. C. militem er altera parte,
teſtatur quod idem dñs rer per aduiſame
tum conſilij curie augmentationum reuen
tionū Coꝛone ſue, tradidit, conceſſit, et ad firmā dimi-
ſit pꝛefato J.C. omnia illa ducenta quarteria oꝛdei et
quadꝛaginta quarteria frumenti boni ⁊ ſuauis grani
que firmarius ſeu firmarij rectoꝛie de O. ⁊ H. in comi
tatu L. parcelle poſſeſſionū nuper monaſterij de N. in
Comitatu Eboꝛ pꝛo et nomie redditus ſiue annualis
firme eiuſdē rectoꝛie dcō domino regi annuatim reddere et deliberare debent ſeu debet. HABEN-
DUM gaudendū et annuatim percipiendū oꝛdeū
et frumentū pꝛedictū pꝛefato J. C. et aſſignatis ſuis
a feſto ſancti Marci Euāgeliſte vltimo pꝛeterito vſqꝛ
ad finem termini ⁊ per terminū viginti et vnius an-
noꝛum ertunc pꝛorimo ſequentiū ⁊ plenarie complen

G iij dozum,

dozum, reddendo inde annuatim dicto domino regi
heredibus et successozibus suis quadzaginta libzas.
riij.s.iiij.d.legalis monete Anglie, videlicet pzo pdi:
ctis ducentis quarterijs ozdei triginta libzas, et pzo
pzedictis quadzaginta quarteriis frumenti decem li:
bzas. riij.s.iiij.d.ad festa scti Marci euageliste et scti
Martini in hieme vel infra vnum mesem post vtrucz
festum festozum illozum ad Curiã pzedictã per equa
les perciones soluendas durante termino pzedicto.
Pzouiso semper quod si contigerit pzedictum redditũ
aretro soze insolutũ per spaciũ vnius mensis post ali:
quem diem solutionis eiusdem superius expzessum,
si debito modo petatur, quod tũc hec pzesens dimissio
vacua sit ac pzo nullo habeatur, aliquo in pzesenti di:
missione contento in contrariũ inde non obstante. In
cuius rei.rc.

¶A lyke fourme in Englyshe.

His endenture made betwene A.B.of
London gent.on thone pte, and C.D.of
N.in the countie of N. yomã on that o:
ther pte.Wytnesseth, that the sayd A.B
hath grãuted, dimised ꝗ to ferme letten
to the fozsayd C. D. all those one hundzeth quarters
of whete, and two hundzeth quarters of Barley of
good and swete grayne, whyche the fermour oz fer:
mours of the personage of N. in the countie of N.
ought yearly to paye and delyuer to the sayd A B. foz
and by the name of rent oz yearly ferme of the sayde
parsonage. To haue, enioye and yearly to perceyue ꝑ
wheate and barley afozsayde to the sayd C. D. ꝗ hys
assygnes frõ the feast of saint M.rc.Yelding ꝗ payng
ther:

therfoze yearly to the fayd A. B. hys erecutours and
affygnes thze fcoze pound.&c.Pzouyded alweys,that
yf it chaunce the fayde yearely rente of. lr.li. to be be
hynde vnpayde by the fpace of one moneth after anye
day of payment of the fame befoze erpzeffed and fpe=
cifyed,yf it be in due maner demaūded, then thys pze
fent leafe,immediatly to ceafe and ftande voyde and
of no fozce ne vertue,any thyng in thys pzefent inden
ture to the contrary herof in any wyfe not wytftan=
dyng. In wytnes wherof the parties afozfayd. &c.

**C The fourme of a very perfecte leafe of fundzy lozd=
chyps wyth diuerfe claufes of couenauntes.**

Hys indenture made the laft day of Apzil in þ
rrriiij.yere of þ reygne of our moft dzad foue=
raygne lozd henry þ eyght by þ grace of God
kyng of Englād fraūce & Pzelād defenfour of þ faith
& in erth vnder Chzift of þ church of Englād & pzelād
the fupzeme head,betwene mayfter John P.doctour
of Ciuile law,deane of the colledge.&c.& the canōs of
the fame Colledge on thone partie & A.D.of T.in the
countie of buk. gentlemā on thother ptye,witneffeth
þ the fayd deane & canōs by theyz hole & mutual affēt
confent,wyl,and agriement haue dimifed,graunted,
and to ferme letten, and by thefe pzefentes do foz thē
and theyz fucceffours dimiſe, graunt, & to ferme let,
vnto the fayd A.theyz manfion oz dwellynge place of
theyz manour oz lozdchyp of T. afozfayd in the fayde
countie of buck. late called the pziozy of T. wyth all
the ftyte and circuite of the fame manfiō,& al howfes,
buyldynges, yerdes, clofes, ozcheyardes gardens,
poundes,

pondes, and stewes conteyned wythin the same stite
oz circuite, together wyth al the demeane landes, leas
ues, medowes, and pastures, wyth all and singuler
thappourtenaunces to the sayde mansion oz dwellynge place manour oz lozdshyppe oz to any parte oz
parcell of them, oz to any of the belongynge oz in any
wyse apperteynyng. And also all and singuler theyz
landes, tenementes, medowes, leasues, pastures, cō-
mens, fyshynges, with al other easementes, pzofites,
and comodities, and all other theyz hereditamentes,
what so euer they be, set lyenge and beynge wythin
the towne and feldes of T. aforesayde. And also all
those theyz two mylles called. ꝛc. wyth all and singuler theyz appourtenaunces, pzofytes, and commodities and all other theyz mesuages, landes, tenementes, medowes, pastures, comens, easementes,
pzofytes, and cōmodities, wyth all and singuler rentes, reuersions, remaynders, and seruices of all the
tenauntes aswell freholders, as tenauntes foz yeres,
oz from yere to yeare, copie holders tenauntes at wil
oz otherwyse, set lyenge oz beynge to be perceyued oz
taken wythin the townes paroches oz feldes of T.
N.P. ꝛc. lately belongynge and apperteynyng to the
sayde late pziozie of T. aforesayd wyth all and singuler theyz appourtenaunces, and al that theyz manour
oz lozdshyppe of T. with al the demeanes of the same
and all and singuler theyz other mesuages ꝛc. and o-
ther hereditamentes whatsoeuer they be set lyeng oz
beyng in T. aforesayde and all and singuler reuersiōs
remayndzes and seruices of all the tenementes aswel
of all the freholders tenauntes foz yeares oz frō yeare
to yere as copie holders tenauntes at wyll to the said
manour

manour oz lozdshyppe of C. belongynge oz appertey=
nyng oz whych be in any wyse to be perceyued re.ey=
ued ꝸ taken out of any landes, tenementes, medowes
leasues, pastures oz other hereditamētes whatsoeuer
they be set lyeng and beyng in C.afozesayd. And also
of all maner of suche glebe landes and tenementes,
tithes, oblacions, fruites, pzofytes, and cōmodities,
whatsoeuer they be, to the churches and parsonages
of N.C.ꝸ L.oz to any of them nowe belongyng oz in
any wyse apperteynyng oz whych at any tyme here=
tofoze haue of ryght apperteyned oz belonged to thē
oz to any of them, and also all and singuler pensions
and pozcions in L.W.ꝸc.wyth all ryghtes pzofytes
and cōmodities aswell spirituall as tempozall toge=
thers wyth all woodes ꝸ vnderwodes warrens and
other liberties what so euer they be to the sayde ma=
nours oz lozdshyppes of T. ꝸ. C. oz to eyther of them
belongyng oz in any wyse apperteynynge oz that be
set lyeng oz being in the townes and fyldes of T.ꝸ C.
afozesayd oz in oz vpon any of the pzemisses . Excep=
ted and alwayes reserued vnto the sayde Deane and
Canons and to theyz successours all such rentes and
fermes pensions and pozcions which be conteined in
a scedule indented thereof made , ꝸ to thys indenture
annexed, amountyng to the yearely value of.xx. poū=
des sterlyng. And also excepted and reserued vnto the
sayde deane.ꝸc. all ꝸ singuler felons goodes.wardes
mariages, excheates, hariettes, aduousons and patro
nages of churches in any wyse to the sayd lozdeshyp=
pes belongyng. To haue, holde, occupie and peasebly
to possede ꝸ enioye the said stite manours oz lozdships
ꝑes ꝸ all ꝸ singuler the pzemisses wyth theyz appur=
H tes=

A clause of
reseruation

tenaunces (except before excepted) unto ÿ sayd A. D. to hys executours & his assignes frõ ÿ feast of saynct Michael tharchangell next & immediatly folowyng the date herof unto the ende & terme of. l. yeares then nexte ensuyng & fully to be cõplete & ended, in as ample & large maner & forme & asmuche for hys cõmoditie & profyte as euer any beyng Priour at T. aforsaid or any other fermer occupier or possessour of the same haue at any tyme heretofore occupied, possessed, or enioyed the premisses or any part or parcell therof. Yeldyng & payeng therfore yearly unto ÿ sayd deane & canõs & to theyr successours foure score poũdes of good & lawful mony of Englãd at two termes of the yere, ÿ is to say, at the feast of thannunciatiõ of our blessed Lady & S. Michael tharchãgel by euẽ porciõs And ÿ said A. couenaũteth & graũteth by these presentes that he the sayd A. his executours or assignes shal at his or theyr ꝑper costes & charges wel & sufficiẽtly repaire, susteyne, mainteyne & uphold ÿ sayd manour place & al other howses, barnes & stables now there beyng & to the same belõgyng, duryng the sayd terme. And also shal repaire uphold & maiteyne wel & sufficiẽtly all maner of tenemẽtes buildynges & edificatiõs of tenemẽtes now builded or herafter to be builded to ÿ said manours of T. & C. or to eyther of thẽ belõgyng or apperteynyng at his ꝑpre costes & charges duryng the sayd terme. And also shal wel & sufficiẽtly kepe scoure & repaire al maner of hedges diches & moundes of & in ÿ said lãdes of ÿ said manours & other ÿ premisses duryng ÿ said terme, & so beyng wel & sufficiẽtly repaired in thẽde of ÿ sayd terme shal leaue & yelde up. And the sayd deane & canõs couenauntẽ & grauntẽ for thẽ & theyr successours to & with ÿ sayd A. hys executours

Reparatiõs

and

¶ aſſygnes to beare ⁊ mainteyne al maner of repara¦
ciõs of chaũcels of al ſuch churches as belong to any
of þ ſaid manours oꝛ þ be now oꝛ that herafter ſhalbe
ſituate,edified,oꝛ builded in any of þ ſayd townes vil
lages oꝛ hamlettes befoꝛe mẽcioned oꝛ vpõ any of the
ſaid lãdes tenemẽtes oꝛ other þ pꝛemiſſes. And alſo to
diſcharg þ ſayd A.D hys executours ⁊ aſſygnes of al
ſuch thinges as are dew by reaſon of a cõpoſitiõ made
betwene þ late pꝛioꝛ of T.⁊ the parochiãs of the ſame
Ꝑ.beryng date the.x.day of Mar.An.dñi.m.cccc.l. as
in the ſame cõpoſitiõ moꝛe playnly is declared.And al
ſo the ſayd A.couenaũteth ⁊ grãuteth foꝛ hym his exe
cutours ⁊ aſſygnes to ⁊ wyth the ſayd deane.⁊c.to ac¦
quite ⁊ diſcharge þ ſayd deane. ⁊c. of ⁊ foꝛ al maner of
quite rentes ⁊ other charges whatſoeuer they be due
oꝛ accuſtomed to be payed out of the ſayd manours oꝛ
loꝛdſhyppes oꝛ out of either of thẽ oꝛ other the pꝛemiſ
ſes oꝛ any parcel therof to our ſoueraigne loꝛd þ kyng
þ chief loꝛd of þ fee oꝛ fees,oꝛ to any other pſon oꝛpar¦
ſons whatſoeuer they be duryng þ ſaid terme hauing
theyꝛ cõmenſemẽt begynnynge ⁊ beyng befoꝛe þ date
of theſe pꝛeſentes,þ tenth oꝛ tenthes out of any of the
pꝛmiſſes due vnto our ſoueraigne loꝛd þ kyng only ex¦
cepted,which þ ſaid deane ⁊ canõs ⁊ theſe ſucceſſours
ſhal beare ⁊ paye.And moꝛeouer the ſayd deane⁊ Ca¦ A clauſe foꝛ
nons by theſe pꝛeſentes do licence and authoꝛiſe the the former
ſayd A.and alſo doth couenaunt and grãt vnto him to kepe cour
hys executours ⁊ aſſygnes þ he the ſaid A.hys execu¦ tes ⁊ letes.
tours oꝛ aſſignes by hys oꝛ theyꝛ ſufficient deputie oꝛ
deputies ſhall kepe the courtes and letes wythin the
ſayd manours oꝛ loꝛdſhyps oꝛ wythin eyther of them
in the name of the ſayde deane.⁊c.when ⁊ as often as
      Ꝑ ij   it ſhall

it shal seme good vnto the sayde A.hys executours oz
assygnes without fee oz other alowaūce demaūdyng
foz the same,duryng the sayd terme, and also the said
A. couenaūteth. ꝛc. to leuy gather ꝗ receyue to thuse
of the sayd deane ꝗ Canōs ꝗ theyz successours ail such
rentes as be excepted ꝗ reserued out of this indenture
ꝗ mencioned in the said scedule indented hereūto annexed at such tyme as they shalbe by ꝑ law recouered
oz by any other wise oz meanes sufficiētly oz lawfully
tried ꝗ pzoued agaynst the sayd tenauntes oz deteyg-
nours ꝗ witholders of ꝑ said rētes ꝗ duties to be pai-
able vnto ꝑ sayd deane.ꝛc.yf the sayd A. may obteyne
oz get any of ꝑ sayd rentes ꝗ dueties without costes
and charges in the lawe to be hadde oz made by ꝑ said
A.foz the same ꝗ foz the collection therof to demaūde
no fee oz other allowaunce of the said deane ꝗ canons
vpō hys accōpte therof to be made befoze ꝑ auditours
of the sayd deane ꝗ canōs ꝗ theyz successours,duryng
the sayd terme. Also the sayd A.couenaūteth ꝗ graū-

❧ A clause
where pay-
mēnt of the
rēat shalbe
made.ꝛc.

teth foz hym. ꝛc. to make paymēt at and wythin the
sayd Colledge of the sayde yearely rent of foure scoze
poundes equally at the termes of paymēt befoze specifyed to ꝑ handes of the treasourers of the sayd Colledge at hys owne pzoper costes ꝗ charges wythout
allowaūce takyng foz the same duryng the said terme.
And the sayd deane ꝗ canons foz them ꝗ theyz successours do couenaūt ꝗ graunt by these pzesentes that ꝑ
acquitaunce made sealed and sygned by the treasourers of the sayd Colledge oz by eyther of them to the
sayd A.oz to hys executours oz assygnes foz the payment of the same yearely rent oz any parte oz parcell
therof in maner and fozme befoze mencioned , shalbe
a good

a good sure and suffycient warraunte and discharge
vnto the sayde A.his executours, and assignes, & to
his or theyr deputie or deputies for ꝑ paymēt therof.
AND yf it happen the sayde yerely rente of.lxxx.li.
to be behynde vnpayed in parte or in all, after anye
feast of payment before specifyed by the space of .x.
wekes,that then it shalbe lawfull to the sayde deane
&c.into the sayde manours and lordshyppes, and in=
to all and singuler the premisses with theyr appurte=
naunces to entre and to distreyne, and the distresse
there so taken,to dryue,leade,and carye awaye, and
them to withholde and kepe, vntyll the sayde yerlye
rent and euerye parte thereof with tharrerages,yf a=
ny be,be vnto the sayde deane.&c.fully satis.yed, con=
tented and payed.AND yf it happen the sayd yerely
rent of foure score pounde, to be behynde vnpayed,
in parte or in all after any of the feastes of paymētes
before mencioned,by the space of.iii.monethes, that
then it shalbe lefull vnto the sayde deane and canons
& to theyr successours, into all and singuler the pre=
misses, and theyr appurtenaunces, and into euerye
parcell hereof, to reentre, and then to haue agayne,
and repossede as in theyr former state, and the sayde
A.his executours and assignes fromthence vtterly to
expell and amoue for euermore,this Indenture or a=
ny thynge therein conteyned to the contrary in anye
wyse not withstandynge. AND the sayd deane and
canons couenaunten and graunten for them & theyr
successours, to and with the sayde A. his executou=
res and assignes,that yf the sayd A.his executours or
assignes shall happen at any tyme hereafter to be e=
uicted or dispossessed of any of the premisses or anye

H.iii.   parte

A clause
distresse.

A clause
reentrie.

A clause f
defaltyng
of the ren
in case of
uiction.&

part oꝛ ꝑcel thereof ẃout couyn oꝛ fraude on þ parte
of the said A.his executours oꝛ aſſignes,þ then þ said
rent of.lxxx.li.ſterlyng ſhalbe appoꝛcioned ⁊ diminiſ‑
ſhed accoꝛdyngly ⁊ after ſuch rate ⁊ poꝛcion as þ quā‑
titie and balure of the ſapde landes and tenementes,
rentes,heriditamentes and other duties,parcel of the
pꝛemiſſes ſo euicted oꝛ taken from the poſſeſſiō oꝛ oc‑
cupation of the ſapde A. his executours oꝛ aſſygnes,
ſhal amount and ariſe bnto,and that it ſhalbe laẃful
bnto the ſapde A.his executours , oꝛ aſſignes , to de‑
A clauſe foꝛ
aſſuraūceto
be made, ⁊c
falke ſo moche of his rent at euery of the ſapd paymē‑
tes,this Indenture.⁊c. notwitſtandynge. ALSO
furthermoꝛe the ſapde Deane and Canons couenaū‑
ten and graunten foꝛ them.⁊c. to do, cauſe, and ſuffre
to be done all and ſinguler ſuche thyng and thynges,
acte and actes , as ſhalbe at any tyme oꝛ tymes here‑
after deuyſed oꝛ aduiſed by the counſell lerned of the
ſapde D.his executours oꝛ aſſignes,by what wayes
oꝛ meanes ſoeuer it be , foꝛ the further aſſuraūce and
ful perfite ſuretie of al and ſinguler the pꝛemiſſes and
euery parte and parcell thereof , yf this graunte and
leaſe be not laẃful,perfyte,and ſufficient, to be had ⁊
made bnto the ſapde A.D . his executours and aſſi‑
gnes foꝛ al the hole terme and intreſt aboue ſpecified
oꝛ foꝛ any parte oꝛ parcell thereof in maner ⁊ ſourme
afoꝛeſapde,bpon conuenyent notice and requeſt ther‑
of , gyuen and made bnto the ſapde Deane and Ca‑
nons oꝛ to anye of theyꝛ ſucceſſours , by the ſapde A.
his executours and aſſygnes at the coſtes in the law
of the ſapde A. his executours and aſſygnes.
AND the ſapde A.couenaunteth and graunteth to
and with the ſapde Deane.⁊c. to fynde houſe, lod‑
gynge,

gynge, meate, stable, heye, lytter, and prouandꝛe foꝛ
the hoꝛses of the sayde Deane and Canonnes, and o-
ther commynge with hym oꝛ them in progresse ones
in the yere, by the space of two dayes and two nygh-
tes, the sayde Deane and Canons and theyꝛ successours, paying resonably foꝛ onelye meate and dꝛynke
so proupded durynge the terme afoꝛesayde. And further the sayd A. couenaunteth and graunteth foꝛ him
&c. that he, his executours and assignes shal at thend
of euery. rii. yeres (durying the sayd terme) delyuer oꝛ
cause to be delyuered vnto the sayde Deane. &c. the **Courte rol-**
Courte rolles, well and truly engrossed in parchemēt **les and tes-**
at his and theyꝛ costes and charges of all suche cour- **ꝛoure to be**
tes as shalbe kept in the sayde manours of T. and C **delyuered.**
durynge anye of the sayde twelue yeres. And also at
thende of euery suche. rii. yeres, he the sayd A. his executours oꝛ assignes, shall (as nere as they can) delyuer oꝛ cause to be delyuered to the sayde Deane. &c. in
maner befoꝛe rehersed, a true tenour of all the landes
and tenementes, rentes, and seruices, beinge parcell,
oꝛ in any wyse appertaynyng to the sayde manours.
AND the sayde Deane and Canons couenaunten
and graunten foꝛ them. &c. that they shall delyuer oꝛ
cause to be delyuered vnto the sayd A. &c. at suche tymes as they shalbe therunto required. i. oꝛ. ii. of their
most trew terours whereby ꝑ sayd A. his exec. oꝛ assi.
may the better come to knowlege of all ꝑ sayd lādes,
tenementes, rētes & seruices apteyning to ꝑ sayd manours. And ꝑ sayd deane & canons, & their successours **Clause of**
all ꝑ sayd manours oꝛ loꝛdships, & al other ꝑ ꝑmisses **warrantie.**
befoꝛe letten with all and singuler theyꝛ appurtenaũces (except befoꝛe excepted) vnto ꝑ sayd A. his exec. &
assignes,

affignes for the fayde yerely rent in maner and form before declared,agaynft al people fhal warraunt and defende,durynge the fayde terme by thefe prefentes. AND alfo where the fayde A. ftandeth bounden vn

A claufe of Defence of the obliga-cion,&c. tothe fayd Deane and canõs,and theyr fucceffours by his dede obligatorye being date of thefe prefentes,in the fume of one.C.li.fterlyng,the fayde Deane and canons couenaunten and graunten for them & their fucceffours to and vo the fayd A. his executours admini ftratours and affignes,that yf the fayd A. his execu-tours,adminiftratours or affignes do well and truly obferue,perfourme,fulfyll and kepe, all and finguler fuche couenauntes,grauntes,promiffes,articles and agrementes comprifed in this indenture, which on ý parte and behalfe of the fayd A. his executours admi niftratours and affignes ought to be obferued, per-fourmed, fulfylled and kept, that then the fayde dede obligatorye to be voyde and of none effecte, or els to ftande in his full ftrength and vertue. IN wytneffe whereof to thone parte of thefe Indentures towar-des the fayde.A. remainyng,the fayd mafter Deane & canons haue fet theyr common feale. And to thother parte of thefe Indentures towardes the fayd mafter Deane and canons remaynynge,the fayde A. hath fet his feale.Gyuen the daye and yere abouewritten.

℟The fourme of a leafe of a bruehoufe, or fuche lyke thynge.

THis Indenture made.&c.betwene A.B.of Lon don grocer on the one partie, and C.D.of the fame,bruer,on thother partie,witneffeth, that the fayde A.B.hath dimifed, graunted, and to ferme lets

letten to the fozesayde E. D. all that his brewhouse
with all and singuler thappurtenaunces called N.set
lying and beinge in F.strete in the paryssche of.ꝛc. be=
twene the tenement pertaynynge to our soueraygne
lozde the kynge nowe in the holdynge of J.K.on the
east parte,ꝗ a tenement pertay.ꝛc.on ꝥ nozth part.ꝛc.
togyther,w al maner vessels ꝗ vtensiles to ꝥsayd bru
house belonging,oz in any manerwise apperteyning
that is to say,two hozse mylles pzice.x.s. two great
leades pzice.ꝛc,one masshefatte,pzice.ꝛ.c.ten barels,
pzice. ꝗ so fozth of the rest : oz els ye maye saye thus,
togyther wyth al maner vessels and vtensils contey
ned in certayne a schedule to these pzesent Indentu=
res annexed. TO haue and to holde.ꝛc. And the
sayde E.D.couenaunteth and graunteth.ꝛc. that he
the sayde E. his executours and assignes shall wel,
truly,and sufficientlye mayntayne, repare, and su=
stayne the sayde brewehouse, vessels, and vtensyles
ꝛc. durynge the sayde terme . Pzouyded alwayes,
that yf anye of the sayde vesselles oz vtensilles shall
nede duryng the terme afozesayd foz default of old=
nesse to be renewed,that thã the sayd A.B.his execu
tours and assignes shal of his and their pzopze costes
and charges, renewe all and euerye suche vessels oz
vtensils so to be renewed as ofte as neade shall re=
quyze duryng the sayde terme.So that the same be
not bzoken oz destroyed by the defaulte oz negligẽce
of the sayde E.oz of his seruauntes. And the sayd
A.B.and hys heyzes, the sayde bruehouse wyth the
appurtenaunces and all other the pzemisses befoze
letten,vnto the fozsayde E.his executours, and assi=
gnes foz the sayde yerelye rent in maner and fourme

J befoze

The boke of fondzy

befoze fpecifyed agaynft all people fhall warraunte
and defende, butyl thende of the fayde terme by thefe
pzefentes. In wytneffe.&c.

An other leafe.

HIS Indenture made betwene John Moz-
ton of Hoznechurche in the Countye of Effex
Gentleman on that one partye. And Henrye
Rofe of the fame Efquyze, on that other partye.
Wytneffeth, that the fayde Johan the daye of makynge hereof, hath graunted, dymyfed, betaken, and
letten to ferme, and by this Indenture doth graunt
dimyfe, betake, and to ferme lette, bnto the fayde
Henrye, all that hys manour place called Mozeton
hall, wyth all landes, Tenementes, douehoufes,
barnes, ftalles, ozchardes, gardeynes, pondes, and
waters, wyth thappurtenaunces to the fayde Manour belongynge oz appertaynynge, fette, lying, and
beynge in the Paryffhe of Hoznechurche afozefayd.
To haue and to holde the fozefayde Manoure, landes, tenementes, douehoufes, barnes, ftalles, ozchardes, gardeynes, pondes, and waters, and other the
pzemyffes, wyth thappurtenaunces to the fayd Hen
rye, to his executours and affygnes, from the feafte
of Saynct Michael nexte commynge after the date
of thys Indenture bnto thende and terme of twentye yeares, from thence nexte enfuynge, and fullye
to be complete and ended. Yeldyng and paying therfoze yearelye durynge the fayde terme, to the fayde
John, hys heyzes oz affygnes, twentye pounde of
good and lawfull moneye of Englande, at foure tymes

mes of the yere. That is to saye at the feast.&c.by eue
po2cyons . And yf it shall happen,the sayde yearelye
rent of twentye pounde to be behynde vnpayed , in
parte o2 in al,ouer o2 after any terme of paymēt ther
of afo2esayd, in whyche it ought to be payed , by the
space of syxe wekes,and lawfullye asked. That then
it shall be leful to the sayde Johan, to hys hey2es and
assygnes,in the sayde Manoure, landes , tenemen=
tes,and all other the p2emysses , wyth the appurte=
nances,to entre and distreyne:and y distresses there
so taken lefullye,to beare , leade, d2yue, and cary a=
waye,and towardes them to reteyne vntyll the sayd
yerelye rent and tharrerages of the same(yf anye be)
to them be fullye contented and payed . AND yf it
shall happen,the sayde yearelye Rente of twentye
pounde to be behynde vnpayed , in parte o2 in all,
ouer o2 after anye terme of paymente, thereof afo2e=
sayde, in whych it ought to be payed by the space of
a quarter of a yere, and lawfullye asked,and no suf=
fycyent dystresse then there can be founde. That then
and at all tymes after it shall be lefull to the sayde
Johan,to hys hey2es and assygnes,into all the sayd
Manour,landes,tenementes, and other the p2emis=
ses,wyth thappurtenaunces,holly fo2 to reentre.
And the same to haue agayne, reteyne, and repos=
sede,as in they2 fo2emour estate. And the sayd Hen=
rye Rose , hys executours and assygnes thereof vt=
terlye to expell,put oute, and auoyde, thys Inden=
ture o2 anye thynge therein conteyned to the contra=
rye notwythstandynge.
  And the sayde John couenaunteth and graunteth
by this Indenture, that he o2 his hey2es , the sayde

manour, landes, tenementes, and other the pꝛemiſ
ſes wyth thappurtenaunces, mete and ſufficientlye
ſhall repayꝛe, ſuſtayne, and mayntayne, and agaynſt
wynde and rayne ſhall make defendable, when and
as often as neade ſhall requyꝛe, durynge the ſayde
teeme. Except dawbynge of walles hoꝛnehygh, and
all hedges, dytches and defences belongynge to the
ſayde manour wyth thappurtenaunces whych ſhall
be at the coſtes, and charges of the ſayde Henry hys
eꝛecutoures oꝛ aſſygnes at all tymes, durynge the
ſayd tyme. And the ſame ſo ſufficiently made, repay
red, and amended, in thende of the ſayde tyme ſhall
ſurrender, and delyuer vp, to the ſayde John, hys
heyꝛes, oꝛ aſſygnes. And the ſayde Henry couenaun
teth, and graunteth, by thys endenture that he, hys
eꝛecutours oꝛ aſſygnes, at theyꝛ lyke coſte & charge,
ſhall bere, and paye all maner of quytrentes and out
charges, whyche ſhall be due, and goynge out of the
foꝛeſayde maner, landes, and tenementes, wyth the
appurtenaunces at all tymes, duryng the ſayd tyme
And the ſayde John couenaūteth and graunteth, by
thys indenture, that it ſhall be lefull to the ſayd Hen
rye to hys eꝛecutoures and aſſygnes, to haue and to
take, in, and vpon the landes befoꝛe letten, compe
tent and ſufficyent fyer bote, carte bote, plough bote
and hedge bote, to be occupyed and ſpente, in, and
vpon the landes and tenementes afoꝛeſayde, at all
tymes duryng the ſayde terme. And further the ſaid
John couenaūteth, & graunteth by thys endenture
that he and his heyꝛes, the foꝛſayde manour, lande,
tenementes, and all other wyth thappourtenaunces
to the ſayde Henrye, to hys eꝛecutours and aſſignes
foꝛ the

foz the yerelye rent afozesayde, and bnder the other
couenauntes aboue rehersed, agaynst all people shal
warraunt and defende,durynge the fozesayde terme
of.twenty yeres, by thys endenture.   In wytnesse
whereof.&c.

¶A lease foz yeres of a house.

Thys Indenture made the.xx.day of January,
in the. xv. yere of the reygne of kynge Henrye
theyght betwene syz Thomas Denys knyght
and dame Anne hys wyfe on that one party and Ni
cholas Sewel citizen and grocer of London on that
other partye : Wytnesseth that the same sir Thomas
and dame Anne hys wyfe the day of makyng hereof
haue graunted, dymysed, betaken, and to ferme let=
ten,and by thys Indenture graunteth, dymyseth,be
taketh, and to ferme letteth,to the sayd Nicholas, al
that theyz mesuage oz tenement, wyth all shoppes,
celers, solers, warehouses, yardes, wyth all, and
synguler theyz appourtenaunces to the same messu=
age, oz tenement, appertaynynge oz belongyng,set,
lying and beynge in the parysche of saynt Myldzede
in the Pultre of London, whych was lately the ten
nure, and holdyng of John Crofte and wherein the
sayde Nicholas nowe inhabiteth : to haue and hold
the fozesayde mesuage,oz tenement , with all shop=
pes,celers, solers, and other the pzemisses wyth the
appurtenaunces, to the sayde Nicholas to hys exe=
cutours and assygnes, in as large and ample maner
and fourme in every thynge, as the fozesayde John
Czofte, the same lately hylde and occupyed from the
feaste of

feaste of saynte Mychael the archangell last past be∽
fore the date hereof vnto the ende and terme of twen
tye yeres from thence nexte ensuynge,and fully to be
complete and ended, yeldynge and payinge therefore
yerely, durynge the sayde terme,to the sayd syr Tho
mas and dame Anne his wyfe, or to eyther of them,
theyr heyres or assygnes.iii.li.vi.s.viii.ð.of good and
lawfull moneye of Englande, at.iiii.termes of the
yere, in the citie of London, vsuel by euen porcions.
And yf it shall happen the sayde yerelye rent of.iii.li.
vi.s.viii. ð. to be behynde vnpayed in parte or in all,
ouer or after any terme of payment therof aforsayde
in whyche it oughte tobe payde by the space of syre
wekes: That than it shalbe lefull to ꝑ sayd syr Tho∽
mas ꝯ dame Anne his wyfe, theyr heyres ꝯ assygnes
in al the forsayd mesuage or tenement, and other the
premysses, wyth thappurtenaunces, to enter and di
streyne,and the distresse so taken lefully to beare lede
and cary awaye, and towardes them to reteyne vn∽
tyl the sayd yerely rent, and tharrerages of the same
be fully contented and payde . And yf it happen the
sayde yerely rent of.iii.li.vi.s.viii. ð. to be behynd vn
payde, in partye or in all, ouer or after any terme of
payment therof aforesayde in whyche it ought to be
payde by the space of a quarter of a yere. That than
it shall be leefull to the sayde syr Thomas and dame
Anne hys wyfe, theyr heyres and assygnes in to all
the foresayde mesuage, and other the premisses with
the appurtenaunces,holly to reenter and the same to
haue agayne, reteyne, and repossede ,as in theyr for∽
mer estate, and the sayde Nicholas, hys executours,
and assygnes, therof vtterly to expel, put oute, and a
moue

moue, thys Indenture oʒ any thynge therin conteyꝫ
ned to the contrarye not wythſtandynge.

And the ſayd ſyʒ Thomas and dame Anne, couenaũ
ten, and graunten by thys Indenture, that they their
heyʒes, oʒ aſſygnes, at theyʒ owne coſt & charge, the
ſayde meſſuage, oʒ tenement, and all other the pʒeꝫ
myſſes, wyth the appurtenaunces, well and ſuffyciꝫ
ently ſhall repayʒe, ſuſteyne, and mayntayne, and aꝫ
gaynſt wynde and rayne, ſhal make defenſyble when
and as often as nede ſhal requyʒe, durynge the ſayde
terme, and alſo at theyʒ lyke coſte, and charge, ſhall
beare and paye, all maner of quyterentes, and outeꝫ
charges whyche ſhall be due, and goynge out of all
the foʒeſayde meſſuage, and other the pʒemyſſes at
all tymes durynge the ſayde terme. And the ſayde
Syʒ Thomas and dame Anne couenaunten, and
graunten by theſe pʒeſentes, the foʒeſayde meſſuage
oʒ Tenement, and all other the pʒemyſſes, wyth the
appurtenaunces, to the ſayde Nicholas, to hys exeꝫ
cutours and aſſygnes, foʒ the yerely rent afoʒeſayde.
And vnder the other couenauntes aboue rehearſed,
agaynſte all people ſhall warraunt and defende, duꝫ
rynge the foʒeſayde terme of twentye yeres, by this
Indenture.

In wytneſſe whereof, the partyes afoʒeſayde to
theſe Indentures interchaungeably haue ſet to their
ſeales, the daye and the yere aboueſayde.

⸿ The fourme and maner howe
   to make Releaſes.

               J.iiij.   ʒe

YE shall vnderstande, that ther be sondry sortes of releases. Some be of a mannes hole right, which he hath in landes, tenementes, or hereditamentes. Other some be of actions realles and personals, and of other thynges, which kynde of Release is vsuallye called a generalle Aquytaunce, the fourme whereof ye shall fynde in the tytle of Acquitaunces. But concernynge the nature of releases, where they take place, and of the strength and vertue of the wordes in the same, I remitte you to master Liteltons boke of Tenures. Myne institute and purpose here is onely to descrybe sondry formes and examples of them.

¶ The fourme of a release made to the tenaunt of the freeholde of a manour.&c.

Nouerint vniuersi per presentes me Thomã R. filium et heredẽ Johãnis R. armigeri defũcti remisisse, relaxasse, et omnino de me et heredibus meis quietum clamasse Richardo D. armigero totũ ius, titulũ et clameũ quam habui, habeo, aut quouismodo in posterũ habere potero, de et in manerio de. R. iuxta A. vel sic.

¶ An other forme of the same.

Omnibus Christifidelibus ad quos preses scriptum peruenerit T. R. filius et heres C. R. armigeri defuncti, saltm in dño sempiternam. Noueritis me prefatum T. remisisse, relaxasse, et omnino pro me et heredib⁹ meis imperpetuum quietũ clamasse per presentes R. D. armigero in sua plena et pacifica possessione existenti heredibus et assignatis

et pacifica possessione existenti, heredibus et assigna=
tis suis imperpetuum totum ius meum, titulum cla
meum, demandam, et interesse, que vnquam habui,
habeo, seu quouismodo in tuturum habere potero,
vel poterint heredes mei, de et in manerio de R.tu=
rta A.in comitatu R. cum omnibus terris, tenemen=
tis, redditibus, seruicijs, pratis, pascuis, boscis, et pa
sturis, vna cum omnibus alijs pertinentijs eidem
manerio spectantibus, nec non de et in omnibus illis
terris et tenementis, cum omnibus suis pertinencijs
vocatis J. iacentibus et existent. in parochijs de. A.
R.et M.in comitatu predicto que quidem manerium
terra et tenementa ac cetera premissa cum omnibus
suis pertinencijs quondam fuerunt M. R. aui mei,
Jta videlicet, qt nec ego predictus T. nec heredes
mei, nec aliquis alius per nos, pro nobis, seu nomine
nostro, aliquc dius titulum clameum, demandam seu
iteresse de aut i predicto manerio de R.cum omnibus
terris, ten.redditibus, seruicijs, pratis, pascuis, boscis,
& pasturis, ac omnibus alijs pertinentijs eidem mane
rio spectantibus aut de vel in omnibus predictis ter
ris et tenementis cum omnibus suis pertinencijs vo
catis J. neq in aliqua parte seu parcella eorundem
de cetero clamare vel vendicare poterimus nec debe=
mus quouismodo in futurum, sed ab omni actione
iuris tituli, clamei, demaunde et interessi in eisdem
simus penitus exclusi imperpetuum per presentes.

   Et ego vero predictus T.et heredes mei predictum
manerium de R. cum omnibus terris, tenementis,
redditibus, seruicijs, pratis, pascuis, boscis et pastu
ris cum alijs pertinencijs eidem manerio spectanti=
bus, ac etiam omnia predicta terras et tenementa cũ

                R   om=

omnibus suis pertinencijs vocat.J.pꝛefato R. here=
dibus et assignatis suis contra omnes gentes war=
rantizabimus et imperpetuů defendemus, In cuius
rei testimonium huic pꝛesenti scripto meo sigillum
meum apposui. Dat.ꝗc.

ℭA release made by dede of tenemen=
tes befoꝛe purchased,wyth a
clause of warrantyse.

Omnibus Chꝛistifidelibus ad quos hoc pꝛesens
scriptum peruenerit.J.L.de Oxon. salutem in
domino sempiternam.Ců.C.F.de N. habuerit
et perquisuerit de me pꝛefato J. vnum tenementum,
situatum et iacens in N.in parochia beate marie vir=
ginis, in alto vico seu platea inter tenementů.w.E.
ex parte oꝛientali et tenementum P.T.ex parte occi=
dentali, cuius vnů quidem caput abuttat super vi=
cum pꝛedictum versus austrum et alterum caput ab=
buttat super pomerium siue gardinů.G.S. versus
boꝛeam quod tenement. cum suis pertinencijs idem
C.modo tenet et inhabitat ibidē. Habendum et tenen
dum eidem C. heredibus et assignatis suis imperpe=
tuum pꝛout per cartam feoffamenti per me eidem.C.
inde confectā cuius dat.est. iiij. die Apꝛilis. Anno re=
gni regis Henrici.vij . post conquestum Anglie deci=
mo septimo,plenius apparet.Noueritis me pꝛedictū
J.remisisse,relaxasse, et omnino pꝛo me et heredibus
meis imperpetuum quietum clamasse,pꝛefato C.he=
redibus et assignatis suis totum ius meum , et cla=
meum,quod vnquam habui,habeo, seu quouismodo
habere potero in futurum in pꝛedicto tenemento , ců
suis pertinencijs. Ita videlicet qd̄ nec ego, nec here=
des mei nec aliquis alius per nos seu nomine nostro
aliquod

aliquod iuris vel clamei in predicto tenemento cum
suis pertinencijs,nec in aliqua inde percella de cetero
exigere, clamare seu vendicare poterimus nec debe=
mus in futurum,sed ab omni actione iuris et clameo
inde simus prorsus exclusi imperpetuum per prese=
tes.Et ego predictus J.et heredes mei predictum te
nementum , cum omnibus suis pertinentijs prefato
C.heredibus et assignatis suis contra omnes gen=
tes warrantizabimus,et imperpetuum defendemus
per presentes.In cuius rei.ic.

¶The fourme of a releafe made by the heyze whych hath ryght in the tayle.

Mnibus Christifidelibus ad quos hoc pre=
sens scriptum peruenerit A.O.frater J.O.
de R.salutem in domino sempiternam.Cum
R. O. nuper antecessor meus videlicet pater P. pa=
tris S.patris mei, et predicti Johannis fratris mei
senior per certam suam feoffamenti quondam dede=
rit et concesserit predicto .P. filio suo vnum teneme=
tum cum pertinentijs suis in villa de D.predicta vo=
cat.O. Habendum et tenendum eidem. P. et here=
dibus de corpore suo legittime procreatis , et pro de=
fectu huiusmodi hered. de corpore suo legittime pro=
creat. predictum tenementum, cum suis pertinen=
tijs,rectis heredibus predicti R. integre remaneret
qui quidem P.obijt, post cuius decessum pdictu.tene
mentum,cum suis pertinetijs prefato S. patri meo
descederi,tet post decessum predicti S. predictum te
nementum cum suis pertinencijs prefato J. fratri
meo seniori,vt filio et hered suo descedit,et p defectu
heredu de corpore pdicti. J.legittime procreat. pdict.

                    K.ij.   tenemen=

tenementum, cum suis pertinenciis mihi pꝛefato I.
vt consanguineo et recto heredi pꝛedicti R. descendere
deberet per foꝛmam donationis pꝛedicte. Noueritis
me pꝛefatum I remisisse, relaxasse, ⁊c. vꝛs.

**¶A release made by the feoffes to
one of them.**

Omnibus Chꝛistifidelibus ad quos pꝛesens scri
ptum peruenerit N. R. et S. T. salutem in do=
mino sempiternã. Noueritis nos pꝛefatos, N.
et S. per pꝛesentes remisisse, relaxasse, et omnino pꝛo
nobis et heredibus nostris imperpetuum quietum
clamasse I. S. de. O. heredibus et assignatis suis to=
tum ius nostrum, et clameum, que vnquam habuimꝰ
habemus, seu quouismodo in futurum habere poteri
mus aut alter nostrum habet, seu habere poterit, in
omnibus illis terris, et tenementis que nuper habui=
mus simul cum pꝛedicto I. in villa et in campis de
I. in Comitatu Oxon. ex concessione et feoffamento
domini I. Bꝛian Capellani et N. D. de I. pꝛedict. in
quoꝛum quidem terris et tenementis idem Ioh. S.
iam existit in plena possessione: Ita videlicet quod
nec nos pꝛedicti N. et S. nec heredes nostri nec ali=
ꝗs aliꝰ noie nostro seu alterius nostri aliquod ius, vel
clameum in pꝛedictis terris et tenementis, cum suis
pertinentijs ◦ nec in aliqua inde parcella exigere, ⁊c.
sed ab omni actione. ⁊c. In cuius rei testimonium. ⁊c.
Anno regni regis Henrici. vii.

**¶A release made by hym whych had
the lande in moꝛgage.**

Omnibus

Vnitus Christifidelibus ad quos presens
c. Noueritis me prefatum. &c. per presentes
remisisse, relaxasse. &c. R. W. de O. heredibus
et assignatis suis imperpetuum totum ius meum, et
clameu q̄ie vnquam habui, habeo , seu qnouismodo
&c. in vno tenemento in O. cum suis pertinencijs, que
nuper habui ex dono et feoffamento predicti R . in
villa de O. predicta situato in parochia Sancti Ced
di inter tenementum H. D. ex parte australi, et tenementum T. A. ex parte boreali, et abuttat super vicū
regiū versus Orientem, per modum morgagij , pro
xx. libris sterlingorū et quas mihi iam soluit et satis-
fecit : quod quidem tenemen. cum suis pertinentijs
idem R. W. in sua plena possessione iam habet . Ita
videltcet quod nec ego, nec heredes mei. &c. sed ab omni. &c. In cuius rei. &c. his testibus &c. Anno regni regis Henrici. vii.

¶ A release of dowrye made by a
wyddowe.

Omnib⁹ Christifidelibus ad quos presens scriptum peruenerit A. H . vidua vel relicta R. H.
de O. salutem in domino sempiternam. Noueritis me prefatam A . in pura viduitate mea et legit-
tima potestate, remisisse, relaxasse. &c. E. J. in sua pos
sessione existenti heredibus et assignatis suis totum
ius meum et clameum, que vnquam habui, habeo &c.
ratione dotis mee in tercia parte vnius tenementi cū
suis pertinentijs , quod idem E . modo inhabitat in
villa de O. predicta, in pochia. &c. qd quidem teneme-
tū cū ptinencijs, prefatus E. nup pquisiuit de prefato
R. quondā viro meo. Ita videltcet, quod nec ego, nec
aliqs ali⁹ noie meo. &c. sed ab oi actōe iuris tituli. &c.

K. iij.   A release

¶ A Release made to the
tenaunte foꝛ terme
of yeres.

Omnibus Chꝛiſtifidelibus.ꝛc.Cum.R.w.de.O
teneat de me pꝛefato.J. vnum tenementū cum
ſuis pertinenciis,quod idem.R.inhabitat in pa
rochia ſancti Michaelis archangeli ad pontem boꝛia=
lem Oꝛonii, ex parte auſtrali hoſpicii vocat.le crown
pꝛo termino annoꝛū. ꝛc. Noueritis me pꝛefatum.J.
remiſiſſe, relaxaſſe. ꝛc.   Ita ꝙ nec ego, nec heredes
mei. ꝛc.   Sed ab omni actione iuris clamei.ꝛc.
    Datum, ꝛc. Anno regni regis Henrici ſeptimi,
Decimo quarto.

¶ A dede of ſale made by the
execucours by vertue
of the teſtament
of theyꝛ
teſta=
toꝛ.

Omnibus Chꝛiſti fidelibus, ad quos hoc
pꝛeſens ſcriptum peruenerit. w.ꝛ.J.ex=
ecutoꝛes teſtamēti.R.w. de ciuitate lon
Don ciuis et mercatoꝛis , ſalutem in do=
mino ſempiternam. Cum pꝛedictus.R
per teſtamentum ſuum lectū, ꝛ pꝛoclamatum in hu=
ſtingis London tentis die.ꝛc,pꝛox. poſt feſtum ſācti
Barnardi anno regni Regis Henr.viii ꝛc.xix.dederit
et ligauerit Johanne vꝛoꝛi ſue tria tenementa ſua cū
pertinent. que habuit in dicta ciuitate, vnde vnum te
nemen

nementum ſituatum eſt et iacet in parochia ſancte ma
rie birginis in ffancheſtrete inter tenementum.R. ex
parte boʒiali, et tenementum. J. de. A. ex parte au=
ſtrali. Et abbuttat ſuper bicum regium, in ffan=
cheſtrete pʒedict. berſus occidentem, et tenementum.
P. C. berſus orientem.
¶Et aliud tenementum de pʒedictis tribus tenemen
mentis ſituatū. eſt et iacet in perochia omnium ſanc=
toʒum in Lombardſtrete inter tenementum.J.B. ex
parte auſtrali et tenementum.H.R.ex parte boʒeali ⁊
abbuttat ſuper bicum regium de. L. berſus occident.
et tenementum. R. S. berſus oʒientem. Et tertium
tenementum de pʒedictis tribus tenementis ſituatuʒ
eſt, et iacet in parochia ſancti Andʒee de eſchepe inter
tenementum. T. A. ex parte auſtrali et tenementum.
J.H.ex parte boʒeali, et bnum caput abuttat ſuper bi
cum regium de.L. pʒedict. berſus oʒientem et alterū
caput abbuttat ſuper benellam de podinglane berſus
occidentem. Habend. et tenend. pʒedicta tria tenemen
ta cum ſuis pertinentibus pʒefat. J. ad terminum bi=
te ſue. Et poſt deceſſū pʒedicti. J.boluit et legauit an
tedictus teſtatoʒ quod pʒedicta tria tenemēta cum ſu
is pertinenciis Agnete filie ſue et heredibus de coʒpo
re ſuo legitime pʒocreatis integre remanerent et pʒo
defectu heredis, de coʒpoʒe eiuſdem Alicie legittime
pʒocreati, boluit et legauit pʒedictus teſtatoʒ, quod
pʒedicta tria tenementa cum ſuis pertinentiis nobis
pʒefato.W. et .J. execucoʒibus ſuis integre remane=
rent ad bendendum,et pecuniam ſuam inde percipien
dam in operibus charitatis diſponendum pʒout in e=
odem teſtamento plenius continetur.

Et quia

Et quia predicta Johanna obiit, et predicta Agnes ſi
militer ſine hered. de corpore ſuo legitime procreat.
deceſſit: Sciatis nos prefatos, w. et. J. executores
dicti teſtamenti prefati. R. auctoritate dicti teſtamen
ti, dimiſiſſe, conceſſiſſe, et hoc preſenti ſcripto meo con
firmaſſe, ac pro quadam pecunie ſumma, inde in com
plementum executionis dicti teſtamenti pre manibus
ſoluta vendidiſſe. R. D. de London ciui et mercatori
london. predicta tria tenementa cum ſuis pertinent.
habenda, ⁊ tenenda, eidem. R. et heredibus et aſſigna=
tis ſuis imperpetuum, de capitalibus dñis feodi illiⁱᵘ
pro ſeruicio inde debito, et de iure conſueto.
In cuius rei teſtimonium, huic preſenti ſcripto no=
ſtro, ſigilla noſtra. ⁊c.

¶ The fourme of the ſame dede
in englyſſhe.

TO al chriſten people, to whome this preſent wri
tynge commeth. w. J. executours of the teſta=
ment of. R. w. of London citizen ⁊ mercer gre=
tynge in our Lorde euerlaſtynge.
Where the foreſayde. R. w. by hys laſt wyl and teſta
ment, redde and proclaymed in the huſtynges of Lon
don holden, the daye nexte after ſente barnabe in the.
xxix. yere of the reygne of our ſouerayne lorde kyng
Henry the. viii. ⁊c. gaue and bequethed to Johan his
wyfe thre tenementes wyth the apurtenaunces whi=
che he had in the ſayde citye. Whereof one tenemente
lyeth in the paryſſhe of our bleſſed lady of fancheſtrete
betwene the tenement of. R. W. on the Northe parte
and the tenemente of. J. A. on the ſouthe part, and it
abbutteth vpon the kynges ſtreete of fancheſtrete to=
warde the weſt and the tenement of. R. Lancaſtre to
warde

warde the easte. And an other tenemente of the sayde
thre tenementes lyeth in the paryshe of alhalowne in
Lombard streate, betwene the tenement of .P .C. on
the south syde and the tenemente of Henrye Parkar,
on the Northe syde, and it abbutteth vppon the kyn=
ges hye strete called Lumbarde strete, towarde the
easte, and the tenement of R .S. towarde the weast.
And the thyrde tenement of the foresayde thre tene=
mentes is set and lyeth in the paryshe of Saynote
Andrewes in Eastchepe betwene the tenemente of
T.A. on the south, and the tenemet of J.H. on p̄ parte
of the north. And the one ende abutteth vpon p̄ kyn=
ges strete toward the weast, ⁊ the other ende abbut=
teth vpō the lane called puddynglane, toward p̄ east.
To haue ⁊ to hold the forsayd .iij. tenementes wyth p̄
appurtenaūces of the same, to the sayde Johā terme
of her natural lyfe, ⁊ after her decesse, p̄ sayde testator
willed and bequethed p̄ the forsayd .iij. tenemētes w̄
their appurtenaūces shulde remayne holly to Agnes
his doughter, ⁊ to the heyres of her body laufully be=
gotten. And for defaute of heyres of the bodye of the
sayd Agnes laufully begotten, the sayd testator wil=
led and bequethed, that the forsayde thre tenemētes
with thappurtenaūces shulde remayne hollye to vs
the forsayd W. ⁊ J. his executours for to sell, and the
money therof cōmynge to bestowe, ordre ⁊ dispose in
workes of charitie as in the same testament it appea=
reth more at large . And forasmoche as the forsayde
Johā is departed out of this present lyfe., and p̄ for=
sayd Agnes also is deed wout heyre of her body law
fully begotten. knowe ye, that we W. ⁊ J. executou=
res of the sayde testament of the abouenamed R .by

L   aucto

auctoꝛitie of the same testament, haue dimised, graū
ted, and by this our pꝛesent wꝛytynge haue cōfirmed
and (foꝛ a certayne sume of money to the accōplishmēt
of the execution of the same testament to vs afoꝛe
hand delyuered by him) clerely bargained and sold to
R.D. of London citizin and marchaunt of London
the foꝛsayd thꝛe tenementes with theyꝛ appurtenaū
ces. To haue and to holde to the sayd R, and his hey
res ⁊ assignes foꝛ euer, of the heed loꝛdes of the fee,
by the seruyce therof due and of ryght accustomed.
In wytnesse whereof we haue set to our seales.⁊c.

⸿An alienation of a reuersion.

Omnibus xpi fidelib⁹ ad quos pñs scriptum pꝛ
uenerit.W.H.de W. salutem in dño sempiter
nam.Cum T.H. pater meus habeat et teneat
pꝛo termino vite sue quondam tenementum, cum su
is ptinenciis in villa de W.pꝛedict. vocat.H.reuersi
one inde post suum decessum mihi et heredibus meis
spectante.Noueritis me pꝛedict.W. dedisse,et in hoc
pꝛesenti scripto meo confirmasse Thome Boner de C.
reuersionem dicti tenementi cum suis ptineñ, cum ac
ciderit post decessum pꝛedicti R.patris mei. Habeñ,
et teneñ pꝛedictam reuersionem cum suis pertineñ,
cum acciderit pꝛefat.T.B. heredibus et assignatis su
is iperpetuū de capit.dñis feodi illius per seruicia in
de debita.⁊c. In cuius rei testimoniū.⁊c. Dat.⁊c. In
no regni Regis Henrici.vij.⁊c.

⸿The foꝛme of the same
in Englysshe.

To all

To all Chriſten people to whome thys preſente
wrytynge commeth ⁊c. W. H. of W. ſendeth gretyng in our Lorde euerlaſtyng. Where Thomas Harries my father hath and holdeth for terme
of hys life a certayne tenement wyth the pertinences
in the towne of W.aforeſayde called H.the reuerſion
thereof after hys deceaſſe, vnto me and vnto myne
heyres apperteynynge. knowe ye, that I the ſayde
W.haue gyuen and graunted, and by this my preſent wrytynge haue confyrmed to T. B. of C.the reuerſion of the ſayde tenement wyth the appurtenaũces whenſoeuer it ſhall happen after the deceaſſe of
the ſayde R.my father.   To haue and to holde, the
foreſayde reuerſyon wyth all the appurtenaunces,
whenſoeuer it ſhal happen as is aforſayd to the ſayd
T.B.his heyres and aſſygnes for euer, of the chefe
lordes of the fee by the ſeruice of the ſame, due and of
ryght accuſtomed. In wytneſſe whereof, we the ſayd
partyes interchaungeablye haue put to oure ſeales.
The daye and the yere.⁊c.

¶A letter of attourney vpon the
ſame alienation.

Omnib⁹ xp̄i fidelibus ad quos preſens ſcriptũ
puenerit, T.H.de w.ſalutē in dño ſēpiternã.
Cum ego predictus T. habeam et teneam ꝑ
termino vite mee bnum tenementum cum ſuis perti-
neñ.in billa de C.bocat.D. quod quidem tenementũ
cũ ſuis ꝑtinencijs ,et reuerſion. cũ acciderit poſt meum deceſſum Thomas Boner de C. perquiſiuit de
wilhelmo Harryes filio meo. Noueritis me predictum T.H. poſuiſſe dictum Thomam B.in plenã et

pacificam possessionem et sesinam de reuersione dicti
tenementi cū oībus suis ptineñ . per solutionem vniˀ
denarij argenti. Jn cuius rei testimonium.⁊c.

℣ The fourme of the same in englysche.

TO all Chꝛisten people to whom this psent wꝛy
tyng cōmeth, Thomas Harries of Woddstocke
sendeth gretynge in our Loꝛde euerlastynge.
Where as J the sayd T.haue and holde foꝛ terme of
my natural lyfe one tenement wⁱ thappurtenaunces
in the towne of Croydon called Downes, which sayd
tenement wⁱ thappurtenaunces and reuersion of the
same, when it happeneth after my decease T.B.hath
acquired and gotten of W.H. my naturall sonne and
heyꝛe. knowe ye, that J the sayde T.H. haue put the
sayd T.in full and peaceable possession, state ⁊ seison
of the reuersion of the sayde tenement wyth all and
singuler the appurtenaunces by payment of one penye of syluer. Jn wytnesse whereof.⁊c.

℣ An alienation of a free rent, with the
homage and seruices.

Sciant pñtes et futuri qð ego W.H.dedi, con
cessi, et hac pñti charta mea cōfirmaui R.M.
totum redditum meū de.xxx.s.homagium et
liberum seruic.exeuntia de vno tenemento et quatuoꝛ
virgatis terre J. S. in dale cum omnibus pertineñ.
qð quidem tenementū et quatuoꝛ virgate terre quon
dam fuerunt E.S.Habeñ et percipieñ pꝛedict.red
ditū.xxx.s. homagium, liberum seruicium, cum suis
pertinentijs exeuntibus de pꝛedicto tenemento, cum
quatuoꝛ virgatis terre pꝛefat.R.M.heredibus et assignatis suis imperpetuum.

Soluen.

Soluend.faciend. et reddend.ijsdem, modo et forma
sicut predictus. J.S. et eius antecessores mihi et an
tecessoribus meis, facere, soluere, et reddere consue=
uerunt. Et si contingat predict.reddit.xxx.s.a retro
esse non solut. in parte vel in toto, ad aliquod festum
quo solui debeat, extunc bene liceat prefato.R.w. he=
redibus et assignatis suis in predicto teneméto,¶ qua
tuor virgatis terre,cum pertinen. intrare et distringe
re, et destrictiones ibidem inuentas capere,abducere
effugare, asportare,et penes se retinere quousq; de to
to predicto reddend.cum omnibus inde arreragijs, si
que fuerint, sibi plenarie fuerit satissactum et persolu
tum.   In.cuius rei testimonium etc. Dat. ꝛc.
   Anno regni regis.ꝛc.

¶The tenour of the same in en=
glysshe.

BE it knowen to all that be present ¶ for to come,
that J w.H. haue gyuen and graunted ¶ by this
my present dede haue confirmed to.R.M.al my
rente of .xxx.s. homage and free seruice due out of one
tenement and.iiii.roddes of ground of John Sutter
ton in dale wyth al thappurtinaúces,which tenemét
and.iiii.roddes of grounde, somtyme were. E.Sut=
tertons . To haue,holde, and enioye the forsayde ye
relye rent of.xxx.s. homage, free seruise and appurte
naúces due out of the sayde tenement, and .iiij.rod=
des of grounde, to the sayde.R. M.hys heyres, and
assygnes for euer to be payed, made and yelded vnto
them in maner and fourme, as the forsayde. J.Sut
terton and his auncestours were wonte to pay make
and yeld, to me and to myne auncestours in tyme pas
sed. And yf it happen the sayde yerelye rent of.xxx.s.
                              to be

to be behynd hande and not payed in parte oz in hole
at any of the vsual termes at whyche it oughte to be
payed, that than it shall be lawfull to the sayd.R.M.
hys heyzes and assygnes into the sayde tenemente, ꝇ
foure roddes of grounde wyth the appurtenaunces,
to enter and dystrayne, and the dystresses so there ta=
ken, to carye, leade, chace, dzyue and beare awaye, ꝇ
in hys custodye to retayne, tyll suche tyme as all the
forsayde rente wyth the arrerages, yf any there be vn
to the same.R.hys heyzes ꝇ assygnes be fully conten=
ted, satysfyed and payed. In wytnesse whereof.ꝛc.

ꝃA graunte of an annuitie oz
yerelye rent.

Omnibus Chzistifidelibus ad quos pzesēs scrip
tum peruenerit.J.S. armiger, salutem in dño
sempiternam. Noueritis me pzefatum. J. de=
disse, concessisse, et hoc pzesenti scripto meo confirmas
se.R.Thozne, de.R.bnum annualem redditum, siue
annuitatem.xl.s. de quodam tenemento siue hospicio
in parochia omniū sanctozum de.R.existent.Habend
tenend.et percipiend. predictum annualem redditum
siue annuitatem.xl.s.de pzedicto tenemēto, siue hospi.
cum suis pertinent. pzefato.R.heredibus et assigna=
tis suis imperpetuum ad festum annunciationis bea
te Marie virginis, et sancti Michael.archangeli per
equales pozciones soluend. Et si contingat pzedictū
ānualem redditum, siue annuitatem.xl.s. ad aliquod
festum solucionum quo solui debeat in parte vel in to=
to aretro esse non solut. quod extunc bene liceat pzedi
cto.R.heredibus et assignatis suis in dictum tenemē=
tum siue hospicium intrare et distringere et districtio=
nes ibidem inuentas seu captas aspoztare ,abducere,

fu

fugare, et penes se retinere quousq̃ de predicto an=
nuali redditu, siue annuitate vna cum omnibus inde
arreragiis si que fuerint, sibi sit plenarie satisfactum
De quo quidem annuali redditu siue ãnuit.te, posui
predict. R. in plenam possessionem et sesinam per so=
lucionem. vi. denari. sterlin. In cuius rei testimoñ. ꝛc.

    The tenoure of the same in englysshe.

To al christen people to whome this present wry
tynge commeth. I. S. squier sendeth greting in
our lord euerlastyng. knowe ye that I the fore
said I. haue gyuen ꝸ graunted and in this my preset
wrytyng haue confyrmed to. R. T. of O. one yerelye
rent or annuitye of. xl. s. vpon a certayne tenement or
ynne of myne in the parissh of alhalowne in. O. due to
be payde. To haue holde and perceyue, the forsayde
yerelye rente or annuitye of. xl. s. of the sayd tenemẽt
or ynne wyth the appourtenaunces to the forsayd. R.
his heyres and assignes for euer at the feast of thanũ=
ciation of our blessed lady the birgin, ꝸ at the feaste of
saynct Mighel tharchaungel by euen porcions. And
if it happen the foresaid yerely rent or annuity of. xl. s
at any of the feastes aboue named at which it ought
to be payd to be behind and vnpayed that than it shal
be lauful for the said. R. his heyres and assignes in to
the sayde tenement or ynne immediatly to enter and
distrayne, ꝸ the distresse so ther found to take, carye,
driue, ꝸ bring away ꝸ in his or theyr custody to retein
til such tyme as al the sayd yerely rent or ãnuyte ꝸ all
and singuler arrerages of the same be fully contẽted
satissfied, ꝸ payd. Of whych yerlye rent or ãnuytye I
haue put y̌ sayd. R. in full ꝸ peasable possession state
ꝸ seyson, by payeng of. vi. d. sterlyng. In wytnes ꝛc.

                   A surren=

¶ A Surrender.

Omnibus Christifidelibus, ad quos præsēs scrip tum peruenerit, Thomas Roger de Barton sa lutem. Cum Johannes Roger pater meus per chartam suam feoffamenti, dederit & concesserit mihi præfato Thome, vnum messuagium cum suis perti tinē. in villa de Barton prædict. situat. inter tenemen tum. R.w. ex parte australi, et stratam regiam vers boream, habend. et tenend. mihi, pro termino vite mee Ita φ post decessum meum, prædict. mesuag. cum su is pertinent. Henrico Roger fratri meo, heredibus et assignatis suis, imperpetuū remaneret. Noueritis me prædictum Thomam, concessisse, et sursum reddidisse præfato Henrico fratri meo totum ius meum et statū que habeo, pro termino vite mee in prædicto mesuag. cum suis pertinentiis. Habend. et tenend. eidem. H. he redibus et assignatis suis imperpetuum. De capita libus dominis feodi illius per seruic. &c.

¶ The fourme of the same in en glysshe.

To all Christen people to whome thys presente wrytynge cometh Thomas Roger of Barton, sendeth gretynge. whereas John Roger my father by hys dede of feoffement, gaue and graūted vnto me the sayde Thomas, one mesuage, woyth the appurtenaunces in the towne of Barton, lyenge be twene the tenement of .R.w. on the southe parte and the strete, towarde the north. To haue and to hold to me for terme of my naturall lyfe. So that after my deceasse the foresayde mesuage woyth the appurtenaū ces shulde remayne hollye to Henrye Roger, my bro ther, hys heyres and assygnes for euer.

knowe

knowe ye, that J the sayde Thomas haue gyuen
and surrendred to the foresayde Harye my ryght title
and state that J haue for terme of my lyfe in the sayd
mesuage wyth the appurtenaunces of the same. To
haue and to holde to the sayde Harye, his heyres and
assignes for euer, of þ chefe lordes of the fee, paying
for the seruice thereof accustomed. Jn wytnesse. ꝛc.

¶ A particion of enheritaunce betwene systers.

Mnibus Christi fidelibus ad quos presēs
scriptum indentatum puenerit Alicia Mo
ris et Maria Moris filie et heredes Ro=
berti Moris nuper de Royston defuncti,
salutem. Cum predict⁹ Robertus pater noster nuper
obierit seisitus in dñico suo vt de feod de duobus te=
nementis, et.rbi.acris terre cum ptineñ. in Royston
predicta iacentibus que nobis prefatis Alicie et Ma=
rie descenderunt iure hereditario post mortem predi=
cti Roberti patris nostri. Noueritis nos bnanimi as=
sensu et consensu nostro per bisum proborū et legali=
um hominū de bicineto nostro diuisionē dictarū terr.
et tenḟ. fecisse sub forma que sequitur bidelicet.qd ego
predicta Alicia senior filia dicti Roberti habeam illd
teñtum situatum in London grene inter.ꝛc. cum oc=
to acris terre arabilis eidem tenemento annex.
Et qd ego predicta M.iunior filia predict. R. habeā
ꝛc. Habend et tenēd nobis hered et assignatis nostris
imperpetuum de capitalibus dñis feod. illorum per
seruicia inde debit. et de iure consueta, quam quidem
particionem siue diuisionem ratificamus et confirma
mus pro nobis et heredibus nostris imperpetuum.
                                          M   Jn

Thys dede
must be īdē
ted accor=
dyng to the
nombre of þ
systers.

Euerye sy=
sters porciō
must be set
in accor=
dyngly.

The boke of sondrye

In cuius rei testimo. vtriₑ parti huius scripti nostri indentati sigilla nostra alternatim apposuimus. Hijs testibus R.M.N.O.P.Q.Dat.⁊c.

⸿ The tenour of the same particion
in Englysshe.

TO al Christen people to whom this preset wrytyng indented commeth, Alice Morys & Mary M. doughters and heyres of Robarte Morys, late of Royston deceffed sendeth gretynge. Where the forsayde Robart Morys our father late dyed seased in his demeane as of fee of two tenementes, and .xvi. acres of lande wyth the appurtenaunces lyinge in Royston aforesayde, whych after the deceffe of our sayde father descended vnto vs by waye of enheritaunce accordynge to the lawe. knowe ye, that we wyth one assent and confent betwene vs by the aduyse of good and lawfull men of our neyghbours, haue made deuysyon and particion of the sayde landes and tenementes, betwene vs in maner and fourme folowyng, that is to saye : that I the foresayde Alyce the elder doughter of the sayde Robarte shall haue that tenemente lyynge in London grene betwene the lande. ⁊c. and .viij. acres of aryable grounde to the sayde tenement annexed, for the due and hole porcion of myne enherytaunce of the premysses. And that I the sayde Marye yonger doughter of the foresayde Robarte shall haue the tenement called Drakes.⁊c. for the iust and hole porcion of myne enheritaunce aforesayde. To haue and to holde to vs, oure heyres and assygnes,

for

foz euer, of the cheſe lozdes of the ſee accozdynge to
the ſeruyce and cuſtome thereupon due and apertey=
nynge. whyche fozeſayde partynge and deuiſion we
the ſayde Alice and Marye, ratifye, allowe, and eſ=
tablyſh foz vs and our heyzes foz euer. In wytneſſe
therof, to eyther parte of theſe wzytynges indented
we haue interchaungeablye ſet oure ſeales, theſe be=
ynge wytneſſe.L.M.N.O.P.Q.R.S.Datum.xx.
die menſis Auguſti.Anno reg.&c.

⸿Aſſignement of dowzye at the churche doze.

Omnibus Chziſti fidelibus ad quos pzeſens
ſcriptum peruenerit Thomas Marham de
walton ſalutem.Noueritis me pzedictum T
dediſſe,côceſſiſſe, & hoc pzeſenti ſcripto meo aſſignaſſe
Petronille vxozi mee in tempoze ſponſaliozum in o=
ſtio eccleſie parochialis de walton pzedict. celebzäd.
vnum tenementum cum vno crofto eidem annex.bo=
cat.C. Habend.et tenend. ſibi et aſſignatis ſuis ad
totam vitam ſuam pzo rata poztione totius dotis ſue
que poſt moztem meam ſibi contingeret.Dat.&c.
In cuius rei teſtimoniü.&c.

⸿The dede afozeſayde in Englyſſhe.

To al Chziſten people to whome thys pzeſent
cômeth, Thomas Marhã of W.ſêdeth gre=
tynge.Be it knowen, that I the fozſayd Tho
mas haue gyuen and graunted, and in this my pze=
ſent wzytynge haue aſſigned to Petronille my wyfe
in the tyme of our eſpouſelles in the churche doze of
walton afozeſayde to be celebzate one tenement with
a crofte to the ſame annexed called C.

M.ij.   To

To haue and to holde to her and her aſſignes all the
terme of her lyfe for the iuſt and hole portion of all
her dowry whych ſhulde happen to her after ꝑ death
of me the ſayde Thomas her huſvande. In wytneſſe
whereof.℈c.Dat.℈c.

¶How the copye ſhulde be made of
landes holden by the yarde.

AD hanc Curiam dñs conceſſit extra manus
ſuas per Johannem Foſter capitalem ſene=
ſcallum ſuum,Thome Dauid et M̃.brori ei⁹
bnum meſuag.et bi.acras terre cum pertineñ.iacent.
apud B . quibus dñs per ſeneſcal. conceſſit ſeſſinam,
heñd.ſibi et hered. ſuis de domino per birgam ad bo=
luntatem dñi ſecundum conſuetuð manerii. Et dant
dño de feoð.pro ingreſſu inde habend.prout patet in
capite,et fecit dño fidelitatem et admiſſus eſt inde te=
nens.℈c.

¶An other forme for certayne rent for
all maner of ſeruyce.

AD hanc Curiã dñs cõceſſit per J.F.ſeneſcallũ
ſuũ T.B.℈ M̃.brori ſue bnum meſuag.cũ.bj.
acris terre.ij.acẽ.boſci cũ pertin.ꝓfatis T.M̃.
hered.et aſſigñ.ſuis ad boluntatem dñi ſecundũ cõſu=
etudinem manerii reddend. inde ãnuatim dño et he=
redibus(bel ſucceſſoribus ſuis) (yf the lorde be a by=
ſhop or ſuche other) bi.s̃. biij.d . pro omnibus et ſin=
gulis ſeruicijs ad duos anni terminos bidelicet ad
feſtũ ſcti Michaelis Archangeli et Annunciationis
beate Marie birginis equis portionibus, et dãt dño
de fine.℈c.et fecet.fidelitatem.℈c.

It is alſo requiſyte to put in certentie in theyr co=
pyes ,all the cuſtomes,rentes,and ſeruices, and that
is in

is in auncient demeane and in all places where the te
nauntes haue their landes by copye to the & their heyres
after the cuſtome of the manoure, for ther they haue
or ought to haue a cuſtomary rolle wherein is euerye
mannes lande conteyned and what rent cuſtomes &
ſeruices euerye man ought to paye and do, and in ma
nye places theyr lawes and theyr cuſtomes be put in
wryttyng and remayne in their owne cuſtodye to put
them in remembraunce whan nede ſhall requyre.
But in caſe there ſhulde be made any newe incroche=
mētes or intackes incloſed or taken in out of the com=
mons or anye myne newe founde as leade, or tynne,
cole, yron, ſtone or other ſuche, yf a copie ſhalbe made
thereof, it is neceſſarye and expedyent to put the rent
therof in the tenauntes copie, for it is a newe thynge
that hath not gone by cuſtume and it wolde be put in
the cuſtomarie rolle, for this newe approuemēt may
fortune eyther to encreaſe or diminiſhe in the rent and
therfore muſte the rentes be contynually expreſſed.
Alſo where a man hath a lordſhyp wherein be many
tenauntes that holde theyr lande of the lord by copye
of courte rolle, for terme of yeres or for terme of lyfe
and haue no ſtate of enheritaunce in the ſame. In all
ſuche cauſes muſte the rentes be declared in the copi=
es. &c.

¶A recognition of a tenaunt what he holdeth of the Lorde.

D hanc curiam venit. A. B. coram. T. P. ſene
ſcallo huius manerii et cognouit ſe tenere de
dño vnū meſuag. decē acr. terr. tres acr. prat.
cū pertinen. in. L. boc. C. libere per cartam in ſocagio
per reddit. xii. d. vel bnā libram piperis et ſect. cur. bis
per an=

num. Et etiam dictus.A.B. cognouit se tenere de do=
mino aliud mesuag cum crosto adiacent. et sex acras
terre arabilis et duas acr.prati cū pertinentiis ad bo=
luntatem domini secundum consuet. manerii, et per
reddit.iii.s. ꝗ fecit fidelitatem, et admissus est inde te=
nens.ꝛc.

CThe fourme of a copye in aunctent
demeane, where thꝛe pꝛocla=
mations shulde be had.

AD hanc cur.tent. ibidem (tali die ꝗ tali anno)
A.B.filius et heres. J.B. venit et sursum red
didit in manus domini vnū mesuag.x.acr.terre, tres
acras pꝛati, cum vno crosto in.D.infra iurisdic.hui⁹
cur.ad opus. T.H.hered,et assignat.suoꝛnm imperpe=
tuum, virtute barganie siue pactionis inter eos fact.
Et super hoc publica pꝛoclamatio in ead.cur.fact. fuit
ꝗ si quis aliquod ius, seu titulum ad eand. mesuag.
terr.prat.ꝗ croft, vel in aliqua eoꝛum percella pꝛeten=
tendere boluit bel haberet, beniret et audiretur ꝗ nul
lus benit ad hanc cur.per ꝗ secundum consuetud.ma
nerii pꝛedict. mesuag. terre, pꝛati, ꝗ crofti, remane=
rent in manus dūi,vsꝗ ad tertiam pꝛoclamationem,
super eisdem fact. et super hoc dies dat. est partibus
pꝛedictis essendi ad pꝛox.cur.manerii pꝛedicti ad audi
end.inde iudicium suum super pꝛemissis.

CEt ad hanc cur.tent.ibidem, (tali die et anno) tam
pꝛedictus A.B.quam pꝛedict T.H. benerunt,ꝗ super
hoc secunda pꝛoclamatio facta fuit super pꝛemissis,ꝗ
si aliquis aliquod ius vel titulum ad pꝛedict mesuag.
ter.pꝛat. ꝛc. haberet aut pꝛetenderet veniret et audire
tur. Et nullus benit et super hoc dies dat. est partib⁹
pꝛedictis essendi ad pꝛox.cur.manerii pꝛedicti ad audi
endum

endum inde iuditium ſuum.

℃Et ad hanc curiam tent.ibidem (tali die.ɾc.) tã pɀe=
dictus I.B.quam pɀedictus T.H.vener. et ſuper hoc
tertia pɀoclamatio facta fuit ſuper pɀemiſſis, ɋ ſi ali=
quis aliquod ius vel titulum ad pɀedictum meſuagi=
um, terras, pɀata, et crofta. vel iu aliqua eoɀum par=
cella haberet, vel pɀetenderet,veniret, et audiretur,ɾ
nullus adhuc venit.

℃Et ſuper hoc dominus per w.H. ſeneſcallum ſuum
conceſſit ſeiſinam de pɀedict.meſuag.terr, pɀat.et croſ
to cum eorum pertinent.pɀefat.T.H.tenēd.ſibi hered.
et aſſignatis ſuis, ſecundum conſuetudinem manerij
pɀedicti, et dat domino de fine pɀo ingreſſu. ɾc. et ad=
miſſus eſt inde tenens, et fecit fidelitatem.ɾc.

       ℃The fourme of a copye in aunci=
           ent demane where the
            wyfe ſhall be exa
             mined.

Dale. Ad cur.tent.ibidem(tali die ɾc)T.B.de N
et E.vxoɀ eius hic in plena cur. ſola examinata
   et confeſſa, ſurſum reddiderunt in manus do=
mini bnū meſuag.ɾ dimidiatã bouatam terre,ac bnã
quatronam terre cum ſuis pertinent.in Dale pɀedict.
vocat. R.ad opus w. C.de O.bnde accidit domino b=
nus equus de heriotto et ſuper hoc venit dictus.w.C.
et cepit de domino dict. meſuagium.ɾc.cum pertinen
tiis, habendum et tenendum ſibi, et Anne vxoɀi ſue,
hered.et aſſign.ipſius. W. imperpetuum, ſecundum
conſuetudinem manerii per redd.conſuetud. ɾ ſeruic.
inde pɀius debit. et conſuet.ɾ dant domino de fine pɀo
ingreſſu.habend.in dictis meſuag.et ceteris pɀemiſ.ɾc
et data eſt eis ſeiſina ɾc.fecer.fidelitatem ɾc.

                        An o=

An other fourme for terme of lyfe.

AD hanc cur. ꝛc. venit. J. D. et. J. vꝛoꝛ eius ipsa
sola examinata coꝛam senescallo et sursum reddi
derunt in manus domini, vnum tenementū cum
pertinentiis in. A. iacent. inter tenemēt. J. C. ex parte orientali et tenement. C. D. ex parte occidentali
et abbuttat super altam viam ex parte australi et super gardinum. E. F. ex parte boꝛeali, ad opus et vsum
G. H. et. A. vꝛoꝛis sue ad terminum vite eoꝛum et alterius eoꝛum diutius biuentis secundum consuetudi
nem manerij, et dant domino de fin. ꝛc. et fecerunt fidelitatem.

ℂAn other fourme vpon con dicion.

AD hanc cur.ꝛc. venit. J. C. et sursum reddidit
in manus domini vnum cotag. iacens ꝛc. ad o-
pus et vsū. J. D. ꝛc. tenend. sibi, et heredibus suis de
domino ad voluntatem domini secundum consuetudi
nem manerii sub condicionibus subsequētibus videlicet si pꝛedictus J. D. soluat, aut solui faciat pꝛefato. J. C. xl. s. ad festa sancti Johannis Baptiste, et
omniū sanctoꝛū pꝛox. futur. post datum huius cur. e-
quis poꝛcionibus, ꝙ tunc pꝛesens sursum reddicio sit
in suo roboꝛe et effectu, et si ipse defecerit in solutione
solutionum pꝛedictarum, in parte vel in toto quod ex
tunc bene licebit pꝛefat. J. C. et assign. suis reintrare,
et rehabere pꝛedictum cottag. ista sursum reddicione
non obstante in aliquo, et dat domino de fin. et fecit fi-
delitatē. etc. et admissus est. ꝛc.

ℂAn other maner of surrender whyche is made vnto the baylye oute of the courte.

AD hanc

D hanc Curiã.ꝛc. compertum est qꝺ T.C.er
tra Curiã sursũ reddidit in manus J.D. Bal
liui in presencia D.R. et aliorum tenentium
domini huius manerij hoc testantium, bnã acr ã ter
re in R.quondam T.R.ad opus W. J. cui dñs inde
concessit seisinam tenend.sibi et hered.ꝛc.de seruic.ꝛc.
et dat.ꝛc.

**¶ An other forme where the lorde graun-
teth a copye of hys specyall graunt.**

D Curiam apud D.A.tent. ibidem (tali die
ꝛc.) preceptum fuit Balliuo seisire in manus
dñi bnũ tentũ siue mesuag. cũ ptineñ. nuper
in tenura J.B. vocat.R. eo quod ipe alie nauerit et
bendidit dictum tenementum cuidã T.U.sine licen
tia dñi.ꝛc.et inde respondebit dño de eritibꝰ quousꝗ.
ꝛc. Et ꝙ in ista eadẽ curia dñs er sua gracia speciali
cõcessit dictũ tenementũ cum pertineñ.prefat.J.b.cui
dñs inde concessit seisinam habend. sibi et hered. ꝛc.
de domino ad boluntatem secundum. ꝛc. Et dat. ꝛc.
Et fecit.ꝛc.

**¶ An other maner for terme of yeres,
where the lorde shall kepe
reparation.**

D hanc Curiã dñs per J.F. senescallũ suum
concessit E.R.bnũ mesuag. cum donubus sup
astantibus et diuersas terras prat. pascuas et
pasturas cum sepibus fossatis et omnibus alijs suis
pertineñ bocat. A. Habend.et tenend.sibi et assignatis suis a festo sancti Michaelis archangeli proximo
futur.post dat . huius curie bsꝗ ad finem et terminũ
quadraginta annorum ertunc proximo sequentium ⁊
        N   plenarie

plenarie complendozum reddend. inde annuatim.xx.
s̄.ad duos anni terminos,videlicet.et cetera.per equa
les poztiones Pzouiso semper ꝙ durante termino
pzedicto pzedictus dominus inueniet meremiũ ma=
teriem, et ligna totiens quotiens necessarium fuerit
dicto tenemento ad emendandũ reparandũ et susti=
nendum, et dat domino de fine.ꝛc. Et fecit fidelita=
tem.ꝛc.

¶In other maner where a man pzeten= deth a tytle,and after relea= seth in the courte.

AD hanc Curiam tent .ꝛc. cumpertum est , quod
cum dominus per T. Ph. senescallum suum ad
Curam tent.apud C.tali die et anno concessit ex=
manus suas Wilhelmo Piers et heredibus suis
bnam petiam terre continentem circa tres acras ter=
re siue plus siue minus habeatur, quondam T.C.in
A.iacentem inter terram A.B. ex parte australi, et
terram W.S.ex parte bozeali.Habend.et tenend.ꝛc.
ad boluntatem domini secundum cõsuetudinem ma=
neril,et postea benit quedam Agneta Wilhelm. co=
ram pzefato T .Ph. senescallo domini , et pzetendit
habere titulum in pzedicta petia terre, et hic pzesens
in curia remisit relaxauit et imperpetuum quietum
clamauit pzefato Wilhelmo Piers ꝛ heredibus suis
per licentiam domini totum ius suum et clameum,
que habet bel habuit , bel in futurum habere poterit,
in pzedicta petia terre ꝛ in qualibet inde percella. Ita
bidelicet quod nec ipsa Agneta nec heredes sui,nec a=
liquis alius nomine eozũ aliquod ius bel clameum
in

in pdicta petia terre de cetero exigere vel vidicare po=
terit,ſed ab omni actione iuris vel clamei ſint exclu=
ſi per pzeſentes.xc.Dat.domino.xc. Et fecit fidelita=
tem.xc.

　　¶A fourme of a copye where the
　　　heyze is admytted to hys
　　　lande,after the death of
　　　　　hys father.

D hanc Curiam tent.xc.compertum eſt
quod J. B. obijt ſeiſitus poſt vltimam
Curiam qui de domino tenuit ſibi et he=
redibus ſuis vnum tenementum vocat.
E.et obijt inde ſeiſitus.Et dicunt qð R.
B.filius eius eſt pzoximus heres,et plene etatis (vel
infra etatem videlicet duodecim annozum,et in cuſto
dia T.W.) (vel R. M. frater eius , vel conſangui=
neus eius eſt pzoximus heres eiuſdem et plene eta=
tis)et pzeſens hic in Curia petit admitti,et admiſſus
eſt inde tenens tenend.ſibi et hered.ſuis de domino,
ad voluntatem domini ſecundum conſuetudinem.xc.
Dat.xc.et fecit fidelitatem.xc.

　　¶An other fourme of a copye
　　　where the landes are made
　　　intayled with a remayn=
　　　　　der ouer.

D hanc Curiam compertum eſt quod R . B.
de A.ad curiam têt.apð E.(tali die ᵹ an.xc.)
ſurſum reddidit in manus domini vnum te=
nementum et tres acras terre vocat.C . ad opus R.
C.filij eiuſdem R. et Alicie vxozis ſue quibus domi=
nus conceſſit ſeiſinam tenend.ſibi et heredibus de coz
pozibus eozum legittime pzocreatis.

　　　　　　　　N.ij.　　　Et

Et ſi pꝛedictus R. et Alicia vxoꝛ eius ſine hered. de coꝛpoꝛibus eoꝛum legittime pꝛocreatis obierint ꝙ tunc pꝛedicta terra et tenementa cum ſuis pertinen. remaneant rectis heredibus ipſius R. B. Et modo curia iſta infoꝛmatur per totuꝝ homagium ꝙ pꝛedictus R. ⁊ A. obierunt ſine heredibꝰ inter eos pꝛocreat et pꝛedictus R. B. ſimiliter, ⁊ ſuper hoc venit J. B. frater et heres pꝛedicti R. B. et petit admitti et admiſſus eſt tenens. ꝛc. Et per licentiam domini pꝛefatus J. B. conceſſit pꝛedictum tenementum et terras que ei remanſerunt poſt moꝛtem pꝛedictoꝛum R. B. et R. C. et Alicie vxoꝛis ſue remanerent W. C. et heredibus ſuis cui dominus inde conceſſit ſeiſinam tenend. ad voluntatem domini ſecundun conſuetudinem. ꝛc. Et dat. ꝛc. et fecit fidelitatem. ꝛc.

ℂ An other maner of copye foꝛ terme of lyfe, wyth dyuers remaynders ouer.

A

Ð hanc Curiam venit R. B. ⁊ ſurſum reddidit in manus domini vnum meſuagium et octo acras terre cuſtomar. vocat. A. vt dominus faciet inde volútatem ſuam, et dominus inde habeat ſeiſinam. Et ex gratia ſua ſpeciali reconceſſit pꝛedictum meſuagium et terras pꝛefato R. B. et J. vxoꝛi eius durante vita eoꝛum, ita ꝙ poſt eoꝛum deceſſum dictum tenementum et terre remaneant B. vxoꝛi A. durante vita ſua, et poſt deceſſum ipſius B. pꝛedictam terram et tenementum remaneant rectis heredibus ipſius R. B. imperpetuum tenend. eijſdem R. B. et J. vxoꝛi eius durante tota vita eoꝛum per virgã

ad

ad voluntatem domini ſecundum &c.in forma predi=
cta ſaluo iure cuiuſlibet.&c. Et predict.R.et J dant do
mino de fine &c. et fecerunt fidelitatem.&c.

    ¶A ſurrender out of the court and a
        remaynder wyth a con=
          dicion.

AD hanc cur.compertum eſt,ꝙ.R.F.languens
in extremis ſurſum reddidit in manus.B.R.
extra curiam per manus J.H.in preſencia.A.C.B.D
tenent.huius manerii hoc teſtantium vnum meſuagi=
um cū pertin. &c. ad opus.A.vxoris predicti.R, F.te=
nend.ſibi, pro ſeruicio inde debit.ſecundum conſuetu=
dinem manerii, pro termino vite ſue.Jta ꝙ poſt mor
tē dicte. A. predict.meſuag.remaneant Johanni filio
predict.R.et. A.et heredibus de corpore ſuo legitime
precreatis.Et ſi contingat dctū.J.obire ſine hered.de
corpore ſuo legitime procreat,ꝙ tūc pdictū meſuagiū
remaneat.R.filio pdict. R.&.A.et heredib⁹ de corpore
ſuo legitime procreatis. Et ſi cōtingat dictū. R.obire
ſine herede de corporeſuo legittime ꝑcreat.ꝙ tūc pre
dict. meſuagiū per executores vtriuſꝙ eorum diuti⁹
biuent.bendatur et denarii inde recepti et prouenien=
tes in pauperes et alias elemoſinas erogentur,diſpo
nentur, et diſtribuentur, prout eis melius videbitur
expedire, quibus dominus inde conceſſit ſeiſinam te=
nend. in forma predicta, ad voluntatem domini,ſecū=
dum conſuetudinē manerii et dant domino de fin.&c.
et fecit fidelitat.&c.

¶And note that yf one of them dye, and the heyre be
wythin age,the fidelitye muſt be differred tyl he come
meth to lawfull yeres,&c.

                           A ſup=

¶A supplicatyon to be exempte from all
maner enqueſtes and iuries
wythin the loꝛdſhyppe.

AD hanc curiam benit R. C. inſtanter ſuppli=
cand.pꝛout ipſe per trāſacta plurima tempo=
ra ſupplicauit,et pꝛofert domino finem annu
alem nomine exemptionis, vt ipſe ex ſua gratia ſpeci
ali et fauoꝛe ob cauſam ſenectutis infirmitatis ꝗ debi
litatis ſue,poſſit exonerari de cetero ab omnibus ꝗ ſin
gulis inquiſicionibus iuramentis et offic. quoꝛꝫcūꝗ,
tam in hac billa , quam alibi infra dominium dn̄i ſibi
obiiciend.ꝗ aſſignand.Quapꝛopter aſpecta bera ſenec
tute bna cum infirmitate et debilitate ſua, ſub fine an
nuali nomine exemptionis inde pꝛolata ac ſuggeſtio=
ne eius per tenentes et biſus beraciter ꝗ congrue teſti
ficata in pꝛemiſſis,modo dominus conceſſit in iſta cu=
ria per.J.P.ſeneſcallum ſuum pꝛefato. R. C. huiuſ=
modi licentiam, fauoꝛem et exemptionem, ad termi=
num bite ſue duratur.Et pꝛedict.R.C.dat domino de
annuali reddit.perſoluend.annuatim.iiii.d.ad termi=
nos bſuales.

YE ſhall bnderſtande that ther is no maner of
eſtates made of fre land by polle deed oꝛ deed
indented,but there maye be made the ſame of
copy landes by copy,yf they be well made and entred
in the courte rolles . And the ſtewarde is bounde by
law and conſcience to be a iudge indifferent betwene
the tenauntes and the loꝛde, and to enter theyꝛ copies
truly in the court rolles of the loꝛde foꝛ that ſhall be a
greate cōmoditie to the loꝛde to knowe his pꝛeſidence
custcmes

cuſtomes and ſeruices and alſo a great aſſuraunce to
the tenauntes,foʒ yf theyʒ copyes ſhulde be loſte they
may bouche and reſoʒt to the court rolles,and the ſte
warde maye make them newe copies, accoʒdynge to
the olde pʒeſident in the loʒdes recoʒdes, euen as it is
of free land oʒ of any other matter at the cõmon lawe
whan it is enrolled accoʒdyng to ÿ ſtatute which ſhal
euer teſtifye the trueth, what chaunce ſo euer happe=
neth to the parties, as ye maye reade in the booke of
ſurueyenge , wherein be many good examples of in=
rollynge and makynge of recoʒdes.

ℂAn endenture of ſale wyth a repur= chace.

Ꮞ Hys Indenture made the.xbii. day of Auguſte
in the.xxxii.yere of our ſoueraygne loʒde kynge
Henry the eyght, by the grace of god kynge of
Englande,fraunce and Irelande, defendoure of the
faythe,and in earth ſupʒeme head of the church of En
glande and Ireland,betwene A.B.of C. in the coũty
of R.yoman on the one party,and R.M.of D.in the
ſayd coũtye gentylmã on ÿ other party, wytneſſeth ÿ
the ſaid A.B.the day of makyng hereof,foʒ ÿ ſumme
of fourtye markes ſterlyng to hym by ÿ ſaid Rychard
well and truelye contented and payde, in hand at the
inſealynge of thys endenture, wherof and wherw
the ſayde A.B. knowlegeth hym ſelfe wel and truely
contented and payde, and thereof and of euerye par=
celle thereof, dothe clerelye acquyte and dyſcharge
the foʒeſayde Rycharde, hys heyʒes,and executours
by the=

by these pꝛesentes.) Hathe bargayned, and solde, and by thys Indenture bargayneth, and selleth, clerely vnto the sayde Rycharde hys heyꝛes and assignes to theyꝛ owne vse foꝛ euer, all those hys messuages, landes, tenementes, medowes, leases, pastuꝛes, and appourtenaunces, sette, lyenge, and beyng, in the towne parysshe and feldes, of Asshefourthe in the countye of leycester, whyche sometyme belonged to Thomas Freman late of Assheforth afoꝛesayde yeman deceassed. And in lykewyse the sayde. A. foꝛ the summe afoꝛesayde, hath bargayned and solde by this endenture vnto the sayde Richarde all, deades charters, euidences, escryptes, scrowes, wꝛytynges and mynymentes, concernynge the pꝛemisses, and anye parte oꝛ parcell therof and the same deades, charters euidences, escriptes, scrowes, wꝛytynges, and minimentes, the sayd. B. couenaunteth by thys endenture to delyuer oꝛ cause to be delyuered to ꝑ sayd Richard hys heyꝛes oꝛ assygnes, befoꝛe the feast of the natiuitye of sayncte John the Baptist, next commynge after the date hereof, to haue and to holde all the sayde mesuages, landes, tenementes, medowes, leases pastures, and all other the pꝛemisses, wyth theyꝛ appurtenaunces, to the sayde. R. hys heyꝛes, and assygnes, to theyꝛ owne vse foꝛ euer.

⁋ And the sayde. A. B. couenaunteth and graunteth, by these pꝛesentes that he oꝛ hys heyꝛes befoꝛe ꝑ feste of sayncte Myghell the archaungell whiche shall be in the yere of oure Loꝛde God. M. fyue hundꝛed. xlii. shall make oꝛ cause to be made to the sayd Rychard, & hys heyꝛes & to suche other ꝑsonnes as he oꝛ they shall name oꝛ assygne to the vse of the same Rychard hys

A clause of estate foꝛ assuraunce of ꝑ bargayn.

his heyzes and assignes foz euer, a good sufficient &
lawfull estate in the lawe in fee symple,of and in the
sayde mesuages,landes and tenementes, and other
the premisses with the a ppurtenaunces by dede fyne
feoffament,recouerie,release, with warrauntie,sur=
rendze oz otherwyse,at the costes and charges in the
lawe of the sayde Richarde,oz his heyzes, as by the
learned counsayle of the sayde Rycharde oz his hey=
res shalbe best deuysed and requyzed. The same me=
suage,landes,tenementes, and all other premysses,
to be then clerely discharged of al former bargaynes
former sales,tytles of enheritaunce, ioynters, dow=
ryes,mozgages,statutes of marchaunte, statutes of
staple of Westmynstre,intrusions, fozfaytures, lea=
ses,iudgementes, condempnations, executions, ar=
rerages of rentes,and of al other maner of charges,
and encombzaunces whatsoeuer they be.The rentes
and seruices from thenceforth due to the chefe lozdes
of the same fees onlye outtaken and excepted.
And the sayde A.B. couenaunteth and graunteth by
this indenture,that all suche persons as now stande,
and be infeffed and seased of and in the sayde mesua=
ges,landes, tenementes and other the premisses, w̄
the appurtenaunces, oz of oz in any parte oz parcell
of the same, shall at all tymes, from the daye of the
date of this indenture fozwarde, stande,remayne,&
be infeffed and seased of and in the same, to the vse of
the same Rycharde, hys heyzes, and assygnes foz e=
uer.And also the sayde A.B.couenaunteth, & graun=
teth by these presentes, that he and his heyzes, and
all other persons hauyng,claymyng,oz pretendynge
to haue any estate,ryght,tytle, vse oz interest of oz in
                                    D   the

the sayde mesuages, landes, tenementes, and other the premisses with theyr appurtenaunces, or of or in any parte or parcell of the same at al tymes, from the daye of the date of these presentes forthwarde, shall do, cause and suffre to be done, all and euerye thynge and thynges whyche by the learned counsayle of the sayde Rycharde or hys heyres shalbe deuysed for the further assuraunce of all and singuler the premisses, to the forsayd R. to hys heyres and assignes, to their owne vse for euer. And in lykewyse the sayde A.B. couenaunteth and graunteth by this indenture, that he the same A.B. the daye of makynge hereof is very true owner and possessour in hys owne ryght, of all the forsayde mesuage, landes, tenementes and other the premisses wyth the appurtenaunces, and that he hath full power, strength and auctoritie in his owne ryght to bargayne and sell the same to the sayde R. and to hys heyres in maner and fourme aforesayde.

The clause of repurchace.

And further it is couenaunted, condescended and a= greed betwene the sayde partyes, and the sayd R. for his ptie couenauteth & grauteth by this indenture, ꝑ yf ꝑ sayd A. his heyres or assignes pay or cause to be payed to ꝑ sayd R. his heyres or assignes .xl. markes of good & lawful money of Eng. (togyther wᵗ al such costes & expenses as ꝑ same R. his heyres & assygnes shalbe at, aswel in ꝑ makig sure of ꝑ same mesuages

If ꝑ seller be agreed to fynde repa= rations du= ryng ꝑ pos= session of ꝑ bier.

landes, ten. &c. as also in repayryng, makyng, & amen dyng of the same) at anye tyme wᵗin the terme of. iiij. yeres next after the date of this indenture: That thã the sayd R. his heyres, or assignes, shall make to the same A.B. & his heyres, in good, sure sufficiẽt, lawful and indefesable estate to there owne vse & their hey= res

res fo2 euer of ꝗ in thefame mefuages , landes, tene=
mētes ꝗ other the p2emiffes with ꝑ appurtenaūces ꝗ
euery part ꝗ parcell of thē.The fame to be thā clerely
difcharged of al fo2mer bargaines,fo2mer fales,ioyn
ters,dowers, ftatutes of the ftaple of Weft.ftatutes
marchaūt,ꝗ of al other charges ꝗ encōb2aūces,what
foeuer they be,by the fayd R. his hey2es o2 affignes,
at any tyme cōmenced,made o2 done. And at ꝑ fayde
affuraūce of the fame to the fayde A.in fourme afo2e=
fayde to be made,the fayd R. couenaūteth and graū=
teth by thefe p2efentes,to delyuer o2 caufe to be dely=
uered to the fayd A.his hey2es o2 affignes al fuche e=
uidences,dedes ꝗ w2ytynges, as he the fame R. his
hey2es o2 affignes fhal then haue cōcernyng the fame
mefuages,lādes,tenemētes,ꝗ other ꝑp2emiffes with
the appurtenaunces , bnder lyke maner and fourme,
as he the fayd Ryc. receyued them without fraude o2
further delaye. In wytneffe wherof.ꝗc.

℃This dede is cōmōly bfed whē a mā layeth his lād
to mo2gage to an other,ꝗ couenaūteth to pay him by
a certayne daye bnder payne of fo2fayture.And fo in
cafe the daye be b2oken, the landes are as fure to the
lender of the money as if it were a playne bargayne
o2 a fale.It is alfo bery good in Wales, where they
bfe to pledge lande,called Ty2 p2yd.

℃An Indenture of fale of wood.

His Indēture made betwene A.B.of. T.in ꝑ
coūtie of D.gent.of ꝑ one partie,ꝗ E.f.of S
in ꝑ fame T.yomā of ꝑ other ptie: witneffeth,
that the fayde A.B.the daye of makyng hereof, hath
bargayned and folde,ꝗ by thefe p2efent Indentures
doth clerely bargayne ꝗ fell bnto the fayd E.al thofe

hys woodes and vnderwoodes , now standyng and
growyng in and vpon hys groues and hedgegroues
called M.in the paryſh of N.in the Countie of Eſſex.
And the ſayde E. doth couenaunt and graunt by this
Indenture,that he,his executours oꝛ aſſygnes,ſhall
leaue ſtandyng in and vpon the foꝛſayde landes cal=
led M. competent and ſufficiente ſtathelles and ſto=
rers,accoꝛdyng to the cuſtome in the ſame countrye,
heretofoꝛe vſed.And alſo the ſayde R. doth couenaut
and graunt by this Indenture,that he,his executou=
res oꝛ aſſygnes at theyꝛ owne coſtes and charges all
hedges and fences belongynge to the ſayde groues
and hedgerowes well and ſufficyently ſhall amende
reſtoꝛe,and repayꝛe,when and as often as nede ſhall
requyꝛe,from the daye of the ſellynge of the ſayd woo=
des,to the ende and terme of.iiij. yeres then next en=
ſuyng,foꝛ the ſauegarde of the ſpꝛynges growynge
vpon the ſame. And the ſayde E. doeth foꝛther coue=
naunt and graunt by theſe pꝛeſentes, that he,his ex=
ecutours oꝛ aſſygnes , ſhall not fell anye of the ſame
woodes,oꝛ vnderwoodes,but in due and ſeaſonable
tymes of fellynge,that is to ſaye, yerely betwene the
feaſtes of Saynct Michael the Archangell , and the
Annunciation of our bleſſed ladye the virgine, from
the feaſte of Saynct Michael the Archangell nexte
commynge after the date hereof to the ende ⁊ terme
of thꝛe yeares , from thence nexte enſuynge , fullye
to be complete ⁊ ended. And the foꝛeſayd A.B.foꝛ his
parte doeth couenaunte and graunt, by thys Inden=
ture,ꝑ the ſayde E . hys executoures,⁊ aſſignes ſhall
haue free ingreſſe,⁊ regreſſe , to ⁊ from the ſayd woo=
des ⁊ vnderwoodes,with hoꝛſe,carte,⁊ cariage,at al
tymes

tymes, accordynge to hys pleasure, for the fellynge, hewyng, cutting downe, & carying away of þ forsaid vnderwoodes, in maner and fourme afore declared, durynge all the foresayde terme, wythout let or interruption of any person or persons. For the sale & bargayne of all whyche woodes and vnderwoodes, the sayde E. doth couenaunt and graunt by these presentes to paye or cause to be payed to the sayde A. hys executours or assignes. xx.li. of good and lawefull money of Englande in maner and fourme folowynge. That is to saye in hande at the sealynge of these endentures.x.li. of whyche.x.li. the sayde A.B. knowelegeth hym selfe well and truly satissyed and payd & therof, and of euery parcell of the same clerelye dothe acquyte and dyscharge the sayde John hys heyres, & executours, by these presentes and at the feast of the natiuitye of our lorde god nexte commynge after the date hereof.x.li. in full payment of the sayde.xx.li. In wytnes wherof &c.

¶ An endenture of bargayne of wheate.

This Indenture made betwene A.B. of w. in the countye of kent yeman on the one parte, and C. D. of Lambehith in the countye of Surr. gentylman on the other parte, wytnesseth that the sayde A.B. the daye of makynge hereof, hath bargayned & solde & by these presentes bargayneth & selleth vnto þ sayde C.D. xx. quarters of wheate and. xx. quarters of rye, good wheate and rye cleane and marchauntable, wyth the beste, accomptynge.viii. busshelles with the heape to euerye quarter. All whyche.xx. quarters wheate, and.xx. quarters rye, the sayde A.B. doth couenaunt and graunte by thys endenture that he hys

executours

executours oz assygnes, at hys oz theyz owne coste &
charge, shall delyuer oz cause to be delyuered to the
sayde C.D.to hys executours oz assignes, franke and
free at the dwellynge house of the sayde C.D.of Lã=
behith afozesayde befoze the feaste of the Natiuitie of
oure lozde god nexte commynge after the date hereof
wythout any further delaye fraude oz contradiction.
And the sayd.C.D.couenãuteth & graunteth by this
endenture that he hys executours oz assygnes shal be
readye and receaue all the same.xx. quarters wheate
and.xx.quarters rye at all tyme and tymes whan soe
uer the fozesayde.A.B. oz hys executours oz assygnes
shall bzynge the same to be delyuered in maner and
fourme as is afoze declared . Foz the bargayne, and
sale of all which twentye quarters wheat &.xx. quar=
ters rye , & foz the delyuery therof in maner & fourme
afozesayd, ý sayd C.D. couenaunteth & graunteth by
these pzesentes to paye oz cause to be payd to the sayd
A.B.hys executours oz assygnes, foz euery quarter of
the sayde wheate.viii.shyllynges sterlynge, & foz eue=
rye quarter of the sayde rye. vi.shyllynges sterlyng in
maner and fourme folowynge, that is to saye &c .

A clause ob=
ligatozye in
the enden=
ture.

To all and synguler couenauntes grauntes, pay=
mentes, articles, and agrementes afoze reherced on
eyther parte of the sayde partyes well and truely to
be obserued and kepte, eyther of the same partyes bin
deth them self to other in the summe of twenty
poundes sterlynge, well and trulye to
be payde, by thys endenture.
In wytnesse wherof &c.
An Indenture of settynge ouer of
a lease.

Thys

Hys Indenture made betwene. A.B. ciſtizen and Mercer of London, on that one partye, and C.D. Citizen and Haſberdaſher of London, on that other partye, wytneſſeth, that whereas E.F Cytyzen and Mercer of London, by hys endenture of a leaſe, bearynge date &c. Graunted, and to ferme dyd lette vnto the ſayde A.B. all that hys tenemente and houſe, wyth ſhoppes, cellers, ſollers, warehouſes, and appourtenaunces, ſette, lyenge, and beynge in the paryſſhe of ſaynct Marga.&c. whyche is nowe in the tenure and occupacion of the ſayde A.B.

To haue, and to holde the ſayde tenemente, ſhopſpes, cellers, ſollers, warehowſes, and appourteſnaunces, to the ſayde A.B. to hys executours, and aſſygnes, from the feaſte of ſayncte Mychaell the arſchaungell laſte paſſed befoze the date of the ſayde enſdenture, vnto the ende and terme, of thyztye yeares, from thence nexte enſuyng and fullye to be complete and ended, yeldynge, and payenge therefoze yerelye, durynge the ſayde terme, to the ſayde. E.F. hys heyſres oz aſſygnes foure pounde of good and lawefull moneye of Englande, at.iiii.termes, of the yere in the cytye of London, vſuall by euen poztions wyth dyſuers other couenauntes grauntes and artycles ſpeciſfyed and compzyſed in the ſayd endentures as by the ſame endentures thereof made, moze playnlye doth appeare.

Wherupon nowe the ſame.A.B. foz the ſumme of twenty pounde to hym in handes by the ſayd C.D. þ daye of makyng herof well and trulye contented and payed, whereof the ſayde A.knowlegeth &c.

Hath

hath bargayned, folde, and fette ouer, and by thys
endenture doth bargayne and clerely fell vnto p̄ fayd
C.D. all hys eftate, ryghte, tytle, vfe, intereft, and
terme of yeres, whyche he hath yet to come in the pre
miffes by the vertue of the indenture, and leafe afoze
mentioned. To haue and to holde the fayde tenement
wyth ſhoppes, follers, celers, warehoufes, and appourtenaunces to the fayde C.D. hys executoures ⁊
affygnes, from the feaft of faynct Mychael the archā
gell, nexte commynge after the date hereof vnto the
ende and terme of all the yeres yet foz to come fpecifyed and compzyfed in the fozmer endenture of a leafe.
The fame C.D. hys executours oz affignes yeldyng
payenge, doynge, and perfourmynge all, and euerye
thynge and thynges, whyche the fayde A. by vertue
of the fozmer endenture is bounde oz ſtādeth charged
foz to do and therof clerelye to acquyte and dyfcharge
the fayd A.B. and hys executours by thefe pzefentes.
And the fayde A.B. couenaunteth and graunteth by
thys pzefentes, that he at no tyme befoze p̄ date hereof hath done, noz at any tyme hereafter ſhal do, caufe
oz fuffer to be done, any acte oz thynge whych ſhulde
oz maye be pzeiudiciall oz hurtefull vnto the fayde C.
D. hys executours and affygnes in hauyng and enioy
ynge all the fayde tenement. ⁊c. oz any parte oz parcel
of the fame, in maner and fourme as is afoze reher-
fed. In wytnes ⁊c.

℣An endenture foz the fale of a
reuertion.

Thys endenture made the fyzfte daye of October
in the .xxxiii. yere of the reygne of our fouerayn
lozde kynge Henry the eyght ⁊c. betwene Bzyan Murell

an Murell of Wakefelde in the Countie of Yozke, of
the one parte ⁊ R. F, citizin and Surgion of Londō
on ÿ other partye: wytnesseth that the sayde Robert,
the day of makyng hereof hath bargayned ⁊ solde, ⁊
by these pzesentes doth bargayne ⁊ sell vnto the sayd
Bzian, and to his heyzes foz euer, all the reuersyon
when it shall happen to come and fall incontinent by
and after the death of Johan Gibson grandmother
to the sayde Robert, of and in all those landes, tene=
mentes, meddowes, leases, woodes, pastures, ren=
tes, reuersions, seruices, with all and singuler the
commodities ⁊ appurtenaūces longyng to the same,
set, lying ⁊ beyng in the toune and feldes of A. in the
countie afozesayde (now in the holdyng of Thomas
Fletcher) and all his ryght, clayme, tytle, vse, posses=
syon, and interest of and in the same.   And also the
sayde R. by this Indenture bargayneth and selleth
vnto the sayde Bzyan, his heyzes, and assignes foz e=
uer, all and singuler dedes, charters, euidences scry=
ptes, scrowes, minimentes, ⁊ wzytynges concerning
the fozsayde landes, tenementes, and other the pze=
misses with the appurtenaūces oz any parte therof,
and the same and euery one of them the sayd Robert
couenaunteth and graunteth to deliuer oz cause to be
delyuered to the sayd Bzian, his heyzes oz assignes,
at al tymes hereafter, as he may them get oz laufull=
ly come by.   To haue and to holde the sayde landes,
tenementes, and other the pzemisses wᵗ the appurte=
naunces, and the right, title, vse, and reuersion of the
same to the sayde Bzian, his heyzes and assignes, to
theyz owne vse foz euer, incontinent after the decease
of the sayde Johan G. And the sayde R. couenaūteth
P   and

and graunteth by this Indenture, that he oꝛ his hey
res within a moneth next after the deceaſſe of the foꝛ
ſayde Johan ſhall make oꝛ cauſe to be made to the
ſayde Bꝛian and his heyꝛes, and to ſuche other per
ſons as he oꝛ they ſhall name and aſſigne to the vſe of
the ſayde Bꝛyan, his heyꝛes and aſſignes foꝛ euer, a
good ſure, ſufficient and lawfull eſtate in the lawe, in
fee ſimple, of and in the ſayd landes, tenementes and
all other the pꝛemiſſes with the appurtenaunces, be
it by dede, fyne, feoffement, recouerie, releaſe, wyth
warrauntie oꝛ otherwyſe, as by the learned coun
ſayle of the ſayde Bꝛyan oꝛ hys heyꝛes ſhalbe aduy
ſed. The ſame to be then clerely diſcharged of all foꝛ
mer bargaynes, foꝛmer ſales, tytles, ioynters, dow
ryes, ſtatutes marchaunt, ſtatutes of the ſtaple, of
Weſtmynſtre, intruſions, fynes, foꝛfaytures, vſes,
wylles, iudgementes, executions, condemnations, ⁊
of all other maner of charges, and encombꝛaunces,
whatſoeuer they be. The rentes and ſeruyces from
thencefoꝛth due to the chefe loꝛdes of the fees of the
ſame, and the ryght ⁊ title of the ſayd Johan duryng
her naturall lyfe, of and in the pꝛemiſſes alonelye ex
cept and reſerued. And further the ſayd R. couenaun
teth and graunteth by this Indenture, that he ⁊ hys
heyꝛes and all other perſons hauyng oꝛ pꝛetendyng
to haue any eſtate, ryght, tytle, vſe, claymie, oꝛ intereſt
of oꝛ in the foꝛſayde landes, tenementes, and other ꝑ
pmiſſes wō the appurtenaũces, oꝛ of oꝛ in any part oꝛ
parcell of the ſame at all tymes from the deceaſſe of ꝑ
foꝛſayd Johan foꝛthwarde ſhall do, cauſe and ſuffre
to be done all ⁊ euery thyng and thynges, whiche by
the learned counſayl of the ſayd B. oꝛ his heyꝛes ſhal
be

be aduyſed foʒ the further aſſuraunce ⁊ ſure makyng
of al the foʒſayd landes,tenemētes, and other the pʒ
miſſes wyth the appurtenaunces to the ſayde B. his
heyʒes and aſſygnes to theyʒ owne vſe foʒ euer.
Foʒ the ſale and bargayne of al which.⁊c.(ſettyng in
the payment as in other eramples here afoʒe.)

¶In other ſale of reuerſion in the ma⸗
ner of a dede in latyne.

Mnibus Chʒiſti fidelibus ad quos pn̄tes li⸗
tere puenerit J.H.ſenioʒ de L.in com̄.midle⸗
ſer yoman.Salutē in dn̄o ſempiternā.Cū C.
M.bidua que fuit vroʒ J.M. de H.in Com̄. A. huſ⸗
bandman iurta boluntatē eiuſdē J. M. habeat et te⸗
neat ad terminū bite eiuſdē C. er dimiſſione traditio⸗
ne et charte indentate cōfirmatione mei dict . J.H.ac
J.B.nuper de B.pʒedict. iam defunct. oīa illa terras,
tenement.redditus et ſeruic.cum pʒatis,paſcuis,pa⸗
ſturis bijs ſemitis ſepibus foſſatis,boſcis,ſubboſcis,
et omnib⁹ ſuis pertineñ. que ego dictus J. H. et pʒe⸗
dict.J.B. quondā cōiuncti habuim⁹ nobis heredib⁹
et aſſignatis noſtris imperpetuum er dono et feoffa⸗
mento dicti J.M. in billa et campis de L. in Comit.
pʒedict.reuerſione omnium pʒedict.terraꝝ.tenement.
reddit.ſeruic.cum pʒatis,paſcuis, bijs, ſemitis,ſepi⸗
bus.foſſatis,boſcis,ſubboſcis , et omnibus ſuis per⸗
tinentijs poſt moʒtem dicti C.mihi pʒefat. J. heredi⸗
bus et aſſignatis meis de iure ſpectante . Noueritis
me pʒefatum J.H . dimiſiſſe,tradidiſſe, liberaſſe ,et
hoc pʒeſenti ſcripto meo confirmaſſe Nicholao S.de
L.pʒedict.dictam reuerſionem omniū pʒedict.terraꝝ.
tenꝭ.reddit.et ſeruic.cū pʒatis,paſcuis, paſturis bijs
ſemitis,ſepib⁹,foſſatis,boſc.ſubboſc.⁊ oīb⁹ ſuis ptiñ

statim cum acciderit post moꝛtem dict.C. Ita ꝙ oīa
pꝛedict.terre,tenementa,reddit.seruicia cū pꝛatis.ꝛc.
et omnibus suis ptineñ.que post moꝛtem dict.C.mi:
hi pꝛefato J H.hered.et assignatis meis reuertere,re
manere, ꝗ descēdere deberēt,statim ꝗ immediate post
moꝛtem dicte Cicilie integre remaneant pꝛefato N.
S.Habenð.et tenenð.dictam reuersionem cum om:
nib⁹ et singulis pꝛemissis, cū ptineñ.post moꝛtē dict.
C.heredibus et assignatis suis imperpetuū de capi:
talib⁹ dñis feodi silius per seruicia inde debit, et de
iure consuet.per pñtes.In cuius pei testio.ꝛc.

CAn Jndenture defesaunt of a foꝛmer
sale of landes.

His Jndēture made.ꝛc.betwene sir Hugh
R.of N.in the Countie of S.knyghte
on the one partye,and R.B.citizin ꝗ mer:
cer of London on the other partie:wytnes
seth, that where the sayde syꝛ Hugh by Jndenture,
bearynge date the.xx.daye of June,the.xxxij.yere of
the rayne of our soueraygne loꝛde kynge Henrye the
eyght.ꝛc.made betwene the same syꝛ Hugh on the
one partye,and the sayde R.B.on the other partye,
foꝛ the sume of.l.li.sterlyng to the same syꝛ H.cōten:
ted and payed,bargayned and solde to the sayd R.al
ꝑ.ij.mesuages wt the shoppes,cellers,sollers,wharf
and al other theyꝛ appurtenaūces set ꝗ lying at Lōd
bꝛydge fote,in the pysh of S.Magnet.of Londō, in
one of the whych.ij.mesuages Wil.Dikons grocer
now dwelleth,and in the other of them R.S.nowe
inhabyteth,and al other landes,tenementes,and he:
reditamentes,with the appurtenaūces,whjch ꝑ said
syꝛ H.oꝛ any to his vse, thā had within ꝑ same parish
And

And alſo all the deedes, euidences, wrytynges, and mynymentes, concernynge the ſame meſuages, landes, tenementes, and all other the premiſſes and euerye parcell of the ſame, wyth dyuers other clauſes co uenauntes and grauntes in the ſame endentures ſpecifyed, and conteyned, as by the tenour thereof more playnlye doth appere. Neuertheles the ſayd Robert for hym, hys heyres, and aſſygnes, wylleth & graun teth by theſe preſentes to the ſayde ſyr Hugh and his executours, that yf the ſayde ſyr H. hys heyres or executours at any tyme wythin the ſpace of thre yeres, next enſuynge the date hereof, well and truelye contente and paye, or cauſe to be contented and payed to the ſayde.R.lr.li.ſterlynge, that then and from thenſ fourth after ſuche paymente made, the ſayde.R. and hys heyres and all and ſynguler other perſons nowe beynge ſeaſed, or that hereafter ſhall be ſeaſed of the premyſſes of or any parcel therof to the vſe of the ſaid Robert and hys heyres ſhall ſtonde and be therof ſea ſed to the onlye vſe of the ſayde ſyr.H. and of hys hey res. And alſo the ſayde Roberte couenaunteth and graunteth by theſe preſentes that he and his heyres, and al other perſones ſeaſed to their vſe of and in the premiſſes, wythin the ſpace of.viii. monethes next af ter ſuch paiment made, ſhal make or cauſe to be made vnto the forſayd ſyr.H. and his heyres or other at his or theyr denomination and theyr heyres, a good ſure ſufficyent & lawfull eſtate, of and in the ſayde meſuages, landes, tenementes, and other the premyſſes, wyth the appourtenaunces, by dede, fyne, feoffemēt releaſe, confyrmation, or otherwyſe as by the coun cell, lerned of the ſayde ſyr H. ſhall be aduyſed at the
onlye

onlye costes, & charges of the sayde syz. H.in the law,
dyscharged of all former bargaynes and sales, statu=
tes of the staple, statutes marchaunt, recognysaun=
ces, ioynters, dowers, and of all other charges, and
encombzaunces, what so euer they be, made, knowe=
leged oz graunted, by the sayd R.hys heyzes oz þ sayd
other personnes . And the sayde R. couenaunteth and
graunteth by these pzesentes that he within þ space of
one yere nexte after that the sayde astate be made shall
delyuer oz cause to be delyuered to þ sayd syz. H. oz his
heyzes,all such euidences, charters,wzytynges,& my=
nymentes whyche he oz anye other to hys vse, to hys
knoweledge, hath then oz afterwarde shall haue con=
cernynge the pzemisses, and euerye parcell of the same
In wytnesse.&c.

    ¶An Indenture of sale of copye holde
landes.

Thys indenture made &c. betwene M.R. wyd=
dowe, late the wyfe of T.R. whyle he lyued ci=
tizen and tauerner of London, and T.R. sonne
and heyze, apparant of the sayde T.on the one parte,
and R.B.sergeaunt at the lawe on the other part: wit
nesseth that the sayde M. and T. the sonne hath bar=
gayned and solde, and by these pzesentes clerelye bar=
gaynen and sellen to the sayde R, B. all that mesuage
cellers, sollers, houses, edifyces, gardens, ozcheyard
and landes, in Putney in the countye of Surrye in þ
whyche the sayde Thomas the father dwelled and oc
pyed togyther wyth all easementes, commodytyes, &
appourtenaunces, to the same belongynge and apper
teynynge, whether they be fre holde oz copye holde, oz
what so euer tenure they be of.

                        And

And the ſayde M.ℸ.T.the ſonne couenaunten ℸ graun
ten foꝛ them and theyꝛ heyꝛes to and wyth the ſayd R.
and hys heyꝛes, that they ſhall make the ſayde.R.and
hys heyꝛes oꝛ hym and other perſons and theyꝛ heyꝛes
at the nomination of the ſayd R. oꝛ hys heyꝛes ſure of
the ſayde meſuage, garden, yarde oꝛcheyarde, landes
tenementes and other the pꝛemiſſes,befoꝛe the feaſt of
ſaynt Andꝛewe next commyng by ſurrender therof in⸗
to the loꝛdes handes to the vſe of the ſayd R. and hys
heyꝛes,oꝛ to the vſe of hym and other perſons by hym
to be named,and to theyꝛ heyꝛes oꝛ other wyſe at the
expenſes,coſtes and charges in the law of the ſaid M.
and T.the ſonne oꝛ of one of them, theyꝛ executoures,
oꝛ aſſignes.And alſo at their like exſpences,as wel foꝛ
the loꝛdes fyne as foꝛ all other thynges, ſhal cauſe the
Loꝛde of the manour foꝛ the tyme beynge of whome
the ſayde meſuage and other all the pꝛemiſſes be holdē
to make a ſure graunte,ſeaſon,poſſeſſion and delyuery
of and in all and ſinguler the ſame to the ſayde.R.and
hys heyꝛes,oꝛ to hym and other perſonnes at hys no⸗
mination and to theyꝛ heyꝛes accoꝛdynge to the lauda⸗
ble vſe, and cuſtome of the ſame maner hertofoꝛe vſed
And furthermoꝛe the ſayd M.couenaunteth and grau⸗
teth ꝑ yf the ſayd R.oꝛ ſuch perſons at his nominaciō
whych ſhal haue the ſayde meſuage, landes,tenemen⸗
tes ℸ other the pꝛempſſes wout coupne oꝛ colluſyon be
laufully euicted , diſpoſſeſſed oꝛ dyſeaſed out of ꝑ ſayd
meſuage landes ℸ tenementes, oꝛ any parte thereof by
reaſon of any foꝛmer right oꝛ tytle that any perſō hath
to the ſame better than the ſayde.M.oꝛ T.the ſonne oꝛ
yf that the ſayde .R. be not made ſure of the pꝛempſ⸗
ſes befoꝛe the feaſte of Eaſter nexte commynge.

A clauſe in
caſe thebier
ſhuld be diſ
poſſeſſed by
a foꝛmer ti⸗
tle then to
recouery of
theſelloure
in aſmuche
other lādes
at his plea⸗
ſure.

                          That

That than the sayde R. and hys heyꝛes shall immedi
atlye wythin the space of thꝛe monethes nexte after a=
ny suche euiction, dyspossession, oꝛ dysseason, haue as
much lādes ⁊ tenemētes, of ꝑ foꝛesayd. M. ⁊ T. which
they oꝛ eyther of them, haue oꝛ hath in their possession
reuersion, oꝛ vse at the election and pleasure of ꝑ sayd
R. as shall amount and be of the clere yerelye valewe
of the sayde mesuage ⁊c. oꝛ of asmuche parte thereof
as the foꝛesayde R. shall be so lawefullye euycted and
dysseased of oꝛ that shall not be assured to the sayde R.
befoꝛe the feast of easter aboue rehersed, to haue and
to holde, all and synguler suche landes, tenementes ⁊
appourtenaunces, whych the foꝛesayd R. shal in case
afoꝛesayd laufully requyꝛe and chose to hym ⁊ to hys
heyꝛes oꝛ to suche other persones as he shall appoynte
in maner effecte and fourme and in as good assuraūce
as he shulde haue had by vertue of thys endenture, in
the foꝛesayde mesuage, ⁊c. and euery parte and parcell
of the same. And also the sayde. M. bargayneth ⁊ sel=
leth to the sayde R. all maner of stuffe, goodes, husti=
limentes, and implementes, to them and eyther of thē
perteynynge, and belongynge beynge in the same me=
suage, garden houses ⁊c. at the daye of sealynge of
these pꝛesentes. And the sayd. M. and T. the sonne do
graunten that they shall dyscharge the sayde landes,
and tenementes, of all arrerages of rentes, and of al
rentes, excepte the yerely rente of .xii. d. And that the
sayde R. shall take the pꝛofytes from the feast of saint
Mychael last past foꝛward. Foꝛ whyche sale and bar
gayne of all and synguler the pꝛemysses on the part of
the sayde M. and T. the sonne to be obserued, per=
fourmed and done, the sayde R. hath contented, and
payde

payed to the sayde M.and T.xl.li.of lawfull money
of Englande: whereof they holden them fully cōtent
and pleased,and therof acquyten & dischargen p̄ sayd
R.by these pſentes. And ouer this the sayde R.coue=
naunteth & graūteth,and him and his executours by
these pſētes byndeth to p̄ sayd M.& T.the sonne that
he shal cōtent and pay,oʒ cause to be cōtented & payed
to the sayde M.& T.oʒ theyʒ assignes.lxxx.li.of good
and lawfull englysh money,at suche tyme and when
the sayd R.oʒ other parsons at his nomination shall
be made sure of the sayde mesuage and other the pʒe=
misses in fourme as is afoʒsayd,on this syde the feast
of Ester next cōmynge . And the sayde R.couenaun=
teth and graunteth,that yf the sayde M.and T.cause
the sayde estate to be made to the sayde R . and hys
heyʒes,oʒ to hym and other persons at hys nomina=
tion in maner afoʒerehersed, on this syde the feast of
Easter aboue mencioned , that then an obligation of
the date hereof,wherein the sayd M.and T. p̄ sonne
stande bounden to the sayde R.in.x.li.sterlynge be
boyde and of none effect. And then the sayde R. shall
delyuer the foʒesayde obligation to the abouenamed
M.and T.to be cancelled. In wytnesse of al whyche
couenauntes,grauntes,and agrementes.&c.

⸿ An Indenture foʒ the fermynge
of a personage.

This Indenture made betwene syʒ S.H. clerke
parson of the paryssh churche of S. in the Coun
tie of Essex on the one partie, and James Hay
warde of D.in the same Countie clerke on the other
partye : wytnesseth that the sayde syʒ S. the daye of
makynge hereof, hath graunted, demised , betaken,

Q and

and letten to ferme, and by this Indenture doeth de=
mife, graunt, betake, and to ferme let vnto the fayde
James, all that his churche and parfonage of S. a=
foꝛefayde, with the manfion place belongyng to the
fame, and alfo all glebe landes, tythes, frutes, pꝛo=
fytes, oblations, obuentions, commodities, emolu=
mentes, aduauntages, and appurtenaunces to the
fayde churche and perfonage belongynge, oꝛ in anye
wyfe apperteynyng (excepte, and alwaye referued to
the fayde parfone and his affignes, onelye the tythe
kyddes of all the fayde paryfh.) To haue and to hold
all the foꝛfayd church, parfonage and manfion, w̃ all
and finguler glebe landes, edifices, tythes, frutes
pꝛofytes, oblations, obuentions, commodities, e=
molumentes, aduauntages, and appurtenaunces to
the fayde churche, parfonage and manfion place in a=
ny wyfe perteynyng and belongyng (except befoꝛe ex
cepted) to the fayde James, to his executoures and
affignes, from the feafte of faynt John the Baptifte
next cõmyng, after the date herof vnto the ende, and
terme of. iij. yeres from thence next enfuyng, fullye to
be complete and ended: yeldyng and paying therfoꝛe
yerely durynge the fayde terme, to the fayde perfone,
oꝛ hys affygnes, eyght pounde of good and lawfull
moneye of Englande at. ij. termes of the yere, that is
to faye, at the feaftes of the annunciation of our la=

dye, and faynct Michael the Archangel by equal poꝛ=
cions. And yf it fhall happen, the fayde yerely rent of
viij. li. to be behynde vnpayed in parte oꝛ in all, ouer
oꝛ after anye terme of payment therof afoꝛefayde, in
which it ought to be payed, by the fpace of. viij. we=
kes, and lawfullye afked, and no fufficient diftreffe
then

then can be founde there. That then and all tymes
after,it shalbe lesull to the sayde person and his assy=
gnes into the sayde churche and parsonage, and all
other the premisses with the appurtenaunces hollye
to reentre,and the same to haue agayne,retayne and
repossede,as in his former estate, and the sayde Ja=
mes, his executours and assignes thereof vtterlye to
expell,put out and amoue. This Indenture or anye
thynge therin conteyned notwithstandyng. And the
sayde S.couenaunteth and graunteth by this Indē=
ture,that he,his executours or assignes, the forsayde   A clause of
reparacion.
personage, mansion places and houses before letten,
well and sufficiently shal repare susteyne, and mayn
tayne,and agaynst wynde and rayne shal make defen
cible,when & as often as nede shal requyre duryng ye
sayd terme. And the sayd syr James doth couenaunt
and graunt by these presentes,that he,or his sufficiēt
deputie shall well and dulye serue the cure of the for=
sayde churche, and shall mynistre all sacramentes &
sacramentalles, to the paryshners of the same at all
tymes when and as often as nede shall requyre, du=
rynge the forsayde terme. And also the sayde syr Ja=
mes at hys owne cost and expences, shall beare and
paye all maner of ordinarye charges, and paymen=
tes,due and goynge out of the sayde parsonage, and
all other the premisses wyth the appurtenaunces at
all tymes durynge the foresayde terme. And the
sayde S.couenaunteth and graunteth by these pre=
sentes, to beare and paye all maner of extraordina=
rye charges and paymentes, whyche shall be due,
and goynge oute of the sayde parsonage, by all the
forsayde terme of .iij.yeares.

                     Q.ij.   And

And the sayde James and his assignes shall mayn=
tayne and supporte all maner tythes, offrynges, righ
tes and customes apperteynynge and belongynge to
the sayd psonage. And the sayd S.H. couenauteth &
graunteth by these presentes, that he at no tyme du=
ryng the sayde terme, shall not resigne, permute nor
by anye other wayes discharge or disinisse hym selfe
of the sayd benefice and appurtenaunces, nor of any
parte or parcel of ye same, neyther shal procure, cause,
or suffre to be done any acte or other thynge, whyche
maye or myght in anywyse be hurtfull or preiudicial
to the sayde James, his executours or assignes in ha=
uynge and enioynge of the forsayde personage, and
other the pmisses wt the appurtenauces, tyl ye forsayd
terme of yeres be vtterly ended & expired. In wit. &c.

¶ An Indenture betwene parteners.

This Indenture made the.b.daye of Marche, in
the.xxviij.yere of the raygne of kynge Henry the
viij.betwene John Terroll and Edward Wil
son citizins and haberdashers of London on the one
partye. And John Bessem and Rycharde James of
the same cytie, grocers, on that other partye: wytnes=
seth, that where as at the daye of the makyng hereof
it is accorded, couenaunted, cocluded, and agreed be=
twene the sayde partyes, and eyther of the same par=
ties by him selfe, & for his owne parte, couenauteth,
graunteth, and byndeth hym selfe to the other, that
they, and eyther of them shall ioyntlye as parteners
occupy togither aswel in byeng & sellyng of al maner
goodes, wares, and marchaundyces, as by factour=
shyp, alienation, exchaunge, and otherwyse, as well
beyonde the see, as on this syde, that is to saye, from
the

the daye of the makynge hereof vnto the ende & terme
of. v.yeres than nexte folowynge, and fullye to be cō=
plete and ended. Durynge whyche tyme oz terme, ey=
ther of the ſayde partyes ſhall be iuſte, faythfull, and
true to the other, in byenge and ſellyng, and otherwiſe
as is afozeſayde. And all ſuche lucre, pzofyte ,and en
creaſe, gayne, aduauntage, and wynnynge as ſhall
come and growe in byenge and ſellynge anye goodes
wares oz marchaundyſes, and otherwyſe duryng the
ſayde terme, ſhall be equallye parted and deuyded, be=
twene the ſayde partyes, that is to ſaye, eyther of thē
to haue hys iuſte and true pozcyon, oz parte of þ gay=
nes afozeſayde . And at all tymes wythin the ſayde
terme, when it ſhall pleaſe eyther of the ſayde parties
to gyue admoniciõ oz warnyng to other, then eyther
of them to make the other a iuſt and a true reckenyng
and accompte of the byinge and ſellynge of all maner
of wares, goodes, marchaundyſes and otherwyſe as
is afozeſayde, and of the encreaſe and aduauntage, þ
ſhall come and growe of the ſame.
℃ And alſo it is couenaunted and agreed betwene the
ſayde partyes, that yf eyther of the ſayde partyes, at
any tyme within the ſayde terme happen to loſe by det
ters, caſualtye, oz otherwyſe, any parte oz parcell of
the occuppinge in byinge and ſellynge of any goodes,
wares, and marchaundices, and otherwyſe in maner
and fourme as is afozeſayde:ſo that it be not by negly
gence, colour oz fayned pzetence, and that immediatly
pzoued : that the ſame loſſe be bozne equallye betwene
eyther of the ſayde parties. And alſo it is couenaūted
concluded, and agreed bytwene the ſayde partyes and
eyther of them by them ſelues, and foz hys owne part
                                        pzompt

pzomytteth couenaunteth and graunteth to the other
that yf any of thē wythin the sayd terme which at this
pzesent tyme are not espoused, happen hereafter to es
pouse and marye a wyfe, that then fozthwyth it shalbe
at the wylle and pleasure of the other whether the par
ty so espoused oz maryed shall any longer contynue as
partener accozdynge to the tenour and fo urme aboue
rehersed.

And also it is agreed that yf eyther of the sayd par
tyes happen (as God defende at any tyme within the
sayde terme to dye, thā the executours oz administra
tours of the goodes aud cattels of the partye so decea
sed shall truly wythout any couyn oz gyle, make a iust
and a true accompte and readye paymente and delyue
raunce of all suche encreases and gaynes as then shal
be remaynynge to the other lyuynge.

And mozeouer, it is couenaunted and agreed betwene
the sayde partyes, that yf eyther of them be found vn
true in hys recepuynge and accompte contrarye to the
true meanynge of thys pzesent endenture, to the value
of twentye shyllynges sterlyng, then the same partye
so founde defectyue, to fozfayte and paye to the other
an hundzed pounde sterlynge wythout any delaye ac
cozdynge to the tenour and true meanynge of thys pze
sent Jndenture. And to al and synguler couenauntes
pzomysses, condicions and paymentes afoze sayde on
eyther partye to be truelye wythoute couine oz fraude
obserued, fulfylled, and kepte in maner and fourme
as is afozesayde, eyther partye foz hym and hys execu
tours byndeth hym selfe to the other in the summe of
thze hundzed poundes sterlynge, well and truely to be
payde by these pzesentes.

In

In wytnesse whereof the partyes aforesayde to these
Indentures enterchaungeably haue sette to theyr sea=
les. Gyuen the daye and yeare abouesayd.

¶An Indenture for a
prentyse.

Ec Indentura testatur ꝗ G.H.filius W.H. de
com.D. husbandman posuit se ipsũ apprenticiũ
E.W.ciui ⁊ Haberdasher London.ad artem su=
am qua vtitur erudiend. et secum more apprenticii sui
commoratur.et deseruitur.a festo omnium sanctorum
anno regni regis Henrici octaui.⁊c.vsꝗ ad finem ⁊ ter
minum octo annorum extunc proximo sequent. ⁊ ple=
ne.complend.Durant.quo termino predictus Georgi⁹
prefat.E.tanquam magistro suo bene ⁊ fideliter deser
uiet, secreta sua celabit, precepta sua licita et honesta
libenter vbiꜭ faciet, damnum eidẽ magistro suo non
faciet, nec ab aliis fieri sciet ad valorem duodecim de=
nariorum per annum vel amplius quin illud pro posse
suo impediet, aut statim dictum magistrum suum in=
de premuniet. Bona dicti magistri sui non deuastabit,
nec ea alicui illicite accomodabit, fornicacionẽ in domi
b⁹ dicti magistri sui, nec extra non cõmittet, matrimo=
nium non contrahet, ad talos seu aliqua alia ioca illi=
cita non ludet.

Tabernas non frequentabit cum bonis suis propri
is aut alienis durante dicto termino, sine licentia dic=
ti magistri sui, non mercandizabit.

A seruicio suo predicto,nõ recedet nec se elongabit, sed
in omnibus tanquam bonus ⁊ fidelis apprenticius be
nigne se geret, ⁊ habebit per dictum terminuu.

Et pre=

Et pꝛedictus E.pꝛefat. G.appꝛenti. suũ cũ in arte sua
qua vtitur melioꝛi modo,quo sciuerit, poterit, aut do
cebit,tractabit ⁊ infoꝛmabit,vel faciet ifoꝛmati debito
modo castigand. Jnueniend.oia sibi necessaria, vt bi᷏
ctum,vestitũ,lineũ,laneũ,calceament. ⁊ lectum suffici
ent.per totũ dictũ terminũ. Et ad istas conuentiones
omnes ⁊ singulas ex parte dicti appꝛent.bene et fide᷏
liter tenend. et perimplend. foꝛma vt supꝛa , idem ap᷏
pꝛenti. firmiter se obligat per pꝛesentes. Jn cuius rei
testimonium , partes pꝛedicte hiis indentu. sigilla sua
alternatim apposuerunt M.D.tunc maioꝛe Ciuitatis
London R.H.H. S .tunc vic. eiusdem ciuitatis. Da᷏
tum London in festo et anno supꝛadictis.

C An Jndenture foꝛ a pꝛentyce in Englysh.

Thys Endenture wytnesseth ꝑ Thomas Smith
the sonne of John Smyth, of Newe Sarũ in
the countye of Wylshyꝛe marchaunt hath putte
hym selfe appꝛentyse wyth wyllyam webbe of newe
Sarũ afoꝛesayd in the county of Wylshyꝛe,taylour ⁊
after the maner of a pꝛentyse wyth hym to dwel from
the feaste of Chꝛystemas nexte commynge, after the
date hereof vnto the ende and terme of. vii.yeres than
nexte ensuynge,and fully to be complete.By al which
sayde terme, the sayde Thomas appꝛentyce, to ꝑ said
Wyllyam as hys maysler welle and faythfullye shall
serue, hys secretes shall kepe, hys commaundmentes
lefull and honest euery where shall do, no foꝛnicatyon
in the house of hys sayde maysler noꝛ wythout he shal
cõmyt,hurt vnto hys sayd maysler he shall not do,noꝛ
consent to be done to the value of.xiii.d. by the yere, oꝛ
aboue,but he to hys power shall lette oꝛ anon hys ma
ster warne. Tauernes of custome he shall not haunte
but

but it be about his masters businesse there to be done
At the dyse,cardes, oz anye other vnlefull games he
shal not playe. The goodes of his sayde master inoz-
dinatly he shal not waste,noz them to any man lende
without hys masters licence, matrimony wyth any
woman within the sayde terme he shall not contracte
noz espouse,noz from his seruice neyther by day noz
by nyght shall absent oz pzolonge hym selfe, but as a
true and faythful seruaunt ought to behaue him selfe
aswel in wozde as in dede . And the sayd Wyllyam
vnto the sayde Thomas in the crafte the whiche he
vseth after the best maner that he can oz maye , shall
teache and enfourme, oz cause to be taught and enfoz
med,as moche as to the sayde crafte belongeth, oz in
any wyse apperteyneth,and in due maner to chastyce
hym,fyndyng vnto his sayd seruaunt meate, dzynke,
lynen , wollen, hose, shoes , and all other thynges to
him necessarye oz belongynge to appzentice of suche
craft,to be founde after the maner and custome of the
cytie of London. In wytnesse wherof the partyes a-
fozesayde to these Indentures , sonderlye haue set to
theyz seales.Gyuen the.xxij.daye of Septēbze,in the
xxxij.yere of the reygne of kynge Henry the.viij.&c.

¶An Indenture of maryage.

THis Indenture made betwixt dame Anne H.
Wo.A.and R.M.&c.of the one partye,and E.
F.esquyer on the other party:wytnesseth that
it is couenaunted,graunted, condescēded and agreed
betwene the sayde partyes, in maner and fourme folowyng,that is to saye: the sayde E.F. couenaūteth
and graunteth , that he by the sufferaunce of God,
			R		shall

shal mary & take to wife Elisabeth E. widow dough
ter of the sayde dame Anne late the wyfe of W. E. &
his executrice, and the same Elisabeth espouse & wed
after the lawe of holye churche, before the feaste of
saynct Michael the archangell next comynge, yf the
same Elisabeth wyll therto agree. And in lykewyse
the sayde dame Anne, W. A. and R. M. couenaunten
and graunten, and euery of them couenaunteth and
graunteth that the same Elisabeth. by the suffraunce
of almightie God, shal mary and take to husband the
same E. F. and hym espouse in lawe of holye churche
before the feast of saynt Michael the archangel nexte
comminge, yf the sayde Elisabeth wyll therto agree.
For whiche maryage so had, done and solempnised, the
sayde E. couenaunteth, graunteth, and agreeth, that
he shall make, or cause to be made, vnto the same
dame Anne, w. A. and R. M. &c. on this syde the feast
of the natiuitie of oure Lorde nexte comynge, after
the date, as good, sure, sufficient, and lawfull estate,
or estates, of and in the manoure of M. &c. wyth the
appurtenaunces, in the Countie of L. &c. & all other
landes and tenementes, rentes and seruices with the
appurtenaunces, which the same E. F. or any other,
to hys vse, hath, haue, or had, in M. aforesayde, be it
by recoueryes, fynes, feoffamentes, confirmation, release, dede or dedes inrolled, wyth warrauntie of the
sayde E. F. and of Thomas F. or J. F. or otherwyse,
as shalbe best aduysed by the learned counsayl of the
sayde dame Anne w. A. &c. at the costes and charges
of the sayde E. F. the same manour, landes, tenementes. &c. with the appurtenaunces, clerely discharged
of all estates, former bargaynes, sales, recognisaun-
ces

res,and all other charges, whatsoeuer they be.
Excepte an annuitie of fourtye shyllynges by yeare,
graunted to E.D.Esquyer foz terme of his lyfe.And
excepte also all suche landes as be in the ioynter of
Marye late wyfe of I f.bzother to the sayde E . F.
and also excepte the rentes , and seruyces to the loz=
des of the fee thereof,due and accustomed.
And also the sayde E . shall further do, and suffre to
be done at all tymes,on thys syde the feaste of the na
tiuitye of oure Lozde afoze rehearsed, all and euerye
suche thynge and thynges that shall in lykewyse be
aduysed by the counsayle learned of the sayde dame
Anne,w.I.&c. and foz to make the sayde dame Anne
and w.I. &c. and theyz heyzes , sure of the sayde ma=
noure,landes,tenementes, and other the pzemysses,
wyth the appurtenaunces.
To haue and to holde the same manoure, and other
the pzemisses wyth the appurtenaunces, to the same
dame Anne w. I. &c. and theyz heyzes , to the vse of
the sayde E.F.and Elisabeth , and the heyzes males
of the bodye of the sayde Geozge by the sayde Elisa=
beth ,to be begotten wythout empechement of wast.
And foz defaute of suche yssue to the vse of the sayde
E.F.and hys heyzes,and to perfourme hys last wil.
And that after the sayde maryage,all personnes sea=
sed of the sayde manoure , and other the pzemisses,
shall stande and be seased thereof,to the vse befoze re=
hecsed. And ouer this the sayde E . F. couenaunteth,
and graunteth , that yf the sayde manour and other
the pzemisses,(excepte befoze excepted),be not of the
clere yerely value of C.li.ouer all charges and expen
ses, that he the same E .at reasonable request of the
             R.ij.   sayde

sayde dame Anne.XX.A.&c.oz any of them shall make
oz cause to be made lyke sure estate oz estates , of and
in other landes and tenementes within the sayd cou=
tye,of as moche clere yerelye value as the sayde ma=
nour and other the pzemisses, except befoze excepted,
is vnder,and lacketh of the sayde yerely value of c.li.
to the sayde dame Anne. XX. C. &c. and their heyzes,
to the vse afoze declared. And also shal suffre the sayd
Elizabeth at her libertye and pleasure to marye one
Elisabeth E . her doughter, and doughter and heyze
of the sayd CU.E.to any persō that it shall please her.
And dispose suche money and pzofytes that shal foz=
tune to be graūted and pzomysed foz the marying of
the sayd Elisabeth the doughter , at the libertie and
pleasure of the fozsayde Elisabeth the mother wout
cōtradiction, let oz disturbaunce of the sayde E.F.oz
any person by his cōmaundement , pcurement oz as=
sent.And that he ꝑ sayd E.shall not receyue noz haue
any money oz rewarde foz the sayd mariage. Moze=
ouer,the sayde E.F. couenaunteth and graunteth by
these pzesentes,that if it foztune the sayd Elisabeth ꝑ
mother after the sayd mariage solempuised betwene
her and the sayd E.F. to decesse out of this wozlde in
the lyfe of the same E. her husbande,that then the foz
sayd E.shal gyue licence, power and auctozitie to the
sayd Elisabeth afoze her death , to make a testament
conteynyng her last wyll,and the same testament, to
gyue and dispose at her pleasure , of the goodes and
catalles of the sayd E. F. amountyng to the value of
an C.li.sterlyng. And that the sayde E.F.shall suffre
suche persons as the sayde Elisabeth shall name , to
haue and do the execution and distribution of ꝑ same
accoz=

accordyng to her mynde and pleasure.

And that after her deceasse, the sayde E.F.shall gyue
delyuer, paye, and execute, to suche personnes as the
same Elisabeth shal bequeth and appoynt, to haue a-
nye thynge of the sayd Edwardes goodes extending
to the sayde somme of.C.li. And the sayd dame Anne
w.A.ꝛc wyllen and graunten by these presetes that
yf the sayde E.F. well and truelye do holde, obserue,
perfourme and kepe all and synguler couenauntes,
grauntes, promysses,and agreinentes afoꝛe rehersed
on hys parte wythout deceyte ꝛc. that than an obliga
tion of CC.li.bearynge date.ꝛc. wherein he stondeth
bounde to the sayde dame Anne ꝛc. be clerelye voyde,
and of none effecte.ꝛc. In wytnesse ꝛc.

⸿A foꝛmall endenture of a playne bargayne
whyche is a good president in all
common sales of landes.

Hys Indenture made ꝛc. betwene G.F. on the
one partye, and R.L,of London mercer, of the
other partye, wytnesseth that the sayde E.hath
clerelye bargayned, and solde, and by these presentes
clerelye bargayneth and selleth to the sayde.R.L.the
manour of L. wyth the appourtenaunces, in the cou̅
tye of Suss.and all landes,tenementes, rentes,reuer
tions,seruyces,medowes,leases, woodes,waters,
mylles, parkes, pastures,feldes and fennes wythal
and synguler theyꝛ appourtenaunces and all maner
proꝛfytes, gaynes, and vauntages arysyng vpon the
same, whyche he oꝛ any other person oꝛ personnes to
hys vse,hath,haue,oꝛ had,in þ townes and paryshes
of Benton bukley,Roydon etc.in the countye of S.as
foꝛesayde. To haue and to holde the sayde manoure,
lau-

landes tenementes, and all other the premisses wt the appurtenaunces to the same R. hys heyres and assygnes for euermore. And also the sayde G. hath bargayned and solde to the sayde R. L. all deades, charters, euydences, wrytynges, escriptes, and mynymentes, whyche he or any other person or persons to hys vse, hath or haue concernynge the premysses or any parte or parcell of the same. And the sayd euydences dedes, charters. &c. couenaunteth and graunteth to delyuer to the sayde. R. hys heyres or assygnes on thys syde ye feast of all saynctes, nowe next com nyng or after as he maye conueniently obteyne and get the͂ &c. whych e manours, landes, tenementes, &c. the sayde George couenau͂teth, grauteth and also waranteth to be of the clere yerelye value of. CC. li. sterlyng ouer and aboue all charges and reprises. And that he hath laufull power and auctoritye to bargayne and to sell the premisses, to the sayde R. and hys heyres, as afore is sayde And also the sayde G. couenaunteth and grau͂teth, by these presentes, that he before the sayd feast of al sayntes nowe nexte commyng shall make or cause for to be made to the sayde R. hys heyres & assygnes vnto such persons and to theyr heyres as the same R. shal name and assygne a good sure, suffycient and laufull estate, in fee simple of and in the sayde manour, landes, tenementes and other the premysses, and appourtenaunces, by fyne, feoffament, recouerye, release, confyrmation, deede or deedes, enrolled wyth warranty or warrantyes, or otherwyse as by the lerned councell of the sayd R. hys heyres or assygnes shall be aduised at the costes and charges only in the lawe of the sayd G. his heyres or assygnes, dyscharged of all former bargaynes,

nes and ſales, ſtatutes, recognyſaunces, annuyties,
fees, ioynters, dowers, leaſes, fynes, iſſues, amerci=
mentes, condempnations, iudgementes, executions,
intruſions, and of all other encumbꝛaunces and char
ges what ſoeuer they be, except the rētes and ſeruices
of the chiefe loꝛdes of the fee therof from hēnſfoꝛth due
and accuſtomed to be payed. And alſo the ſayd G. co=
uenaunteth ⁊ graunteth to dyſcharge the ſayd R. of al
arrerages of rentes growyng eand beyng due befoꝛe
ꝑ date of theſe pſentes. And ouer thys ꝑ ſayd George
couenaunteth, ⁊ graunteth ꝑ he and all other perſons
at any time ſeaſed to the bſe of the ſaid George of and
in ꝑ ſame manours ⁊c. ſhal at al tymes befoꝛe the feaſt
of Candelmas in the yere ⁊c. ſuffre ⁊ cauſe to be done,
and ſuffred all and euerye ſuch thyng and thynges as
ſhall be deuyſed by the councell lerned of the ſame .R.
wyth waratẏ of the ſame agaynſt all men, and with
out warantye of the ſayd other perſons foꝛ to make
the ſame manoure, landes, tenementes ⁊c. ſure to the
ſayde R. and hys heyꝛes, oꝛ to ſuche other perſons, ⁊
to theyꝛ heyꝛes, as the ſame. R. ſhall name ⁊ appoynt
therbnto at the coſtes ⁊ charges in the lawe of ꝑ ſayde
G. and hys heyꝛes, ⁊ that the ſame R. ⁊ his heyꝛes oꝛ
ꝑ ſaid other perſōs ⁊ their heyꝛes whom ꝑ ſaid R. ſhal
therbnto aſſigne after ꝑ ſayd eſtate had oꝛ made ſhalle
haue ⁊ enioy ꝑ ſame manour ⁊c. wꝰout any lawfull ex=
pulſiō euiction oꝛ interruption of ꝑ ſayd G. oꝛ his hey
res oꝛ any perſon oꝛ pſons by reſon of any tytle had oꝛ
growen befoꝛe the date of theſe pꝛeſentes. Foꝛ whiche
bargayne, ſale, couenantes, grauntes, and agremen=
tes, on the behalfe of the ſayde George to be perfour=
med, obſerued, and done.

                              The

The sayde Rycharde hath well and truely contented
and payde in hande to the sayde George before þ date
of these presentes.MMMM.lriii.li. of lauful moneye
of England in full contentation and payment of and
in the sayde bargayne and sale and other the premis=
ses, whyche sayde somme &c.the sayd G.knowlegeth
hym selfe fullye contented and payed and thereof ac=
quyteth &c. In wytnesse &c.

¶And yf the monye be not payed in hande ye must er=
presse the dayes of payment of the same and the clau=
ses of dystres or reentrie,or any other penalties accor=
dynge to the couenauntes of the partyes.

¶An Indenture of particion of lan=
des deuyded amonge
systers.

If it be be=
twene.iii.si
stersit must
be tripar=
tyte or inde
ted acordig
to the num
ber of þ par
tyes.

Hys Indenture made the tenth daye &c.be=
twene H.w. citizen of London, and Anne
hys wyfe, one of the daughters and hey=
res of W.R. late of London,mercer, & one
of the systers and heyres of T. R.whyche was sonne
and heyre of thesayde. w. R. whan he lyued on þ one
party, and Johan Roys wyddowe sister of the sayd
Anne, and an other of the doughters and heyres of
the sayde w.R. and another of the systers and heyres
of the sayde T.R. and Simon R. citizen and mercer
of London. W.w. draper and J. B. draper whyche
were of late enfeffed by the sayd Johan of the moytie
of a great tenement or meswage &c. sette and lying to
gythers in the parysche of S.B. to the vse of the sayd
Johan and her heyres on the other party.Witnesseth
that it is couenaunted, graunted, condescended, and
agreed betwene the sayde partyes for a particion be=
twene

twene them, to be had and made of the enheritaũce
of the ſayde tenement and other the premiſſes in the
ſayde paryſh, which deſcended to the ſayd Anne and
Iohã in coparcenery, by and after the death of ꝑ ſayd
W.R. aſwell as doughters and heyres of the ſayde
W.R. as ſyſters and heyres of the abouenamed Th.
R. in maner and fourme enſuyng. Fyrſt it is couenaũ
ted and agreed betwene the ſayde partyes, and the
ſayde Iohan, and her feoffees, graunten by theſe pre
ſentes, that the ſayd R. and Anne in the ryght of the
ſame Anne ſhal haue for her part and purporte of the
forſayd landes and tenementes ꝛc. iij. dwellyng tene
mẽtes of the yerely value of. iiij. li. In one of ꝑ which
ſayde tenementes Thomas D. barbour nowe dwel=
leth and inhabyteth, conteynyng in it ſelfe. lx. fote. aſ=
ſyſe, ſquare. ꝛc. And in the other tenement of the thre
tenementes, dwelleth one M. A. wydowe, and it con
teyneth. ꝛc. And the thyrde tenement in poſſeſſion of
A.R. ꝛc. whiche ſayde. iij. tenementes, wyth the yar=
des, kytchins, chaumbres. ꝛc. in as ample and large
maner and fourme as the ſayd perſons now in them
dwellyng haue, or occupy, or they or any other afore
tyme haue had or occupyed. The ſayde Philip and
Anne, as in the ryght of the ſame Anne, ſhall haue &
enioye, to her and to her heyres, in full recompence &
and allowaunce, of and for, her parte and purporte
that to her belongeth, or ought to belonge of all the
ſayde meſes, landes, tenementes. ꝛc. by and after the
deceaſſe of the forſayd W. and T. and eyther of them
as one of the doughters and heyres. ꝛc. And it is a=
greed betwene the ſayde partyes, and the ſayd Iohã
and her feoffees ben contente & pleaſed, to accept and

                S   take

take in full recompence and allowaūce of and for the parte of the sayde Johan, of all the meses, landes. &c. and other the premisses afore rehearsed, to the vse of the sayde Johan and of her heyres one greate tene= ment lying by the sayde thre tenementes conteyning &c. wyth the appurtenaunces, in as ample and large maner as T.C. gentlemā now dwelleth in the same or any other. &c. And it is furthermore fully agreed couenaūted & graunted betwene the sayd parties by these presentes, that at all tymes conuenient it shall be lefull to eyther of them to entre into others parte, to them allotted, to do reparations and other beho= fes necessaryes, vpon the meses, landes and tenemē= tes to them seuerally allotted, and in amēdyng, buyl= dyng or repayryng or otherwyse, of and vpon theyr owne partes of the sayde landes, tenementes. &c. to them alotted and appoynted by these presentes.
And ouer that it is agreed, couenaunted and graun= ted betwene the sayd partyes, ꝑ all annuall rentes & seruice due to the lorde or lordes of the fee. &c. shalbe equally borne betwene the sayd A. & Johan and their heyres and assignes, enhabiters of the same tenemē &c. that is to saye, eyther of them for theyr parte, and portion afore allotted. &c. In wytnesse. &c.

¶ An Indenture of sale of plate vpon a condition and in defaute of repayment for euer.

This Indenture made the. xxv. daye of. &c. be= twene. W. Y. of London Gentleman, en the one partye, and T. H. of H. in the Countie of H. on the other party: wytnesseth that the sayd Tho. being possessed of a cuppe wyth a couer of syluer par= cel

cell gylte, waying.xxij.ounces, and an halfe a quar=
tron of Troye weyght. Item a playne pece of syluer
parcell gylt with a starre on the botome, waying.xij.
ounces, thre quarters of the same weyght, and two
greate goblettes .xc.hath bargayned, solde and dely=
uered all the sayde plate of goldsmythes worke, the
daye and yere aboue rehersed, within the cytie of Lō
don in playne and open market, to the sayde W .P.
for the summe of fyftye pounde sterlyng, whereof the
sayde Thomas knowledgeth hym selfe fully conten
ted and payed by these presentes. Neuerthelesse, the
sayde (W.wylleth and graunteth by these presentes,
that yf the sayde Thomas wel and truly content and
paye, or cause to be contented and payed, vnto the
sayde W.hys executours or assygnes wythin þ sayd
cytie of London fyftye pounde sterlyng, in the feaste
of Chrystmasse next commyng, after the date of these
presentes, wythout any further delaye, that then the
sayde Wyllyam shall delyuer, or cause to be delyue=
red to the sayde Thomas, his executours, or assyg=
nes so makynge payment of the forsayd fyfty pounde
all the sayde plate of goldesmythes worke, and eue=
ry parte and parcell of the same, the sale and bar=
gayne aforesayde notwythstandynge.
And yf defaute be made of or in payment of the sayde
fyftye pounde in parte or in all at the daye and place
afore mencioned, that then the sayde Thomas wyl=
leth and graunteth, and hym and his executours byn
deth, by these presentes, for to warraunt all the sayd
plate and the sale and bargayne of the same, to the
sayde wyllyam, his executours and assygnes agaynst
all persons for euermore. In wytnesse whereof. xc.

Thus moche is sufficient for the trade of makynge of Indentures.

¶Awarde.

Unto all trewe Christen people to whome this
present awarde shall come, or it shal rede, se, or
heare, J. P. grocer & J. A. poulter, citizins of
Londo. Sende gretyng in our Lord God euerlastig:
where as dyuers variaunces, controuersies, & debates heretofore haue ben had, moued & dependyng betwene Raufe. R. citizin and grocer of Lond on the one
partie: and J. L. citizin & fysshmonger of Lod on that
other ptie for seasyng & pacifying whereof either of
the same pties hath compromitted & bounde the selues to
other by obligation in the sume of. xx. li. sterlynge, w
condition therupon endorsed to stande and abide the
awarde, ordynaunce and iudgement of vs the sayde
J. P. and J. A. of theyr comen assentes indifferently,
elect and chosen. So alwayes that our sayde award
ordynaunce and iudgement, of and vpon the premisses were made and gyuen vp in wrytyng on this side
the feast of all saynctes next commyng, after the date
herof, as by the same obligations thereof made, bea-
ryng date the daye. &c. more playnly it doth appeare:
wherupon now we the sayd arbitratours after the ma
ner of varyans by vs suspectly knowen aperceyued,
and wyth good & due deliberatio therupon had & taken we haue made and gyuen vp our awarde in that
behalfe, in maner & fourme folowyng. That is to say
fyrst and principally we the sayd arbitratours do a-
warde, ordeyne, and iudge by this our preset award
that

that eyther of the same parties at thensealyng of thys
present awarde, shall enseale, and for theyr dede delyuer the one to the other, a good sure, suffycyente, and
laufull acquitaunce generall, of all and all maner of
actions, as well reall, as personall, sutes, quarelles,
trespasses, dettes, debates, accomptes, and demaundes, what soeuer they be, betwene the sayde parties,
at any tyme before the date hereof,they haue ben had,
moued or dependynge.

Also we awarde, ordeyne and iudge, by thys our present awarde, that the sayde Raufe shall paye, or cause
to be payde to the sayde J. Lynet, to hys executoures,
or assygneys. iiii. pounde of good and laweful moneye
of Englande, in maner and fourme folowynge, that
is to saye in hande at thensealynge of thys our present
awarde twentye shyllynges sterlynges, and in ꝑ feast
of Easter nexte commynge after the date hereof.rl.s.
in full contentation and paymente of the sayde.iiii. li.
And that vpon the payment therof, the same partyes
to contynue and be louers, and frendes, as they were
before the date hereof. In wytnesse ꝛc.

The fourme of makyng all kynde of obligations.

Nouerit vniuersi ꝑ ꝓsentes me w.G.de R.in
Ccm.S.gentleman teneri et firmiter obligari. w.G.in decem libris sterlingo. sol-
uend.eidem w.aut suo certo attornat. vel
executoribus suis, in festo sancti Michaelis archangeli prox.futur.post dat. ꝓntiu,ad quamquidem solutionem

tionem bene & fideliter faciend obligo me heredes & ex
ecutores meos per presentes sigillo meo sigillatas dat.
tertio die Octobz. Anno regni regis Henrici octaui &c
tricesimo tertio.

¶An Obligacyon where two are
bounde to twayne.

Nouerint vniuersi per presentes, nos .W.M. de
C. in Com. L. yoman, et T, R. de R. in Comi.
predict. Tayler, teneri & firmiter obligari S. J
& C.R. gentylmen, in .xii. li. sterlyng. soluend. eisdem
S. J. et C. R. seu eorum alteri, vel eorum cert. attur:
nat. heredibus vel executoribus suis, in festo omnium
sanctorum prox. post dat. present. Ad quam quide so:
lutionem bene & fideliter, faciend. obligamus nos, et
vtrumq nostrum per se, pro toto et in solid. heredes
et executores nostros per presentes sigillis nostris si:
gillat. Dat. &c.

¶Where .iii. are bounde to one.

Nouerint &c. nos. A.B. C. D. E. F. milites, tene
ri &c. G.H. gentylman in xx. li. sterlynge soluen:
dis eidem. G. H. aut suo certo atturnato vel exe:
cutoribus suis in festo omnium sanctorum prox. futur.
post dat, present. Ad quam quidem solutionem bene &
fideliter faciend. obligamus nos, et quemlibet nostru
per se & pro toto & in solid. hered. & executores nostres
per presentes. Sigillis nostris sigillat. &c.

¶An obligation where two owners of
a shyppe are bounde to two
marchauntes.

Nouerint

OUerint vniuerſi per preſentes nos Johan
Barnes, ⁊ Robertum T. de villa Hull mari
narios ac poſſeſſores, ſiue proprietarios cu
iuſdam nauis voc.⁊c. The Johā of Hulle,
teneri et firmiter obligari w. C. ⁊ J. C. mercatoribus
ville Calic. in.xl. li. ſterlinge ſoluend. eiſdem w. etc.
J. C. ſeu eorum alteri vel eorum certo atturnat. hered.
ſeu executoribus ſuis in feſto Paſche prox. futur. poſt
dat. preſentium. Ad quam quidem ſolutionem bene ⁊
fideliter faciend. obligamºnos ⁊ vtrumcz noſtrum per
ſe pro toto ⁊ in ſolid. ac nauem predictam cum toto ap-
paratu eiuſdem heredes ⁊ executores noſtros ac omni
a bona noſtra tā vltra mare cī citra, vbicumcz fuerint
inuenta per preſentes. In cuius rei teſtimonium etc.
℅And ye ſhall vnderſtande that in obligations wyth
condicions it is commonly accuſtomed to ſet no day of
paymente of the forſayte for than it ſhall be due at all
tymes whan it is requyred yf ſo be the cōdicion be not
kepte.

℅An obligation wherin thre are bound
to the kynge and other.

OUerint ⁊c. nos A.B.C. ⁊c. mercatores de ve
netia teneri, ⁊ firmiter obligari excellentiſſimo
in Chriſto principi et domino noſtro, domino
Herrico oct. dei gratia Anglie Francie et Hibernie ⁊c.
ac Thome B. et Hugoni C, collectoribº cuſtom. ⁊ ſub-
ſid.d. eiſdem domini Regis in portu Colceſtre. in.xx.li.
ſteriiig, ſoluend. eiſdem domino regi et cuſtomar aut
eorum vni vel eorum certo attournato ad quamquidē
ſolutionembene et fideliter faciendi, obligamus nos
et vtrumcz noſtrum per ſe pro toto ⁊ in ſolid. heredes ⁊
executores noſtros per preſentes ⁊c.

　　　　　　　　　　An obliga-

The boke of condʒy

¶An Obligation of dyuers dayes of
payment wyth expʒeſſynge
of a foʒſayte yf de
faut be made.

Nouerint ꝛc.nos I.B.C.D.ꝛc.teneri ꝛc.G.H.ꝛc
in.CC.li. ſterlyng.ſoluend.eidem.G.ꝛc.in foʒma
ſubſcripta, videlicet in feſto annuntiationis be
ate Marie virginis pʒox.futur.v.li.in feſto Paſche tūc
pʒox.ſequent, v li. in feſto Natiuitatis ſancti Johan=
nis Baptiſte tūc pʒox.futur.v.li et ſic de fe ꝛo ad feſt.ꝛc.
videlicet in feſtis pʒedictis.v.li. quouſcꝫ dictas.CC.li.
plenarie ſic perſoluantur, ad quas quidem ſolutiones
ꝗ quãlibet eoʒum et pʒemittitur bene et fideliter faciēd
obligamus nos et quemlibet noſtrum ꝛc.
Et ſi contingat nos pʒefat.I.B.C.D.ꝛc. deficere in a=
liqua ſolutione ſolutionum pʒebictar.in parte vel in to
to contra foʒmam pʒedictam, tunc volumus ꝗ concedi
mus nos teneri et quemlibet noſtrum,per ſe pʒo toto ꝗ
in ſolid.per pʒeſentes firmiter obligari pʒefat.G. in p̃=
dictis.CC.li. ſterling ſoluendis eidem G.aut ſuo certo
atturnat.executoʒibus aut aſſignatis ſuis.ꝛc.
In cuius rei teſtimonium ſigilla noſtra ꝛc.

¶A ſure obligation in a caſe where the
detter is miſtruſted, foʒ fleynge in
to ſanctuarye oʒ beyonde the ſea, to
ſuffer to be ſued, oʒ ſuche lyke cau=
ſes, wyth expʒeſſynge of reſtitution
of all coſtes, and charges, of the
ſute.ꝛc.

Noue

NOuerint vniuerſi per pñtes, qð ego A.B.non
coactus, non compulſus, nec aliqua alia mala
imaginatione ad hoc induct⁹,ſed mera propria
et ſpontanea voluntate , et certa ſcientia recognoſco,
ac palam et publice confiteor me teneri et p pñtes fir
miter obligari D.E.in.l.li.ſterling.ſoluend . et reſti‑
tuend.eidē D.E. aut ſuo certo atturnat . procurator.
nūtio hered.vel execut.ſuis, aut latori pñtium in feſto
Paſchę .px.futur. ſine dilatione vlteriori. Ad quam
quidem ſolutionē bene et fideliter faciend ꝗ p implēd
in forma predicta, obligo me,heredes , et executores
meos,ac omnia bona mea mobilia et imobilia preſen
tia et futur.tum vltra mare quam citra in quocuncꝫ
loco vel iuriſdictione inuent. fuerint capiend et diſtri
gend.Et ſi qð abſit defectus fiat in ſolutione predict.
vltra feſtum ſiue terminum ſuperius limitat. tunc ꝗ
cuncꝫ dampna ſumptus, et intereſſe dictus E.D.
patietur aut pati poterit vel debet, pro tēpore eiuſdē
defectus.ꝛc.illa omnia et ſingula ego dictus A.B.te‑
neor et firmiter obligor per pñtes ſoluere et fideliter
ſatiſfacere ſicut de debito principali ſtatutis , priuile‑
giis, ac cōſuetud.quibuſcūcꝫ ciuitatis Lōdon,ſeu cu‑
iuſcuncꝫ alterius ciuitatis ville patrie vel loci ad hoc
contrariis,non obſtantibus.Reuoco etiam et renūtio
omnes protectiones, defenſiones , ſanctuaria, fran‑
cheſias,libertates,ſubuētiones et priuilegia quecūcꝫ
per que ego poſſem i hac parte tueri aut cautelas ſeu
dolum miniſtrare in dampnum et preiudicium pre‑
dicti E. creditoris mei de premiſſis.ꝛc. In cui⁹ rei te‑
ſtimonium.ꝛc.

⸿After this maner may ye make all obligations.

                                    ℂ   Con‑

¶ Conditions of dyuerse sortes.

Oz asmoche as there be dyuers fourmes of endozsemētes called cōmely conditions, some in latyne, some in Englysh, accozdynge to the sondzye pleasures of the wzyters, lest I shulde be o= uer tedyous to the reader, I thought it moost conue= nyent to set only thē that be cōmonly vsed in Englysh yf anye be disposed to traduce them into Latyne, he maye : do it easely after the examples that here vnder folowe.

¶ A condition foz perfourmyng of awarde
in a matter of landes.

He condition of this obligatiō is such that yf the within boundē H. J. and I M. do stande to, obeye, pfourme, kepe and fulfyll the awarde, arbitrement, ozdenaunce, rule, and iudgement of B w. gentleman. &c. and O. M. sergeaūt at the lawe, arbitratours indifferently named, elect, and chosen, aswell on the parte of the wythinnamed R. as on the parte of the sayde H. J. to arbitre, ozdeyn and deme, aswell of and vpon the ryght, tytle, inte= rest, vse, and possessyon of a garden, lyinge. &c. as of, and vpon all actions, trespasses, quarelles, sutes, de= bates, dettes, demaundes, and all other grefes, and inconuenyences, had moued, styzred, oz dependynge betwene the sayde partyes concernyng the same gar= den. And also yf the sayd H. J. befoze the feast of Ea= ster nexte cōmynge. &c. shewe vnto the sayde arbitra= tours, all suche wzytynges as they haue in theyz possessyon concernyng theyz ryght, tytle, vse, interest,

O z

oz poffeffion of the fozfaydgarden, in such wyfe, that
the fayd arbitratours be not delayed to gyue an ar=
bitrement of and in the pmiffes, foz want of fyght of
the euidence of theyz partye. And the same awarde,
arbitrement,ozdynaunce,rule, and iudgement of the
fozfayde arbitratours the fayd H. J.and J M.do on
theyz partye, well and trulye perfourme and kepe.
So that the same awarde,arbitrement.⁊c.of ⁊ vpon
the pzemiffes,be made and yelden vp in wzytyng on
this syde the feaft of Eafter next cōmyng,wythin ly=
mited. That then this pzefēt obligation to be voyde
and of none effect:oz els to remayne in his ful ftrēgth
power and vertue.

⸿ A condition to delyuer cozne at a cer=
tayne daye and place.

He condition of this obligation is suche, that
yf the wythin bounden J. S. well and trulye
delyuer,oz cause to be delyuered vnto the with
in named J. M. hys executours oz affygnes at the
dwellyng place of the same J. M. set ⁊ beinge in the
towne of Holme.rr.quarters of wheate, whyte and
redde,swete,cleane,dzye and marchaūdable,wyth ⁊
beft,on this syde the feaft of all saynetes within wzit
ten:that then this obligation to be voyde, and of no
value, oz elles to abyde in his full strength, vertue,
and effect.

⸿ A condition to mayntayne the poffiffion
in a sale of landes.

He conditionof this oblig. ⁊c. that yf the wyth
in named A. maye wel and peaceablye haue,
holde,enioye, ⁊ poffeffe, from the date of these
pfētes,to him and to his heyzes and affignes foz euer

all and singuler those landes,tenementes.ꝛc.wyth al
the appurtenaunces,set,lying,and being.ꝛc. (whych
late were the landes of the wythin bounden R. and
whych the sayde A. lately had to hym and to his hey
res and assignes,of the gyfte and graunt of the sayde
R.as by a certayne dede by the same R.to the foꝛsayd
A.thereof made,and vnder hys seale of armes sealed
and subscrybed wyth hys owne hande moꝛe openlye
doth appeare)without any molestation,interuption,
eiection,expulsion,oꝛ recouery of the same,oꝛ any par
cell thereof by the sayde R. hys heyꝛes oꝛ assignes,oꝛ
by any other person by reason of anye ryght oꝛ tytle,
to hym oꝛ them befoꝛe the date wythin mencioned,
had,growyng,oꝛ accreasyng, that then this pꝛesent
obligation.ꝛc.oꝛ elles.ꝛc.

¶ An other fourme vpon the same.

He condicion ꝛc. that yf the wythin named .A.
haue holde and peasablye possesse to hym and to
hys heyꝛes and assygnes foꝛ euer all those.v.mes
suages, wyth thappourtenaunces whyche sometyme
were the wythin bounden Wyllyam Haukyns wythout any dyfference, let, interruption, eiection, expulsion, impleadynge, molestynge, vexation oꝛ grefe, other by the sayde.C. oꝛ hys heyꝛes oꝛ any other person
oꝛ persons what soeuer they be hauynge oꝛ pꝛetēdyng
any maner right,title,vse,clayme oꝛ interest of ꝛ in the
sayd.v.mesuages, oꝛ any parte oꝛ percell of the same,
that than thys pꝛesent obligation ꝛc.

¶ A condicion foꝛ the warrantye of woad oꝛ any lyke thyng.

The

The condicion &c. that where the wythin=
bounden F. hathe bargayned ſolde and
deliuered to the within named.R. one hū
dꝛed bales of Tholouſe woad, of ꝑ mar
kes of foure knottes euerye bale, ⁊ hath
pꝛomyſed, and waraunted vnto the ſame R. that eue=
rye ſet of the ſame woade ſhall make whan it is ſette
and pꝛoued.iiii.li. ſterlyng: If it ſo be that euery ſet of
the ſame woad whan it is ſet ⁊ pꝛoued make the ſayde
warantye of.iiii.li.ſterlyng, that than this pꝛeſent ob=
ligation ſhalbe voyde and holde foꝛ nought.
And yf any ſet of the foꝛeſayde woade (reckenyng .iii.
C. foꝛ a ſet) make not, whan it is ſette and pꝛoued,the
ſayde warantye of .iiii.li. ſterlynge. And then , yf the
foꝛſayde F. from tyme to tyme, vpon due knowelege
therof to hym made and gyuen by the foꝛſayd R.oꝛ by
hys aſſygnes, well and trulye delyuer oꝛ do to be dely
uered vnto the ſayde R.oꝛ to hys certeyne attourneye,
oꝛ to hys executours,at the bꝛydge foote in the citie of
London,as moche Tholoſe woad of the goodnes and
warrauntie afoꝛeſayde after.xvi.ſ. ſterlynge foꝛ euery
hundꝛeth weyght therof, as ſhall lacke in any ſet of ꝑ
foꝛeſayde warrautye of.iiii.li.ſterlynge that than alſo
thys obligation be voyde.&c.

¶A condicion vpon an Indenture of apꝛentyſhyppe.

The condition of thys obligation is ſuche , that
where A.B. the ſonne of the wythinboūde C.D
by hys certayne Indenture whoſe date is the.x.
day &c.hath put him ſelfe apꝛentyſe to the wythin na
med R . M. to be learned in the crafte oꝛ myſterye of
payntynge, and to dwell wyth hym &c. froɱ the ſayd
date

date to the ende and terme of.viij.yeres then next en=
suinge,and fully to be complete and ended, as in the
sayde Jndenture thereof made moze openlye doeth
appeare.Pf the sayde J. well and truly serue the foz=
sayde E.M. hys master in the maner of appzentyse,
from the daye of the date within wzytten,to the ende
and terme of the sayde.viij. yeres , accozdynge to the
tenour, purpozte and effecte of the sayde Jndenture,
in all poyntes and articles.xc.that then.xc.

¶ A condition where a man hath bought
an others ryght,and hath a letter of at=
turneye,to sue foz the same,byndyng
the seller,that he shal not gyue a=
ny quytaunce to the partye in
daunger of the byer.xc.

THe condition of this obligation is suche , that
where as the wythinbounden A.B. made and
ozdeyned the within named C.D.hys especial
good & lawfull atturney, to axe, leuy. xc.to the vse,
pzofyte and comoditie of the sayde C.D. of one E.F.
cytizin of London grocer.xx.li.sterlyng,in which the
sayde E.F.by hys obligation thereof made,standeth
bounde to the sayde A.B.as in a certayne letter of at=
turney,by the sayd A.to the abouenamed C.D. ther=
of gyuen,moze euidentlye appeareth.   Pf the sayde
A.B. from the date of this pzesent obligation do not
call agayne,reuoke , oz disanull the fozsayde letter of
atturneye , noz any maner sale, plee, oz action by the
fozsayde C.D. in the name of the fozerehearsed A. a=
gaynste the abouewzytten E.F. oz his executours in
any

any courte hereafter to be comenced oʒ depenbyng noʒ
by any other meanes wythstande, let, oʒ interrupt the
tytle of the same.C. of and to the sayde summe of.rr.li
noʒ gyue vnto the sayd E. F. noʒ to hys erecutours a=
ny maner quyttaunce, dyscharge oʒ release of oʒ vpon
the sayde summe oʒ any parte oʒ poʒtion of the same,
that than thys pʒesent oblygation ꝛc.

¶A conditiõ foʒ to kepe the peas and to be of good abearynge.

T   He Condicion of thys obligation is suche that
yf the wythinbounden S. and Elisabeth hys
wyfe, do kepe the peas agaynst all the kynges
lyege people, and especiallye agaynst.A.B.C.D. ꝛc
and beare hym selfe honestlye and duelye, bothe in his
woʒdes and deades agaynst the sayd A.B .ꝛc.noʒ dy=
sclaunder thẽ oʒ any of them, of oʒ vpon any such mat
ters touchyng the death of I. M. oʒ the sute about the
triall of the same.wherein the sayde A.B.ꝛc.are by the
kynges lawes ecclesiasticall and tempoʒall clerelye de
clared innocent and free that than ꝛc.

¶ A Condition to warraunt the sale of a Shyppe.

T   He condicion of thys oblygatyon is suche that
where the wythin bounden A.B. solde vnto þ
wythin named C. D. a certayne shyppe called þ
Marye of Calice, and all maner of battell instrumen
tes, furnymentes, and apparell of the same shyppe,
wyth the appurtenaunces,foʒ a certayne somme of mo
ney betwene them accoʒded as in a bylle of sale therof
made playnlye dothe appere.

                                If the

If the fayde.C.D.well and peafably may haue,hold,
enioye and poffeffe, to hym hys heyzes and affignes al
the fayde fhyppe, battell inftrumentes, furnimentes,
apparell, and appourtenaunces afozefayde, wythout
contradiction, let, oz dyfturbaunce of any perfon oz per
fons, by reafon of any clayme oz intereft in the fame be
foze the date of thefe pzefentes had oz made accozdyng
to the tenoure, and effecte of the fayde Indenture that
than.&c.

C A condicion to caufe a man to feale
an obligation by a cer=
tayne daye.

He condition.&c. that yf the wythin boun=
den I. C. befoze the feafte of N. nexte com=
mynge after the date hereof caufe W. C. of
the towne of B. to be bounde by his wziting
oblygatozye fuffycient in the lawe and wyth hys feale
infealed vnto the wythin named T.in.x.li. fterlyng to
be payde the.x.daye of Augufte &c. and alfo befoze the
fame feafte, caufe the fayde w. to delyuer the fame ob
lygation clerelye foz hys dede and duetye in the towne
of B.vnto J.K.of H. clothyer, to the vfe of the fayd T
that than.&c.

C A condition to delyuer oyles by a
daye fyxed.

He condition of thys obligation is fuche that yf
the wythin bounden I. at anye tyme befoze the
feaft of faynt Mychael the archaungel next cõ=
mynge after the date wythin wzytten, delyuer oz caufe
to be delyuered in the citye of London to w.R. wythin
named, oz to hys certeyne attozney, heyzes, oz execu=
tours, tenne tonnes of oyle of cyuyle, good, fwete,
and

swete and marchaundable, full and well bounde ac=
cordyngly:that then this present obligation.ꝛc.

¶A condition to make astate to an
other,by a certayne daye.

The condition of this obligation is such, that yf
the wythin bounden A.before the feast of Ester
next cōmyng,make vnto the wythin named R.
and to suche other persons as the sayde R.shall ther=
vnto name and assygne , to haue and to holde , to
them , theyr heyres and assygnes , a good sure suffy=
cyent and lawfull estate of and in , all those landes,
tenementes.ꝛc . by dedes and euidences sufficient in
the lawe,or by fyne or recouerye, yf nede shal requyre
or by any other sure and lawfull meanes as shall be
aduysed by the learned counsayle of the sayde R. hys
heyres or assygnes,that then.ꝛc.

¶A condicion to saue a man harmelesse,
that is bounde for an other man
by recognisaunce.

The condition of this obligation is suche , that
where the wythin named A.B.C.D.at the spe=
ciall instaunce,petition and request of the with
in bounde E.F. and for his dette , by a certayne obli=
gation of recognisaunce made before w.M. recorder
of the cytie of London,and J.R. knyght Alderman
of London ,the tenth daye.ꝛc. stande bound vnto the
Chambre of London,in the summe of.xx.li.sterlyng
by waye of a recognisaunce,as in the same obligatiō
playnelyer appeareth. If the sayde E.F. hys heyres,
executours and assygnes, paye vnto the sayde cham=
U   berer

berer all the foꝛesayd summe of twenty li.and also saue
and kepe harmeles the aboue named A.B. ꝛc. from all
maner indempnityes, costes, and charges, of foꝛ and
concernynge the sayde obligation of recognysaunce ꝺ
all other thynges concernynge the same, that than ꝛc.

¶ A Condicion to paye a rente ac-
coꝛdyng to an Indenture
of a lease

He condicion. ꝛc. That where the wythin
bound A.B.hath lately taken in ferme foꝛ
the terme of.vi. yeres of ꝑ wythin named
C.D. one tenement, set, and lyinge in the
towne of W.ꝛc foꝛ the rent of.xl. s.yerely to be payde
as in a payer of endentures thereof made, whose date
is ꝛc. playnlyer appereth.

If the sayde A.B. and hys executours well ꝺ truely paye oꝛ cause to be payde to the sayde C.D.hys hey
res and assygnes, the foꝛesayde yerely rent fourty shyl
lynges at the dayes and termes accustomed accoꝛding
to the tenour and effecte of the sayde endenture ꝛc.that
then.ꝛc.

¶ A condition vpon an Indenture of
sale,to make good the summe.

He condition of thys obligation is suche, that
where the wythin bounden A.B. the day of the
date wythin wꝛytten , foꝛ the summe of . xx. li.
sterlyng,bargayned, solde and delyuered to the with
in named C.D . dyuers goodes, plate and icwelles,
in a certayne Inuenture compꝛehended , bearynge
date

date.&c. vnder a condition in the same Jndenture spe
cifyed.yf the sayde A.B.make defaute of payment in
the sayde Jndenture mencioned and compzised.

And then yf al the fozsayde goodes plate and iewel=
les indifferentiy pzysed, be founde of lesse value then
twentye markes sterlynge of readye money, so the
sayde A.B.immedyatlye paye, oz cause to be payed,
to the abouenamed C.his heyzes oz assig.&c.as moch
good and lawfull moneye oz other ware as shall a=
mount to the summe of all that shalbe lackyng of the
sayde twentye pounde in the goodes, plate, and i e=
welles afoze reherced, that then this pzesent obliga=
tion be of no value.&c.

¶A condition in a ioynter,to gyue astate
in certayne landes to the wyfe,where
there is none other indenture made
betwene the partyes.

The condition of this obligation is suche , that
yf the wythin bounden W.R.&c.oz his heyzes
at their owne pzopze costes and charges befoze
the feast of Easter next after the date wythin wzitten
make oz cause to be made vnto A . B. &c. a good sure
suffycient and lawfull estate in the lawe, of and in al
and singuler those landes,tenementes.&c.wyth thap
purtenaunces, in the cytie of London,of the yerelye
value of.xl. li. sterlyng , ouer and aboue all charges,
and repzises. To haue and to holde, all the sayde
landes and tenementes, wyth the appurtenaunces,
vnto p̓ sayd A.B.C.D.foz terme of life of M. G.to p̓
vse of p̓ same M.G.& her assignes foz term of her life

the whyche M. by the grace of God shall mary and take to husbande the sayde W.R. And also yf þ sayd w.R. after the sayde estate of and in the landes and tenementes aforerehearsed, do suffre and cause to be done, all and euerye thynge and thynges as shalbe aduysed by the learned counsayle of the sayde A.B. C.D.&c.theyr heyzes and executours, to make the forsayde state sure to the aboue named A.B. to the vse of the same M.for terme of her lyfe, be it by reco= uerye, fynes, feoffamentes, release, confirmation, and dedes enrolled, wyth warrantie, oz wythoute warrantie,oz any of them,that then.&c.

A condition to perfourme a payze of Indentures.

The condition.&c.that yf the wythin bounden J.w.well and truly obserue,fulfyl,& kepe,all and singuler grauntes, promyses, and agre= mentes,on the partye of the sayde J.w. and A.hys wyfe,to be obserued and kept,conteyned, declared & specifyed in a payze of Indentures, bearynge date the.x.daye.&c.betwene the sayde J.w.of the one par= tye,and the wythin named R.S. on the other parte therof made;sealed,and delyuered,that then.&c.

A condition to saue a man harmelesse,beinge suretye for an other in a simple obligation.

The condition of this obligation. &c.that yf the wythin boundē J.B. fromhenceforth,do saue and kepe harmlesse from al indēpnities, losses actions,troubles & vexations,the win named w.J. his heyzes and executours, agaynst Th.L.R.G.&c.

and

& euery of them, theyr heyres &c. of and for a certayne
wryting obligatory of the summe of.rl.li. wherin the
sayd W, I. standeth bounde as suretye for the sayde
I.B.togyther with M.A.of D.draper, ioyntlye and
seuerallye, as by the same obligatió playnlyer appea=
reth, that than &c.

       ¶ A condition of the peace, or the good
                aberynge.

The Condition &c. yf the wythinbounden.S.T.
personallye appere in the custodye of the baylye
wythin wrytten or of hys depute, before the iu=
styces of our soueraygne Lorde the kyng &c. the mon=
daye next after the Natiuitye of saynt John the Bap
tyst &c.at the towne &c. to fynde there before the sayde
iustyces good and suffyciēt suerties of the peace, & to be
haue and beare hym selfe well and peasablye agaynst
our sayde soueraygne lorde and all hys lyege people &
specyallye agaynste. A.R. and in the meane tyme kepe
the peace of our saiv soueraygne lorde. And so frō hens
forth saue and kepe harmeles the wythin named bay=
lye.&c. for and concernynge the premisses or any parte
of them that than.&c.

       ¶ A condition to be true pryfoner.
      The Condition &c.that yf I.H.marchaūt of Lu=
 T kas whyche nowe is in the kynges pryson vn=
      der kepynge of the shyryffe wythin wrytten as
well by reason of a wryt of our soueraygne Lorde the
kynge of the statute of the staple conteynyng the sūme
of.C.li.sterlynge as also for certeyne other actiōs cau=
ses ,and suytes, on the behalfe of R.S. &c moued &
commenced, be from hensforth true and faythfull priso
                     ner ta=

ner tariynge and remaynynge wyth the sayd shyryfe
and his deputyes tyl the same. J.B. be fully at an end
dyscharged and acquyted of the sayde actions & than
content and paye to the sayde shyryffe &c. all and synguler costes, charges, fees, and other dutyes in such
cases heretofore accustomed to be payed, that than &c.

A Condition for the sealynge of acquyt
taunce or release of
landes &c.

The Condicion of thys oblygatyon is such, that
yf the wythin bounden A.B. do cause J.M. fer
geaunt at the lawe and E. hys wyfe before the
feast of Easter nexte commynge at the costes & charges in the lawe of the sayde A. by theyr sufficiente
dede in the lawe, to release, remyt, and quyte claym
to the wythin named C.D. &c. and theyr heyres, all
theyr ryght, tytle, dower, and interest whych þ said
J.M. and E. hys wyfe, or eyther of them haue had,
or maye haue, of and in all suche landes, tenementes. &c. that than. &c.

Hereafter foloweth the maner of makynge of acquytaunces in latin
and in Englysshe.

Acquittaunce of a percell of a summe
Querint vniuersi per presentes me. A.B. &c. recepisse et habuisse die confectionis presentium,
de. W. J. &c. xx.s. sterling. pro festo omniū sanc
torum anno domini &c. in partem solutionis. xx. li. ster
ling. in quibus idem W. per scriptum suum obligato
rium cum conditione in dorso eiusdem conscript. super eod. confect. mihi prefat. A. tenetur et obligatur.
De

De quibus quidem.xx.s. in partem solutionis maio=
ris sum.in eadem conditione specificat. fateor me be=
ne et fideliter esse solut.dictumqz W.heredes et execu
tores suos inde esse quiet. p presentes. In cui⁹rei testi
monium,sigillum meum presentibus apposui,dat.ꝛc

¶ The fourme of the same in Englysſhe.

BE it knowen to all men by these presentes, that
J A.B.ꝛc. haue receyued, and had the daye of
makyng of these presentes of W.J.ꝛc.xx.s.ſter
lyng for the feaſte of all saynctes laſt before the date
wythin wrytten in part of paymēt of.xx.li.ſterlig in
which the sayd w.by hys wrytyng obligatory wyth
a conditiō in the backe therof ſtandeth holde and boū
den to me the sayde A.B. for the payment of ꝑ same
Of whyche. xx. s. in parte of paymente of the more
somme in the sayd condicion mencioned , J confesse
my selfe well and trulye contente and payed, and the
sayde W.hys heyres and executours clerelye acquy=
ted and dyscharged therof for euer. In wytnes ꝛc.
¶ Acquietaunce of annuytie.

NOuerint ꝛc. me J.K.ꝛc. recepisse ꝛc. de H.R.
per manus J.D. firmarij manerij sui de R.x.
li. in partem solutionis cuiusdam annuitatis
xx. li. mihi ad terminum vite mee, per dictum H con
ceſſ. percipiend.annuat.ad terminos duos,viz ad fe=
ſtū N.et.N.equis portionibꝰ, de quibus.x.li.fateor
me content.ꝛ solut. et ipsum inde hered. et executores
suos imperpetuum esse quietum per presentes ꝛc.
In cuius rei.ꝛc.

CAcquyttaunce foꝛ the tenthes and sub-
sidye payed to the collectour.

Resens scriptū testatur ꝙ ego magist. Henricus
Hoskins decimarū et subsid. dñi nr̄i regis super
oēs personas ecclesiasticas in et ꝑ totū diocesim
M.ꝑcipiend.collectoꝛ et receptoꝛ generalis, sufficienti
autoꝛitate episcopali fulcit⁹,⁊ legittime cōsuet⁹ recepi
be magistro G.Willims rectoꝛe de bꝛidell pꝛo decimis
et subsid. eiusdem ecclesie sue dicto illustrissimo nostro
Regi, pꝛo anno dñi millesimo, quingen . ⁊c. ad festum
natalis domini,bltimo pꝛeterit.debitis.ꝛbiii.s̄.⁊.ꝛbi.s̄
ti. ꝺ. De quibus quidem pecuniis , fateoꝛ me ad bsum
dicti dñi Regis solut. et ipsum et ecclesiam suā pꝛedict.
penitus liberam et qui etiam per pꝛesentes manu mea
subscript. dat ⁊c. Anno regni.⁊c.

CA generall quitaunce.

N   Querint bniuersi ⁊c. me T.H. remisisse,relaꞃas
se et omnimodo pꝛo me, hered. et eꞃecutoꝛibus
meis imperpetuum quiet.clamasse K.M.de N
omnes et omnimod. actiones tam reales quam perso-
nales sect. querelas, debita, eꞃecutiones, transgressio-
nes , et demaund.quasbel que bnquam habui , habeo
seu in futur.quouismodo habere potero vers⁹ pꝛedict.
R.ratione aut causa quacunꞯ ab oꝛigine mundi bsꝗ
in diem confectionis pꝛesentium. In cuius rei ⁊c.

CThe fourme of the same in
Englysshe.

Be it knowen to al men by these pꝛesentes that I
T.H. haue remised, released, and foꝛ. me myne
heyꝛes, and eꞃecutours perpetually quyte claymed

med to R.M.of N. all and all maner of actions, as
well reall as perſonall ſutes,quarelles,dettes,execu=
trons,treſpaſſes,and demaundes whych J the ſayd
T.myne heyꝛes oꝛ executours haue had oꝛ myght
oꝛ ought to haue agaynſte the ſame R.by any maner
of cauſe oꝛ colour,from the begynnyng of the woꝛld,
tyil the daye of the date of theſe pꝛeſentes. Jn wyt=
neſſe whereof.ꝛc.

    ❡ Aquytaunce made by a vycar oꝛ a par=
       ſon,to the pꝛoctours of hys vy=
        carage oꝛ parſonage.

Nouerint vniuerſi.ꝛc. me . A.B. vicariũ ec=
cleſie parochialis de S.recepiſſe et audiuiſſe
die cōrectionis pꝛſentiũ compotũ finalem et
totalem ꝛꝛ.P. pcuratoꝛis vicarie me pꝛedicte de oi=
bus receptis,exitibus,ſolutionibus,et liberationib⁹
pꝛedict. vicare mee ſpectant. de toto tempoꝛe quo di=
ctus ꝛꝛ.fuit pcuratoꝛ meus ibidē. Jta qd computa=
tis computandis et allocatis allocandis ipſum ꝛꝛ.et
executoꝛes ſuos de quocũꜣ vlterioꝛi cōpoto ratione
pmiſſoꝛũ mihi reddend vſꜣ in diem dat.pñtiũ acqui=
eto libero et exonero per pꝛeſētes ſigillo meo ſigillaꝛ.

    ❡A fourme of the ſame in Engly ſ.

BE it knowen to all men by theſe pꝛeſentes,that
J A.B.vicare of the paryſh churche of S.in the
countie of H. haue receyued and harde the daye
of makynge of theſe pꝛeſentes,the hole,ful,and final
accompt of ꝛꝛ.P.my pꝛoctour of the ſayde vicarage
of and foꝛ all ,and all maner receytes, yſſues,paymē=
tes,and delyueryes, vnto my ſayde vycarage in anye
wyſe pertaynyng , foꝛ al the tyme and ſpace that the
                X   foꝛſayde

foꝛsayde W.P.hath ben my pꝛoctour there. So that
all thynges accounted that ought to be counted, and
all thynges allowed that ought to be allowed. I
do release, acquyte and discharge the foꝛsayde W.P.
hys heyꝛes and execu tours, of all maner further re=
kenynges concernyng the pꝛemisses, oꝛ any parcell of
the same, from the begynnyng of the woꝛlde, tyll the
daye of the date hereof.ꝛc. In wytnesse.ꝛc.

℧Letters of manumission foꝛ a bond=
man, in latyne and English.

Uniuersis et singulis chꝛisti fidelibus pntes li=
teras in specturis T.R. miles, dns S.ꝛ M.co
mitissa R. bꝛoꝛ eius salutē in dno sempiternā.
Cum J.B.alias dictus J.B.natiuus nr,filius R.B.
alias dicti R.B. natiui nri spectant. siue appendent.
manerio nostro de P.in Com.C.in billenagio pꝛocre
atus fuerit, est et ac pꝛo tali et bt talis cōmuniter di=
ctus tentꝰ habitꝰ et reputatus palam publice et pꝛi=
uate. Noueritis nos T.R. ꝛc.certis de causis beris et
legittimis nos ꝛ animos nros i ea parte mouētibꝰ p
nobis et heredibꝰ nris imperpetuū manumisisse, libe
rasse et ab omni iugo seruitutis et billenagij exone=
rasse, put per pꝛesentes nras literas patentes manu
mittinus, liberamus et exoneramꝰ pꝛedict. J.B. cū
tota sequela sua pꝛocreata et pꝛocreand bonis et ca=
tellis terris et tenementis suis perquisitis siue impo
sterū perquirendis quibuscunꝗ. Sciatis etiam nos
pꝛefatos T.et M.ꝛc.Remisisse, relaxasse ac omnino
pꝛo nobis,heredibus et executoꝛibus nostris imper=
petuū quietum clamasse sicut p pntes nostras literas
re

relaxamus, remittimus et quiet . clamamus eidem
J.B.alias dicto J.B. et heredibus suis et toti seque
le siue oẽs et oĩmodas actĩoes reales, ɽ psonales, se
ctas querelas, seruicia, calũpnia, transgref.debita, et
demand quecunꝗ quas versus eundem J . B . ali
as dictum J. B. vel aliquos heredum seu sequelarũ
suarum aut eoꝛum aliquem habemus, habuimꝰ seu
quouismodo habere poterimꝰ aut heredes nr̄i habe
re poterunt infuturũ ratione seruitutis et villenagii
pꝛedict.vel aliqua quacunꝗ de causa ab oꝛigine mũ
di vsꝗ in diem confectionis pꝛesentium . Ita videli
cet quod nec nos pꝛedict.T.dominus S.et M.comi
tissa R.nec alter nostrum, nec heredes nostri, nec ali
quis alius per nos, pꝛo nobis, seu nomine nostro aut
alterius nostrum aliquam actionem, ius, titulum,
clameum, interesse , seu demaundam villenagii vel
seruitutis per bꝛeue domini Regis seu aliquo modo
quocũꝗ versus dictum J.B. aliter dictum J.B. aut
sequelam suam pꝛocreat.seu pꝛocreand bona aut ca
talla, terras, aut tenementa sua pquisita vel impo
sterũ ꝓpquirẽd de cetero exigerᵉ, clamare, seu vĩdicare
poterimꝰ, poterit, aut vnquã poterint in futurũ, sed
totaliter simus imperpetuum exinde penitus auer
si et exclusi per pꝛesentes.   Et nos vero pꝛedicti T.
S.et M.et heredes nostri pꝛefat. J.B. alias dict.J.
B.cũ tota sequela sua pꝛocreat.seu pꝛocreãd liberos
erga gentem omnem warrantizabimus imperpetu
um per pꝛesentes.In cuius rei.ꝛc.

¶The fourme of the same lettre
of manumission in
Englysh.

                 X.ij.   To

TO all Chrysten people that shall se thys pre=
sent wrytynge. T.S. knyght, lorde S ꝸ M.
Ccuntesse of R. his wyfe, sendeth gretyng in
our Lorde God euerlastyng. Where as J. B. other=
wyse called J.B. our bondeman or villayn, the sone
of R.B. otherwyse called R. B. our bondman or vil=
layne belongyng and appendaunt to our manoure of
P. in the Countye of C. was and is borne in pure vil=
lenage, and for and as a bondeman or vyllayne was
and is comonly called, taken, had, accompted, and re=
puted priuyly, and apertly. knowe ye, that we ꝑsayd
T. ꝛc. for certayne good and lawfull consideratí=
ons, mouyng our myndes, haue for vs and our hey=
res manumissed, and from the yock of seruitude and
vyllenage, delyuered, and discharged, as we nowe
by these oure letters patentes, manumitte, delyuer,
and discharge for euer the sayde J.B. otherwyse cal=
led J.B. wyth all hys sequele and progenytie gotten
or to be gotten, and all and singuler goodes, catalles
landes and tenementes, and other perquisites which
the sayde J.B. otherwyse called J. B. nowe hath or
at any tyme shall haue or get hereafter. And ye shall
vnderstande also, that we the forsayd T.S.M. haue
remised, released, and for vs, and our heyres for euꝛ r,
quyte claymed, as we nowe by these presentes do re=
mitte, release, and quyte clayme to the same J. B. o=
therwyse called J.B. and all hys heyres sequele and
progenitye gotten or to be gotten. ꝛc. all and all ma=
ner actions, reall, and personall, sutes, quarelles,
seruyces, trespasses, dettes, and demaundes whatso=
euer they be, whyche we the sayde T.M. ꝛc. or oure
heyres hadde, haue, or hereafter maye or shall haue
in any

in any maner wise agaynst the sayd J.B. otherwise
called J.B. oz any of his heyzes, sequeles, oz progeni
tye be reason of the villenage oz seruitude aforesayd
oz by any other cause, pretence oz colour from the be=
gynnynge of the wozlde vntyll the daye of makynge
of these presentes. So that neyther we the sayde T.
M.&c.noz any of vs noz our heyzes,noz any other by
vs, foz vs, oz in our name, shall oz maye from hense=
fozth haue, exacte, sue, clayme, oz chalenge any ma=
ner ryght,tytle, action, interest,oz demaunde of ville
nage oz bondage,agaynst þ sayd J.B.otherwise cal
led J.B.oz hys heyzes,sequele,oz progenity,goodes
catalles, landes, tenementes &c. oz anye of them by
wzytte of our souerayne lozde the kyng oz by any o=
ther maner, but therof be clerely excluded and auoy
ded, foz euer by these presentes And we the sayd T
S.M.and our heyzes the sayde J.B. otherwyse cal
led J.B. wyth all hys sequele and progenitye gottē
oz to be gotten agaynste all people, shall warraunte
free foz euer. In wytnes whereof &c.

¶ An other fourme of manumyssyon in Englysshe.

TO all chzysten people to whome thys pre
sent commeth, Antony Erle.R. lozde.S.
and of R. sendeth gretynge in our Lozde
God euerlastynge.

Be it knowen vnto all people, that where as we
by the infozmacyon of certayne persons,haue made
tytle, and clayme, to one J.T. of Lynne, in the coū
tye of Nozff. and to one W.T. bzother of the same
J.T.of S. in the countye of R.and all theyz issues
of their

of theyz bodyes commyng to be billaynes and bond
bnto bs, as appendaunt to our manour of J. in the
countye afozesayde. And foz as moche as we fynde
neyther pzofe noz fuffyciente grounde, whereby we
maye bnderftande that the fayd J.and W.oz any of
theyz iffue fhuld be bylleyns oz bonde to bs but by e=
uydent pzofe in fondzy wyfe bzought and fhewed to
bs we rather bnberftande the contrarye to be true.
Therfoze we beynge defyzous to fette all doubtfull
matters aparte and wyllynge alfo the fayde John
and w. to be no further greued oz molefted wzogful
lye wythout fuffycyent caufe and that they may fro
henffourth lyue in furety of þ fame, haue remifed re=
leafed.ꝛc.bt fupza.

Here foloweth the makynge of dy=
uers letters of atturneys.

A generall letter of atturneye to re=
couer dettes.

Ouerit bniuerfi þ pzefentes me T.C.de
W.in Com E. gent.fecifle,conftituiffe
et loco meo pofuiffe dilectum mihi in
Chzifto J.N. meu berum et legittimu
attoznatum ad petend.exigend.leuand.
recuperand.et recipiend. bice ꝭ nomine meo ꝯ pzo me
omnes ꝯ fingulas pecuniarum mearum fummas et
debita mea quecumqʒ, que mihi quacumqʒ de caufa a
perfonis quibufcumqʒ,infra bniuerfnm regnum An
glie debentia,fpectantia,fiue pertinent.fut.Dand. et
per pzefentes concedend.pzedicto attoznato meo ple=
nam et integram poteftatem meam et auctozitatem
in pze

pmissis querendi, agendi, dicēdi, prosequendi, impla
citād, arrestandi, imprisonandi, condempnari faci=
endi, et extra prisonam liberandi. debit.predict.recu
perandi.& recipiendi, et de receptis et recuperatis ac
super sine & concordia, acquietandi, seu alias exone=
rationes nomine meo componendi, sigillandi et deli
berand.& attornat.alium vnum vel plures sub se con
stituend, & reuocand.necnon & omnia alia et singula
que in premissis seu circa ea necessaria fuerit & oppor
tuna vice & nomine meo faciend. exequend.exercend.
expediend.et finiend. adeo plenarie et intregre prout
facere possem, siue deberem si in premissis per sonali=
ter interessem. Ratū & grat. habens & habiturus to=
tum et quicquid dictus attornatus meⁿ nomine meo
fecerit, seu fieri fecerit in premissis per presentes.
In cuius rei testimonium.&c.

The fourme of the same in Englysshe.

Be it knowen to al men by these presentes, that
J T.C. of W. in the countye of E. gentylman
haue made, constitute and in my place set and
ordayned my well beloued in Christ J.N.my trewe
and lawfull atturney to axe, requyre, leuye, recouer,
and receyue, in my name for me and to myne vse all
and singuler sommes of moneye, and dettes whatso
euer they be of all maner persons in any wyse to me
due, perteynyng or belongyng in any parte or place
wythin thys realme of Englande. Gyuyng & graun
tynge to my sayde atturney my full and hole power
and auctoritye in the premisses, to playnt, arrest, sue
declare, implede, imprisō, cause to be condempned, &
release y sayd detters, recouer & receyue, & therbpon
fynallye

fynally accorde and acquite, letters of quitaunce and
other discharges for me & in my name to compound
seale and delyuer, attourney or attourneys one or
moo vnder hym to ordeyne and set & at his pleasure
agayn to reuoke and morouer to do, execute, pforme
conclude, and finysshe for me & in my place as is men
tioned afore, al and singuler thynges whych shal be
expedient and necessarye concernynge the premysses
as throughlye, holly and surelye as I my selfe shuld
do, yf I were there in myne owne person present.
And all that euer my sayde atturney shall happen
to do or cause to be done, in and for the premisses. I
promise to allowe, perfourme, ratifye, and stablish
and therto I bynd me, myne heyres, and executours
by these presentes. In wytnes whereof &c.

℀ A letter of atturney for speciall det.

Ouerint vniuersi per presentes me. I. C.
de W. in Com. K. yoman, fecisse ordinasse
et loco meo posuisse dilectos mihi in Christo R. B. et R. M. meos veros et legittimos attornatos coniunctim & diuisim ad petend. leuand. recuperand. & recipiend. vice et nomine meo, et
pro me de T. H. et de executoribus suis, illas. x. li.
sterling. quas idem T. mihi debet, et iniuste a me de
tinet. et in quibus ipse per scriptum suum obligato-
rium mihi tenetur et obligatur. Dand. et per presētes
concedend. dictis attornatis meis et eorum vtriq̃ cō
iunctim et diuisim plenam potestatem meam, et au-
thoritatem in premissis et in singulis ea tangent. pre
dictum T. & executores suos si necesse fuerit pro non
solutione dictarum. x. li. et cuiuslibet inde parcelle im
placitand. arrestand. condempnari faciend. impriso-
nand.

nanð et extra pꝛiſonam ðeliberanð ac per quēcunꝗ
pꝛoceſſū iuris verſus eoſdem pꝛoſequenð.Necnõ ðe ꝓ
ſuper receptis et recuperatis . ꝗc. anð ſo lykewyſe af=
ter the fyꝛſt example.

¶A letter of atturney to ðelyuer poſ=
ſeſſyon of landeṣ.

Ouerint bniuerſi per pꝛeſenteṣ me W .R.ꝗc.
aſſignaſſe,ſeciſſe,et loco meo poſuiſſe ac conſti=
tuiſſe per pꝛeſētes ðilectum mihi in chꝛiſto A.
R.meum berum et legittimum atturnatū að intrāð.
pꝛo me bice et nomine meo,in omnia illa meſuag.ter
raṣ,tenementa,pꝛata , paſcua, paſtuꝛ. ac cetera pꝛe=
miſſa cum ſuis pertinencijs que nuper fuerūt R.W.
generoſi ðefuncti. Et poſt talem intratū að ðeliberāð
pꝛo me bice et nomine meo plenam et pacificam poſ=
ſeſſionem et ſeiſinam ðe et in pꝛedict. meſuag.terris.
ꝗc.cum omnibus ſuis pertinentijs J.B.ðe L.in coꝛſt
S.Generoſo , aut ſuo certo atturnato, heredibus et
executoꝛibus ſuis ſecundū bim foꝛmā tenoꝛem ꝓ eſſe=
ctum cuiuſdam charte mee per me pꝛefat. W . ante=
ðicto J.B.et alijs fact.cuius ðat.eſt. ꝗc. pꝛout per in=
ſpectionem eiuſdem plenī⁹ apparebit. Ceteraꝗ om=
nia et ſingula que in pꝛemiſſis bel circa ea neceſſaria
fuerint ſeu quomodolibet opoꝛtuna pꝛo me bice ꝓ no
mine meo facienð excercenð.ꝗc.aðeo plene.ꝗc.Rat.ꝗc
aṣ afoꝛe.

¶A letter of atturneye to receyue
poſſeſſion of landeṣ.

Ouerint.ꝗc.ðileitū mihi in chꝛiſto C.D.ðe W
meum berum et legittimū atturnatum að in=
tranð pꝛo me bice et nomine meo in bnum me=
　　　　　　　　　　　ꝑ　　　　ſuagiſ

suagium cum gardino et suis pertinentijs, in villa de N. continent.per estimationem duas acr.terre &c. que nuper fuerunt A.B. defuncti ac plenam & pacificam possessionem et seisinam inde capiend.& post huiusmodi seisinam & possessionem sic inde receptam & habit. eandem ad meum proprium vsum retinend. & custodiend.secundum vim,formam,et effectum cuiusdam charte mihi & alijs fact. per E.F. generosi,vt p eandem chartam inde confect. cuius dat.est &c.manifeste liquet et apparet.Cetera& omnia et singula &c.

And ye shall vnderstande that thys is the vse in takynge of season and possession. Fyrste ye must expell all persons out of the house & call vnto you certayne neyghbours to wytnes at the former dore,thã cause one to reade the deade of feoffement, and yf it be latyne, some bodye must interprete and declare it to wytnes in the mother tongue, then let one of the atturneys, he that gyueth the possession, take the dore or the rynge thereof in hys one hande, and sette the hande of the receyuer of possession, vpon the dore in lyke maner, sayinge.

By the auctoritye of thys deade of feoffemente, I make vnto you lyuerye and season of thys tenement and landes.&c. accordynge to the effecte of the same deede, and therein I sette you in fyrme and peasable possession, than cause the feoffyes to enter &c.

Thys done,it is good to wryte the names of thẽ that be present to beare wytnes, on the backe of the dede, as thus. Data et deliberata fuit seisina, et pacifica possessio I.B.&c.iuxta formam et effectum huiᵉ charte,per W.M. attornat.&c. in presentia I.B.C.D
de vill

De billa pꝛedict.iii.die maii.⁊c.

℀Ind yf ꝓ possessiō be gyuen of a maner, it is good
to haue a courte holdẽ immediatlye in the name of
the newe Loꝛde, and there lette the euidences, and
deedes be ſhewed to the tenauntes, and they to be re
quyꝛed to returne and agree to the ſame aſtate, and
as many as returne, lette theyꝛ names be entred in
the courte rolle.

Lyuerye and ſeaſon of landes, is cōmonly made
by a pece of the ſame earthe taken by the feoffer and
gyuen to the feoffye togyther wyth the deede in maner afoꝛeſayde ⁊c.

℀A letter of attourneye generall and
ſpeciall, in a matter
of landes.

Ꝺiuerſis ⁊c.P.H. de B. in Com.E.yoman fi
lius ⁊ heres R.H. defuncti dum bixit de.C.in
   Com.pꝛedicto yoman, ſalutem in Domino ſẽ
piternam.   Ꝺoueritis me pꝛefatum P. feciſſe oꝛ
Ꝺinaſſe, conſtituiſſe, et loco meo poſuiſſe dilectum mi
hi i Chꝛiſto T.G.meum berum et legit.attoꝛnatũ ad
pꝛoſequend. implacitand. et defendend. bice et nomi
ne meo et pꝛo me in omnibus et ſingulis curiis et pꝉi
tis ac coꝛam quibuſcunqꝫ iudicibus et iuſticiariis.
berſus omnes et ſingulas perſonas, erga quas be
quam, aliqua actio tam realis quam perſonalis, mi
hi quouiſmodo dat ius, ſectam aut defenſionem pei
legem,de et pꝛo omnibus illis terris, et tenementis
meis cum ſuis pertinẽtiis bniuerſis bocat.W.ſitu
atis, iacentibus,⁊ exiſtent. in billis et campis de.C
P.ii.   pꝛedic

V

predict.que mihi dicto P. iure, hereditario descende=
bant per et post moztem predicti R.patris mei et que
in presenti a me iniuste detinentur. Necnon in omnia
dicta terras et tenementa, cum suis pertinencijs vice ex
nomine meo ad intrand ac plenam et pacificam pos=
sessionem et seisinam de et in eisdem pzo me et nomi=
ne meo capiend ac omnes et singulas personas quas=
cunqz firmarios siue occupatozes eozundem abinde
expellend et a mouend et super huiusmodi possessione
sic capta et habita, omnia dicta terras et tenementa,
cum pertinentijs, ad vsum dicti T. custodiend guber=
nand, occupand, et ministrand. Dand et per presentes
concedend predicto atturnato meo plenam et integrã
potestatem meam, auctozitatem et mandatum specia
le predictas personas et earum quamlibet occasione
iniuste detencionis custodie vel occupationis predi=
ctarũ terrarum et tenementozum cum pertinentijs,
aut alicuius inde partis seu parcelle attachiand et
arrestari faciend ac cozam iudicibus et iusticarijs pre
dictis comparere faciend et pzoducend ac versus ip=
sas personas et earum quamlibet occasione predict.
omnes et singulas actiones, sectas, placita et pzo=
secutiones licita, requisit. et necessaria in cur predict.
vbicunqz videbit opoztunũ foze, vice ac nomine me=
is leuand affirmand capiend et attaminand et eas
vel ea secundum iuris exigentiam cum quibuscunqz
inde circumstantijs interplacitand et pzosequend ac
ius et titulum mei predict P.cozam predict.iudicibus
et iustic. declarand exponend et notificand dictasqz
psonas et earũ quamlibet p legis vigozem arrestand
impzison. et côdenari faciend, extra pzisonã deliberãd
ac dampna et expensas in ea parte habit . et h abêd de
ipsis

ipsis persons et de earum qualibet recuperand. ꝸ re
cipiēd. Et de receptis et recuperatis ac super fine ꝗc.
as in the other.

   CA letter of attouꝛney bppon a
     patente.

Uniuersis ꝗc. J.P. bnus armigeroꝛum pꝛo coꝛ
poꝛe illustrissimi domini nostri regis ꝗc.salutē
in domino sempiternam.

Cum idem dominus noster rer, per suas gratiosas
literas patentes quarum dat. est apud westm̄. deci
mo die Febꝛuarij. anno regni sui. rrri. in consideratione veri ꝸ fidelis seruicij ꝗ ego dictus J.P. eidem
illustrissimo domino nostro ante hec tempoꝛa impēdi
ꝸ durante vita mea impendere intendo, concesserit,
ꝸ licentiam dederit mihi pꝛefato J.P. ꝗ ego per me
aut deputatum siue deputatos meos indigenas siue
alienigen. numerum ꝸ quantitatem ducentoꝛum do-
lioꝛum Jsatis, anglice bocat. woad, de Tholosa in
partibus bltra marinis emere et pꝛouidere, ac eadē
ducenta dolia de woad,in bna naui, siue diuersis na
uibus de obedientia dicti domini regis aut obedien-
cia aliquoꝛum amicoꝛum et confederatoꝛum suoꝛum
carcari et imponere ac in quemcunꝗ locum seu quecunꝗ loca huius regni sui Anglie bna bice bel diuer
sis bicibus ibidem ad meum marimum pꝛoficuum ꝸ
auantagium impoꝛtand.conducend.ꝸ inducend.ben-
dend ꝸ distribuend. conduci et discarcari facere pos-
sim,ꝸ baleam licite ꝸ impune,aliquo actu,statuto,re
strictione, pꝛohibitione, aut pꝛoclamatione in contra
rium fact. non obstant.pꝛout in pꝛedictis litteris pa-
tentibus inde confectis plenius continetur.

Noueritis me pꝛefat. J.P. birtute ꝸ auctoꝛitate dic-
         tarum

tarum literarum patentium feciſſe, oꝛdinaſſe, conſtituiſſe et in loco meo poſuiſſe dilectos mihi in chꝛiſto A.B.C.D.mercatoꝛes de hiſpania,meos veros et legittimos deputatos et factoꝛes,irreuocabiles, coniunctim, vice et nomine meo ad faciend. exequēdum, et adminiſtrand. ad vſus, commoda, et pꝛoficua pꝛopꝛia eoꝛundem A.B.C.D. omnia et ſingula in dictis literis patentibᵍ content. Ꞇ ſpecificata videlicet in tam amplis modo et foꝛma pꝛout ego dictus J.P. facere potuiſſem ſeu deberem vigoꝛe pꝛedictarum litterarum patentium,ſi ibidem pꝛeſens p ſonaliter intereſſem. Et deputatum ſiue factoꝛem v num ſeu plutes,ſub ſe conſtituend.Ꞇ ad libita ſua re uocandum.Quibus quidem A.B.C.D.et eoꝛum v trieꝫ coniunctim, ego dictus. J.P. do, concedo, et tranſpoꝛto per pꝛeſentes omnimodam poteſtatem meam, et auctoꝛitatem in pꝛemiſſis.

℧Rat. et grat. habens, Ꞇ habitur. totum et quicquid dicti deputati et factoꝛes nomine meo fecerint ſeu fieri pꝛocurauerint, aut eoꝛum aliquis fecerit, ſeu fieri pꝛocurauerit in pꝛemiſſis,et in quolibet pꝛe miſſoꝛum per pꝛeſentes. Jn cuius rei Ꞇc.

℧A lyke fourme of a letter of attutney vpon a patent in Englyſſhe.

B

Ɛ it knowen to all men by theſe pꝛeſentes ẏ where the kynge oure ſoueraygne Loꝛde by his gracious letters of licence enſealed wyth hys ſignet beryng date at W.the.xii.daye of maye in the.xxx.yere of hys reygne foꝛ certayne conſideracions, hys hyghnes mouing, hath licenced vs .W. C.ſergeant of ẏ Catery of his honoꝛable houſhold and P.L. yoman of hys garde his welbeloued ſeruauntes

nauntes, that we by our ſelues our factours oʒ at=
tourneys ſhal and may puruey and bye in ony place
oʒ places wythin thys his realme of England wher
it ſhal beſt lyke vs.iiii.C.quarters of wheate,and the
ſame to conueye and carye oʒ do to be conueyed and
caryed out of any poʒte, hauen, oʒ creke of hys ſayd
realme, that ſhall pleſe vs in the partyes of Flaun=
ders,Holande, Bʒabant,oʒ ʒelande, there to be vt=
tered and ſolde foʒ our moſte pʒofittes and auaunta=
ges as in the ſayde letters of lycence thereof made,
moʒe playnlye is conteyned.knowe ye that we the
foʒſayd w.C.and P.L. by vertue of the ſayd gracy=
ous letters of licence haue commytted, oʒdeyned, z
deputed,our welbeloued in God A.B. of Parmouth
in the countye of Noʒff. marchaunte and R.S. ſer=
naunt of me the foʒeſayd w.C.our ſuffycyent attur
neys z factouʒs ioyntly z ſeuerally to erecute by the
ſelfe oʒ by theyʒ ſufficiet deputy oʒ deputies the hole
tenure, purpoʒt z effect of the ſayd gracious letters
z euery clauſe z article of the ſame, as vnto the oʒ a=
ny of them ſhalbe thought moſt conuenient and ne=
ceſſarye that is to ſaye in all thynges and by al thyn
ges, in as ample and large maner as we the foʒſaid
w.C.oʒ eyther of vs myght do, ſhulde do, oʒ oughte
to do by vertue of the ſayde gratious letters yf we
our owne ſelfes were perſonallye pʒeſente.
And what ſo euer that our ſayde atturneys oʒ theyʒ
ſufficient deputy oʒ deputyes ſhal do and miniſtre in
the pʒemyſſes oʒ any thynges concernynge the ſame
we the ſayde I.P. and R.S, bynde our ſelfes to ra
tyfye and allowe by theſe pʒeſentes.
　　In wytnes whereof.zc.

　　　　　　　　　　　　　　　A let=

¶A letter of attourney in Englyſſhe.

B
 Be it knowen to al men by theſe pꝛeſentes that J.G.of B. in the countye of Surrey yoman, haue made, conſtitute, oꝛdeyned, and put in my place, my ryght welbeloued in God R.M.gentil man my true and laufull attourney in thys behalfe, to ouerſee, rule and gouerne foꝛ me, and in my name all my landes and tenementes, as well fre holde, as coppe holde, ſette and lyenge, in the towne and pa=ryſſhe of Croydon in the countye of S. And alſo to receyue foꝛ me and in my name all the rentes, iſſues, conmodytyes, and pꝛofyttes, commynge and gro=wynge of the ſame landes, and euery percell thereof And the fermours of the ſame landes, foꝛ none pay=ment to expell, put oute, and amoue and them to let to ferme to other, at hys owne pleaſure and diſcreti=on gyuynge and grauntynge vnto my ſayde attour=ney my full power and auctoꝛytye by the tenoure of thys pꝛeſentes to do and execute all and ſynguler the pꝛemiſſes, as fullye,hollye,and ſurely as J the ſayd John S. myght oꝛ ſhulde do yf this my pꝛeſent woꝛ tynge had not ben made &c. Jn wytnes &c.

¶A letter of ſubſtitucion where the attoꝛney maketh a de putye vnder hym.

V
Niuerſis &c.S.f. &c. ſalutem in domino ſem piternam.
Cum J.T.&c.per quoddam ſcriptum ſuum de attoꝛnat. fecerit, oꝛdinauerit, conſtituerit, et in loco
ſuo

suo posuerit me prefat. S. suum verum & legittimū
attoznat. ad petenð. &c. vice et nomine dicti J. et ad
meum propzium vsum de H. C. r.li.in quibus dict⁹
H. per obligationem suam prefato J.tenetur et obligatur dictusq̄ J. per dictum scriptum suum de at
toznato dederit & concesserit mihi prefato S. atturnato suo plenam et integram potestatem suam et au
thozitatem in premissis tangenð.agenð. psequenð.&c

Et de receptis et recuperatis, ac super fine et cōcoz-
dia acquietant. seu alias exonerationes nomine dicti J.componenð.sigillanð. et liberanð.Et atturnat.
alios vnū vel plures sub me constituenð.& reuocanð
pzout in eodem script. de attoznat. inde confect. plenius continetur. Noueritis me prefat.S. bigoze et
auctozitate dicti scripti de attozn. mihi sic fact.ozdi-
nasse, posuisse.&c. E.W. meum verum et legittimū
substitutum ad petenð. &c. ad vsum cōmodum & pzo
ficuum dicti E.De prefato H. r.li. necnon omnia alia
et singula. in premissis et circa ea necessaria ad facienð. excercenð. expedienð.et finienð.adeo plene & in
tegre,sicut ego predictus. T. bigoze antedicti
scripti attornat. facere possem, seu deberem si prefens personaliter ad
essem. Ratum,gratū
&c. In cuius rei
testimo.&c.

Accozdynge
to the tenoz
of pletter
of atturney

Here foloweth the manner to make
letters patentes in dyuers
and sondzye four-
mes.

¶ Pa-

¶ A patente of an offyce for terme of
lyfe, wyth a fee assigned to
the same.

Mnibus Chrifti fidelibus ad quos præ
fens scriptum peruenerit, R.G. comes
L.falutem in domino sempiternam.
Sciatis me præfatum comitem dediffe,
et per hoc præfens scriptum meum con
ceffiffe w.H.generoso, officium rec eptoris c mnium
exit. proficuorum et denariorum summarum, cres
cent. et prouenient. de omnibus maneriis, terris, et
tenementis, redditibus, et hereditamentis meis qui
buscunque in Com.de B. &c. Ac etiam officium super
uisoris omnium prædictorum maneriorum tert. tene
ment. et hereditamentorum meorum quorumcunque.
Ac ipsum w.H. receptorem ac superuisorem maneri
orū, terrarum,&c. constituisse et ordinasse, prout per
præsentes ordinamus, et constituimus. Habend.te
nend.& occupand. officia prædicta, et eorum vtrumque
per se vel per suum sufficientem deputatum aut de
putatos suos pro termino vite eiusdem w. H.cum ō
nibus proficuis, comoditatibus, et præeminentiis,
vel fic durā quibuscunque, eifdem officiis seu eorum alteri de anti
re plito mei quo spectant.siue pertinent. in tā amplis modo et for
dicti comi= ma, prout aliquis alius vel aliqui alii officia prædi
tis. cta, seu eorum alterum ante hec tempora vs⁹ fuit aut
gauisi fuerunt.
Et vlterius sciatis me præfat.C.dediffe, et hoc præfen
ti scripto meo conceffiffe præfato w. H. pro executio
ne & occupacione officiorum prædict. quandam annu
alem reddit. xl. marcarum sterling. exeunt. de omni=
bus

nibus predictis maneriis, terris, tenementis, &c. ha=
bend.leuand.et percipiend.eundem annualem reddi=
tum.xl.marcarum prefato.xx. pro termino vite sue
naturalis, per manus suas proprias de exit. & profi=
cuis maneriozum, terrarum,&c. ad duos anni termi=
nos videlicet ad festa.&c.per equales poztiones.
Et si contingat predictuin ãnualẽ redditum. xl.mar=
carum. a retro foze &c

as ye se in o
ther graun=
tes and an=
nuites here
befoze.

¶ A graunte of the kepynge of a ma=
nour, parke, and lodge.

¶W. Erle of O. Lozde S.&c. to al Chri=
sten people to whome thys presente wzy=
tynge commeth gretyng in our lozd God
euerlastynge.

¶Wheras. J.late erle of O. myne aũcestour whose
cosyne & heyze J am by his letters patentes dated &c
gaue and graunted vnto J.w. the offyce and keping
of the parke of L.wythin the countye of S.& of the
lodge within the same and also by hys sayde letters
patentes made constitute and ozdeyned the sayde J.
w.to be hys offycer and keper of the sayde parke and
lodge, To haue occupye and enioye the sayde offyce
of keper and lodge to the fozesayde J.w. and to hys
assygnes foz terme of hys lyfe,by hym self oz his suf
fycient deputye oz deputyes, wyth all maner of fees
wages, pzofyttes and commodytyes to the sayde of=
fyce due, oz apperteynyng in as large and ample ma
ner, as any person oz persons befoze that tyme had,
occupyed, enioyed, oz perceyued in the same.

z.ii.   Knowe

knowe you that I John W.nowe erle of O. for
dyuers consyderations me mouing haue gyuen graū
ted, and by thys my present wrytynge do gyue and
graunte to my welbeloued frende T.P.gentilman
seruaunte to the reuerende father in God &c. the ke
pynge of the manour of L. and of the sayd parke of
the dere nowe therein, or that hereafter at any tyme
shall be immediatlye after the death of the sayde I.
W.and as sone as the sayde offyce whych the aboue
named I.W. doeth nowe enioye shall happen to be
voyde by surrender of the sayde I.W. or by anye o
ther lawfull wayes, and meanes. And the same T
P.ordeyne, make, & constitute by these presentes,to
be keper of the same manour, parke, lodge,and dere
whan so euer it shall fyrste happen to be voyde as is
afore rehersed.
And furthermore knowe ye that I the sayde I.W.
erle of O. do gyue and graunt vnto the foresayd T.
P. for the exercysyng and occupyeng of the sayd of
fyce the yerelye fee and wages of.iiii.ƀ.a daye imme
diatlye after the death of the sayde I.W. wyth all
profyttes,fees wages rewardes, auauntages, and
commodytyes to the same offyce in anye wyse due &
appertaynynge in as ample maner and fourme, as
the sayde I.W. or any other hauynge or occupying
the same offyce had, or euer vsed and enioyed.
And also the herbage and pannage, of the sayd park
of L.immediatlye after the death of the foresayd I.
W. and as sone as the sayd office shall happen to be
voyde by surrender of the abouenamed I.W.or by
any other laufull wayes or meanes. To haue, hold,
occupye and enioye the same offyce of kepyng of the
sayd

ſayde manour, parke, lodge and dere immediatly af
ter the death of the ſayde J. W. and as ſone as the
ſame offyce ſhall happen to be voyde, to the ſayd T.
P. foz terme of hys lyfe, by hym ſelfe oz hys ſuffyci=
ente deputye oz deputyes. And to haue and to holde
the ſayde wages and yerelye fee of.iiii.d. a day and ᵽ
ſayde herbage and pannage togyther wyth al other
commodytyes, pzofyttes and auauntages, appertey
nynge to the ſame immedyately after the deathe of
the ſayde J. W. in as large and ample maner as the
ſayd J. w. oz any other perſonnes heretofoze hadde
oz occupyed, foz terme of lyfe of the ſayde T.Philip
pes, the ſame yerelye fee, oz wages, of foure pence a
daye to be payed by the handes of the baylye of the
towne of L. foz the time beynge of the iſſues, pzofyt
tes, and reuenues of the manour of.L. at.ii. feaſtes
in the yeare, that is to ſaye, at the feaſtes of ſayncte
Mychaell the Archaungell : and the Annuntiation
of our bleſſed ladye ſayncte Marye the virgine by e=
uen poztions.

The fyzſte payment therof accozdynge to the rate to
begynne at the fyzſte feaſt of the ſayd. ii. feaſtes next
immediatly, after the death of the ſayde J. w.

And yf it happen the ſayde yerelye fee oz wages of
iiii.d. a day to be behynde and not payed by the ſpace
of one moneth next after any of the feaſtes afoze re=
herſed at whyche it oughte to be payed, that than it
ſhall be lefull to the ſayde. J. w. into the fozeſayd ma
nour of L. &c. to entre and dyſtrayne, and the diſtreſ
ſes there founde to dzyue, carye, and beare awaye ᴈ
wyth hym to holde, kepe, and reteyne, tyl ſuch tyme
as all the poztion of the ſayde yerelye fee oz wages,
of

of.iiii.ð.a daye, so due and behynde hande be sullye
contented and payed wyth the arrerages yf any ther
be. In wytnes whereof ꝛc.

¶A peticion to the kyng foꝛ a pooꝛe scholer.

¶To the kynge our soueraygne Loꝛd.

Pleaseth it youre hyghnes of your moste noble
and aboundant grace, in the waye of charytye
foꝛ and towardes the exhibition of your dayly
oꝛatour and pooꝛe suppliaunt. T.M. master of arte
and student in your bniuersitye of Oꝛenfoꝛde beyng
mynded to contynue in hys studie and lernyng there
whych he shal not be able to do bnles your most gra
cyouse fauoure be shewed to hym in thys behalfe, to
gyue and graunt bnto your sayde oꝛatour the penti
on goynge out of the colledge oꝛ felowshyppe of N.
beynge of your moste noble foundacyon, whych pen
tion the dean of the sayde colledge is bounde to giue
at your nomination by reason that the same colledge
was latelye voyde of a deane and mayster, and the
sayde nowe deane is by your grace to the same pꝛefer
red and called. And that your sayde oꝛatour maye b
pon thys byll sygned wyth your most gracyous hād
haue and obteyne suche and as many your necessary
wꝛytynges, as in thys behalfe shall be to hym expe
dyent. And your sayde oꝛatour shal daylye pꝛaye to
God foꝛ the pꝛeseruacion of youre royall estate long
to contynue in felicitye.

¶A letter patent of a yerely annuytye
wyth dyuers other clauses of fees.

Lykewyse
ye maye ma
ke i ꝑ name
of all other
loꝛde ꝛc.

Ex ꝛc. Omnibus, ad quos hoc pꝛesens scriptū
peruenerit, salutem. Sciatis ꝙ nos in conside
ratione boni et fidelis seruicij per dilectum nobis in

bis in Chriſto.N̄. ante hec tempora impenſ, dedimꝰ
conceſſimus.ac per preſentes damus et concedimꝰ eiſ
dem N̄.quandam annuitatem, ſiue annualem reddi
tum.l.li.ſterlingorum annuatim habend.percipiend
gaudend.et recipiend. de exitibus, reuentionibus, ⁊
proficuis hanaperij noſtri predicti per manus cūci,
vel cuſtodis eiuſdem hanaperij noſtri, pro tempore
exiſtent. habend.⁊ annuatim percipiend. annuitatē, vel mancrū
ſiue annualem redditum.l.li. prefato N̄.pro termino noſtri de N̄
vite ſue naturalis,de exitibus,reuentionibus ⁊ pro o: as ꝑ mat
ficuis eiuſdem hanaperij per manus clerici, vel cu- ter is.
ſtodis dicti hanaperij pro tempore exiſtentis ad feſta annuntiationis beate Marie virgin.et ſancti Mi
chaelis archangeli, equis portionibus, ſuper ſola de
monſtratione harum littecarum noſtrarum patentium ſeu earum irrotulamēt.in dicto hanaperio noſtro
fact. vel alibi prefat.cuſtodi pro tempore exiſtent.oſ-
tenſ. abſqꝫ aliquo breui,vel aliquibus breuibus ſiue
mandat. extra cancellariam noſtram, ſuper eaſdem
litteras noſtras patent. proſequend. ac prefato cleri- A clauſe for
co aut cuſtodi aliquatenꝰ dirigend.Dedimus etiam a tonne of
et conceſſimus ac per preſentes damus et concedimꝰ wyne.
eidem M̄. pro termino vite ſue, bnū dolium vini va-
ſton.annuatim percipiend. durante vita ſua per manus pincerne noſtre anglie pro tempore exiſtentis de
liberand. de illo vino ꝙ idem pincerna noſter pro tēpore exiſtens,habebit et recipiet ad vſum noſtrum ra
tione officij ſui predicti.
Necnon damus et concedimus eidem N̄.pro termi- A clauſe for
no vite ſue annuatim tantum ſerici anglice veluet de a tec gown.
ſerico noſtro de garderoba noſtra et tantum penul.de
ead.garderoba noſtra annuat.ꝑcipiend.⁊ deliberand
per

per manus magistri Garderobe nostre predicti pro
tempore existentis quantum satis erit, et seruiet ad
faciend predict. vnam togam de serico anglice veluet
penulatam annuatim pro termino vite sue de illis se
ricis angl. beluet et penulis de quib⁹ idē ihr de garde
roba nostra pro tempore existens annuatim recipiet
et habebit ratione officii sui predict. Ic etiam damus
et concedimus eidem. N. annuatim durante vita su
a, duas damas idoneas, videlicet vnum anglice a
bucke of season in estate, et aliam anglice a doo of se
ason in hieme, in magno parco nostro, de w. in Com̄
nostro de S. annuatim capiend. ɛ habend . tam per
se ipsum quam per aliquem alium siue aliquos alios
per ipsum assignand. per custodes in parco nostro p
tempore existent. eidem. N. deliberand. Et volumus
ɛ concedimus ꝗ bene liceat et licebit prefato M. ɛ assignatis suis durante vita sua predicta annuatim be
nari ɛ fugare in eodem parco nostro pro predictis du
abus damis capiend. ɛ interficiend. et eas abinde ca
riand. asportand. et habend. vbicūꝗ placuerit ad voluntatem suam sine impedimento nostri et heredum
nostrorum forestariorum, parcariorum et aliorū of-
ficiariorū et ministrorū nostrorū quorumcunꝗ du
rante vita sua. Et vlterius damus et concedimus eidem N. Centum libras sterling. de dono et regardo
nostro de exit. reuentionibus et proficuis hanaperii
nostri predict. prouenient. siue crescent. per man⁹ pre
dicti clerici, eiusdem hanaperii pro tempore existent.
soluend. et deliberand. indilate post ostensionem sibi
harum litterarum nostrarum patent. absꝗ compoto
seu aliquo alio inde nobis vel hered. nostris reddend
seu soluend. pro premissis seu aliqua premissorum.

Et

A clause for
a fee bucke.

Pardon the
barbarouse
latyn of al
thys booke
for the com
mon woor-
des of istru
mētes may
in no wyse
be altered.

Et volumus et concedimus ꝙ predictus clericus de ꝺ clause of
hanaperio nostro pro tempore existens, et predictus allowance.
magister de garderoba nostra predict. pro tempore
existens, habeant plenam allocationem, coram quibuscunꝗ auditoribus et iudicibus nostris,in quibuſ
cunꝗ curiis et locis super specialibus compotis suis
faciend. de exit. reuentionibus, et proficuis separa-
libus ratione officiorum suorum nobis emergen.siue
crescen. videlicet dictus clericus hanaperij nostri pro
tempore existens,tam pro annuali solutione predict.
annuitatis siue annualis redditus.l.li.quam pro pre
dictis centū libris de regardo nostro prefato M. vt
premittitur per nos conceſſ. Et predictus magister
garderobe nostre predicte pro deliberatione dicte an
nualis serici siue veluet, et penularum annuatim ad
faciend. prefato .M. vnam togam penulatam.

Eo ꝙ expreſſa mentio de vero annuo valore aut a-
liqua alia certitudine premiſſorum, seu eorum alicuius, aut de alijs donis, siue conceſſionibus per nos
aut aliquem progenitorum nostrorum, prefato .M.
ante hec tempora fact. in presentibus minime fact.
existit, aut aliquo statuto ordinatione actu, restricti,
one, prohibitione siue prouiſione aut aliqua alia re,
causa vel materia quacunꝗ in aliquo non obstante.
In cuius rei testimonium ꝛc.

℟A letter patent of the kynge or a lorde,
concernynge the gyfte of a steward-
shyppe, and constable. ꝛc.

REX Omnibus ad quos ꝛc. salutem. Sciatis
ꝙ nos considerantes fidelitatem et industriam
predilecti ꝗ fidelis consanguinei nostri.G.ꝛc.
ex gracia nostra speciali et ex certa scientia, et mero
Aa.i. motu

motu nostris concessimus pꝛefato G. officia senescal∣
li siue senescalcie honoris nostri de N. in com. Derb.

Oꝛ of other loꝛdeshyp⁊ and landes. ⁊ Suff. Necnon castri ville dominij et manerij noui castri, super tinam dñioꝛum et manerioꝛu de W. ⁊ B ac omnium alioꝛum castroꝛum, dominioꝛum, mane∣rioꝛum, terratum, et tenementoꝛum nostroꝛum in e∣ijsdem com. cum pertinent. percellis ducatus nostre Lancaster ac eundem G. senescallum omnium offici oꝛum pꝛedict. per pꝛesentes oꝛdinamus, facimus, et costituimus.

Ac etiam concessimus eidem G. officia constabu∣laria castrorum nostroꝛum de T. M. ⁊ P. magistri **A clause of deputation.** foꝛestar. chacee nostre de K. ac balliuoꝛum noue liber∣tatis nostre in com pꝛedict. Necnon magistrum de∣ductus ferarum omnium foꝛestar. chaceatum, parco∣rum, boscoꝛum, et warennoꝛum, iu com. pꝛedict. Ac etiam concessimus eidem G. plenariam auctoꝛita tem, et potestatem facienð. nominanð. et assignanð. de tempoꝛe in tempus, omnes et omnimoð. foꝛesta∣rios et custodes dictarum foꝛestarum, ferarum, cha∣ceaꝛum, parcoꝛum, et warennoꝛum. Ac insuper dedi mus et concessimus eidem G. officium magistri capi talis senescalli, honoris pꝛedict. ac ceteroꝛum pꝛemis soꝛum omnium cum pertinent. Habenð. occupanð. et exercenð. omnia pꝛedicta officia et eoꝛum quodlibet bna cum authoꝛitate et potestate pꝛedict. pꝛefato. G. per se bel per suos sufficientes deputatos ant depu∣tatum suum pꝛo termino bite ipsius. G. percipenð. S∣nuatim in ⁊ pꝛo officijs pꝛedictis, et eoꝛum quolibet C. li. sterling. bna cum feoð. et vað. ab antiquo debit. et consuet. tam eijsdem officiis et eoꝛum cuilibet quã omnibus alijs officijs occupanð. per offic. fiendis et nomi∣

nominand. per pꝛefat.G. auctoꝛitate et poteſtate ſu⸗
pꝛadict.et de eꝛitibus, pꝛoficuis et reuentionibus ho
noꝛis pꝛedict. et ceteroꝛum pꝛemiſſoꝛum,et eoꝛum cu
iuſlibet pꝛouenient.ſine creſcen. per manus fiꝛmario
rum, tenentium, receptoꝛum ſeu alioꝛum officiario⸗
rum et occupatorum eiuſdē pꝛo tempoꝛe exiſtent. ad
terminos ſancti Michaelis archangeli et paſche, eꝛ
quis poꝛtionibus, bna cum omnibus et omnimodis
aliis feod. pꝛoficuis, commoditatibus et libertatib⁹
et emolumentis quibuſcunqꝛ officijs pꝛedictis et eo⸗
ꝛum cuilibet qualitercunqꝛ pertinent. in tam amplis
modo et foꝛma, pꝛout aliqui alij, ſiue aliquis ali⁹ of⸗
ficia pꝛedicta, ſeu eoꝛum aliquod ante hec tēpoꝛa ha⸗
buerunt ſiue habuit, occuparunt bel occupant, ac in
eiiſdem et in eoꝛum quolibet, perceperunt ſiue perci
pit. Eo q͏ꝛ expꝛeſſa mentio de bero annuo baloꝛe ꝛc.
aꝛ ye ſe in the other.

   ¶A letter patent foꝛ kepynge of a na⸗
    turall ideote oꝛ lunatike.

Eꝛ.Omnibus ad quos ꝛc. ſalutem.Sciatis q͏ꝛ
cum T.B. filius et heres H. B. nuper de G. in
com.E.fatuus et idiota exiſtit a natiuitate ſua
et ratione ſui ipſius et regimine terrarum,tenemen⸗
toꝛum, bonoꝛum,et cattalloꝛum ſuoꝛum omnino ba
cat et caret, pꝛout coꝛam nobis fide dignos pꝛobatū
eſt teſtibus.

   Nos bero de gratia noſtra ſpeciali, et eꝛ certa ſci⸗
entia, et mero motu noſtris, bolentes eidem T.de bi
te neceſſariis ꝛ coꝛpoꝛis ſui cuſtodia ſecura ꝑuidere:
Dedimus et conceſſimus ac per pꝛeſentes damus et
      Za.ii. conced/

bel lunatic⁹
et demens
trencticus,
lethargus.
oꝛ othe⸗
wiſe as the
perſon is.

concedimus dilecto nobis in Christo H.J. militi pro
corpore nostro custodiam ipsius T.ac omnium terra
rum et tenementorum reddit.et seruic. cum pertinen
tiis que nuper fuerunt predict.H.B.et que tam per si
ue post mortem eiusdem H. quam ratione fatuitatis
et ideocitatis dicti T.ad manus nostras deuenerunt
seu deuenire debuerint aut debent.Habend.gaudend
tenend. et occupand. custodiam corporis dicti T. ac
omnium maneriorum, terrarum, tenementorum et
aliorum premissorum etc. prefato H.J. heredibus et
assignat. suis pro termino vite naturalis dicti T.B.
absq̃ aliquo compoto seu aliquo alio, nobis vel here
dibus nostris inde reddend.vel faciend.Prouiso sem
per q̃ dictus H. J.heredes et assign.sui de exit.mane
riorum, terrarum, tenementorum, et ceterorum pre
missorum, inueniat predicto T.victualia z cetera om
nia vite sue necessaria,prout decet in tali casu,z quod
terre et teñta.etc. predicta manuteneantur sine vasto
vel destructione. Eo q̃ expressa mêtio de vero annuo
valore etc.

Marginal notes:
Dementie, lethargie frenesis etc.

vel quam di u in predict dementia, frenesi,leth argiaca.du rauerit siue extra mentê suã fore con tigerit z do nec ad pristi nam suam mentem, ra tionê,z me moriam per uenerit.etc.

¶A letter of saufe conduyte for a certayne yeres.

TO all true chrysten people to whome these pre
sent letters shall come A.B.of D.z E.F.citizẽs
of London, sende gretynge in our lorde God e
uerlastynge. Where as one G.H.citizen of London
in dyuerse sommes of money to vs seuerally is indet
ted, whyche sommes of money the sayd G.H. is not
ne by lykelyhode shall be of abilitye to paye and con
tent, onelesse we gyue z graunte vnto hym, oure fa
uoure z

uour and reſpyte, in payment of the ſame. Therfoze
knowe ye ꝑ we the ſayd creditours al abouenamed,
and euerych of vs moued wyth pyttie in conſydera=
tyon of the pzemyſſes, and of the good wyll and de=
ſyze that the ſayde G. H. hath to the contentacion of
the ſayde duetyes, haue gyuen and graunted, and
by theſe pzeſentes gyue ⁊ graunt vnto the ſame G. H
oz by whatſoeuer name oz addiciō that he be named
oz called, and ſo to all them whyche foz the ſayd G.
H. to vs, oz to anye of vs, ſtanden oz ſtondeth boun=
de, oz charged: our ſure, free, and hole lycence, lyber=
tye and ſafeconduyte as moche as is in vs.
So alwaye that the ſayde G.H. and all they whych
foz hym oz wyth hym, to vs oz any of vs ſtande boū=
den oz charged: and ouer that the ſeruauntes and aſ
ſignes of the ſayde G.H. wyth all the goodes, catal=
les, marchaundyſes, dettes, duttes, and other thyn
ges of the ſame G.H. in all maner of places frelye,
quyetly, well and peaſyblye at theyz large and lyber
tye, may and ſhall by day ⁊ nyght, go, come, abyde,
ſoiourne and dwell, paſſe and repaſſe, in, to, oz from
anye cytye, towne, vyllage, oz other place oz pla=
ces, wythin thys realme of Englande, oz elles
wythout. And all the ſame goodes, wares marchan
dyſes, and all other thynges as ben aboue reherſed,
to dyſpoſe as it ſhall lyke and pleaſe the ſame G. and
all thoſe perſon and perſons the whyche wyth oz foz
him to vs oz any of vs, ſtonde bounde and charged:
at all tymes and ſeaſons from the daye of makynge
hereof, vnto the ende and terme of.v. yeres than nexe
and immedyatlye ſuyng after the daye and dayes of
payement ſpecyfyed in the ſpecyaltye oz ſpecyaltyes
                          wher

wherein the sayde G. oz any other perſon oz perſons
foz the ſame G. in any wyſe ſtandeth bounde τ char⸗
ged vnto vs, and that we noz anye of vs, ſhall in no
wyſe purſue, arreſt, attache, hurte, wholde, lette, oz
greue, ne any other perſon oz perſõs foz vs oz any of
vs oz in the name of vs, oz of any of vs, by the auc⸗
tozytye, aſſent, wyll, oz agrement, of vs oz of anye
of vs, the ſayde G. oz thoſe perſon oz perſons noz a⸗
ny of them whyche foz the ſame G. to vs oz anye of
vs in any wyſe ſtandeth bounde oz charged by theyz
bodyes, as fugytyues, noz otherwyſe noz by theyz
goodes, cattelles, marchandyſes, oz any other thin⸗
ges of theyzes oz of any of them, foz payment to be
made to vs oz any of vs of our ſayde duetyes oz any
parte oz parcell of them oz foz to ſynd to vs oz any of
vs, any other oz better ſuertye oz ſuertyes foz conten
tation τ payment of the ſame oure dutye, other thã
we and eueryche of vs nowe haue and hath foz the
ſame payment of our ſayd duetyes oz any otherwiſe
durynge the terme afozeſayde by reaſon oz occaſſion
of anye dette, accompte, dyſceyte, treſpace, byinge,
ſellynge, contracte, oz of anye other thynge mat⸗
ter, oz cauſe, oz grounde of cauſe, what ſo euer it be
befoze the date of theſe pzeſentes, betwene vs oz a⸗
ny of vs, and the ſayde G. and thoſe perſons which
wyth oz foz the ſame G. to vs oz any of vs, ſtanden
bownde, charged oz chargeable, had made, mouing
oz dependynge. And yf it happen wythin the ſayde
terme, any moneye, oz goodes, to be attached oz ar⸗
reſted in the name of vs, oz anye of vs, by anye o⸗
ther perſonne oz perſonnes in the handes of the
ſayde

sayde G. oz of them oz any of them, whych foz hym
to vs oz any of vs standeth bounde oz be charged, oz
chargeable by foꝛce of any bylle oꝛ bylles, playnt oꝛ
playntes,agaynst thē oz any of thē to be leuyed oz at
tamined. That than we,he, oz they of vs, in ꝑ name
of whome any such byl oz billes,playnt oz playntes,
shall be made oz affyꝛmed, shall put in suretye to the
sayde byil,oꝛ bylles playnt oꝛ playntes and so vtterly
dissolue and dyscharge the sayde attachement and at
tachementes,when ꝗ as sone as we they oz he of vs
i ꝑ name of whome the sayd attachement oz attache
mentes, shall be made oz affyꝛmed, shall therto due
lye be requyꝛed by the sayde G. oz by them oz any of
them, whyche foz hym to vs oz any of vs stand boūd
oz charged. And euery of them thereof we and euery
of vs shall clerelye dyscharge, as often as any suche
occasion oz cause shal happen to fall duryng ꝑ terme
afoꝛesayde.

And moꝛeouer we all the credytours aboue speci
fyed, wylle and graunte, and euerye of vs foꝛ hys
owne parte, wyll and graunteth to the sayde G. by
these pꝛesentes that yf it happen the sayde G. oz thē
oz any of them whyche foz hym to vs oz any of vs,
stonde bounde,oz charged,in theyꝛ owne personnes
oz in the personne of them oz any of them oz in oz by
the goodes, catalles, oz marchaundyses, of theym
at any tyme wythin the terme afoꝛesayde by vs, oz
any of vs oz by any other personne oz personnes by
the commaundemente, wylle, pꝛocurynge, authoꝛy
tye, consente, oz knoweledge of vs oz of anye of vs,
agaynste the tenour,foꝛme and effect of thys our pꝛe
sente

Thinke not ꝑ repeticiō of ꝑ woꝛdes to be super fluous it is made foꝛ an example yf there be ma nye credit tours,and ī suche case it cannot be to curiouse.

sent letters of safecōduyt in any wyse to be arrested
sued, impleded, hurte, greued, attempted, vexed, oz
hindzed, and therof after the fozme abouesayd be not
releued noz defended, that than the sayd G. and those
whyche foz hym to vs oz any of vs stande bounde oz
charged: and theyz heyzes and executoures by these
pzesentes shall be fozeuermoze quyte and dyscharged
agaynste hym oz them of vs by whome the sayde G.
and those persons whych foz hym to vs oz any of vs
stande bounde oz charged, shall so agaynst ƥ fozme,
tenoure and effect, of these our pzesent letters of safe
conduyt, be attempted, vexed, oz hindzed, oz any of
them be attempted. &c. and thereof not released, dys
solued, noz defended, accozdynge to the fozme aboue
sayde, of all maner accions, sutes, quarelles, chalen
ges, reconysaunces, executions, & demaundes what
so euer they be, from the begynnynge of the wozlde,
vnto the daye of suche attemptyng, vexation, grefe,
oz hyndzynge. In wytnesse whereof. &c.

¶ A bzyefe commission of a stewarde. &c

Omnib⁹ chzisti fidelib⁹ &c. A. B. &c. salutē. No⸗
ueritis me pfat. A. B. cocess. & p pzesetes cōfir
masse C. D. gent. officia senescalli, supuisoris
& gubernatoris maner. ter. & tenͭ. reddit. & seruic. me
ozū cū ptiñ. in A. B. C. D. &c. cū suis membzis, & pti⸗
nen. vniuers. eundēƈ A. B. senescallū superuis. et gu
bernat. oim & singulozū pzemiss. & quozꝗcūƈ ea tāgeñ.
ozdinasse, cōstituisse, & deputasse, p psentes. Dād &
per pñt. concedend. pzefat. A. B. plenā tenoze pzesen.
potestatē. et auctozitē. vice & noie meo omnes cur. le⸗
tas & dies. &c. pzout aliquis ali⁹ vnꝗ habuit aut ha⸗
bere consueuit &c. after the maner of other grauntes.

¶ A patent of annuitye oʒ yerely fee, gyuen by
a gentleman to his ſeruaunt foʒ
pʒomotion of a maryage.

Chʒiſtianis bniuerſis p̅n̅s ſcriptū iſpecturis ſiue
audituris R.M.armiger,ſalutē i authoʒe ſalu
tis ꝫ fidē idubiā p̅n̅tib⁹ adhiberi. Cū nonnulla
ſpes matrimonii inter Robertū A. famulū meū ꝫ A
gnetē O.annuēte deo futuri affulget.Scitote me eū
dē R.bt qui cōmodū ꝫ btilitatē dicti famuli mei pʒo
pter obſequiū mihi i famulatuſuo ingenue ꝫ diligen
ter pʒeſtitū,plurimū auctā belim,quo cōmodius iu
ter eos biueretur,dediſſe,conceſſiſſe, et hoc p̅n̅ti ſcri
pto meo cōfirmaſſe,pʒefatis Roberto A.et A. quan
dā annuitatē ſiue annualē redditū .ꝗ.li. bone et lega
lis monete Anglie,exeunt.de manerio meo de M.cū
pertiñ.in Cōm.Uigoʒñ. Habend,gaudend,et perci
piend, dictā annuitatē ſiue annualē redditū.ꝗ.ꝯ.eiſ
dē R,A.ꝫ A.ꝫ eoʒū btricꝫ diutius biuēti et aſſignaꝝ.
ſuis durāte.bita mei pʒefati Richardi , et ad feſta ſā
cti Michaelis archā.ꝫ annuntiatiõis btē M.Eginis
equis poʒcionibus ſingulis annis ſoluend . Et ſi ac
quotiēs cōtingat dict.annuitatē ſiue annualē reddit.
ꝗ.ꝯ.aretro foʒe in parte bel in toto, poſt aliquod feſt.
feſtoʒū pʒedictoʒū quo bt pferꝫ ſolui debeaꝫ. Tunc ꝫ
toties bene licebit pfatis R. A. ꝫ A. et eoʒū btricꝫ et
aſſigñ.ſuis in pʒedict.maneriū cum pertiñ. et in quā
libet inde pcellā intrare,et diſtringere. Diſtrictiões
qꝫ ſic ibid.captas licite abide fugare,abducere,aſpoʒ
tare,ꝫ penes ſe detinere , quouſcꝫ eis de eodē reddit.
ſic aretro exiſteñ.plenarie fuerit ſatiſfactū et pſoluꝫ.
bna cū dampnis et expenſis ſuis in ea parte ſuſtinē

Bb. Dis.

dis.Pꝛouiso semper q̄ si dict.nuptie non successerit,
nec consūmate fuerint, aut si iidē R.A.ꝯ A.per me,
aut mea causa aliquo modo pꝛomoti fuerint siue ob-
tinuerint, aut pꝛomoueri siue obtinuere possint,aut
eoꝛum alter potest, aliquam annuitatem, seu annualem redditum,terras,tenementa,seu hereditamen
ta,aut aliam certitidinem victus, habend.eis dura-
te dicta vita mea annui baloꝛis ,x.li. aut maioꝛis,
q̄ extunc pꝛesens scriptū penitus irritū erit , pmissis non obstantibus.In cuius rei testimoniū huic pꝛesenti scripto meo , ego pꝛefatus Richardus M.si-
gillum meum apposui.dat.ꝛc.

¶Here folowe dyuers and sondꝛye kyndes of sup-
plications,bylles of cōplaynt,answers and other
petitions to be put foꝛ any matter in
the kynges courtes.

¶To the kynge our moost dꝛad so-
ueraygue loꝛde.

For a tytle
of lande.

M Ost lamētably complayneth vnto your
hyghnesse, your pooꝛe faythfull and obe-
dyent subiect T.S. of H. in the Countye
of Kent.vncle and heyꝛe vnto R.S.late of
the cytie of London Tyler, that is to wyte, bꝛother
of W.S. father of ꝑ sayde R.S. That where the
sayd R.in his lyfe was seised in his demeane as of
fee,of and in two messuages.xxx.acres of lande era-
ble,wood and pasture seuerally set , lyinge, and being in the paryshes of L.M.N.O.in the sayde coun
tye,

tye. And he so being seased thereof dyed seased, so ẏ
the sayde .ii. mesuages ⁊ other the premysses descen=
ded, and of ryght ought to descende vnto your poore
subiect, as vncle and heyre vnto the sayd R. S. So
it is moost gracyous soueraygne lord, that certayne
wrytynges, euydēces, escriptes ⁊ minimentes cōcer
nyng the premisses which your sayd poore ⁊ fayth=
full subiecte shulde proue hys true tytle by vnto the
premysses, bene cōmen to the handes and possessyon
of w. T. and S. w. of H. aforesayde, by the hauynge
whereof the sayde w. and S. haue conueyed dyuers
and sondrye craftye estates vnto them selues and
therby haue obtayned the possessyon of the premys=
ses, and the same ⁊ profites therof, by the space of .rr
yeres, wrongfully haue wythholden, and yet do, cō=
trary to all ryght and good cōscience. In consydera
tion whereof, and for somoche as youre sayde poore
subiect is in extreme myserye ⁊ nede, ⁊ not hauynge
wherwyth to lyue, but dryuen by necessitie vnto his
dayly labour. which he can not intermyt wythout ẏ
vtter vndoyng of hym and all hys chyldren , and so
of no maner of abilitie to sue for the pmisses by your
lawes. It maye therfore please youre hyghnesse of
your moste aboundaunt grace and pytie, to graunte
your moost charytable and fauourable letters or cō
missyon to be directed vnto such honourable men as
your hyghnesse shall name thereunto, cōmaundyng
them by the same to examyne the premysies, ⁊ fur=
ther to set suche direction ⁊ fynall ende therin, as iu=
styce ⁊ truthe wolde, and ẏ as they wyll answer be=
fore the iudgement of almyghty God, vnto whome
youre sayde poore subiecte wyll (accordynge to hys
BB.ii.   moost

mooft bounden dutye) praye for the preferuation of
your royall eftate.⁊c.

¶ A byll of complaynt vpon certayne grefes, requyrynge a wrytte of Cerciorari.

IN mofte lamentable wyfe fheweth vnto your
good lordfhyppe, your dayly poore oratour. J.
w. of London, that where one Andrewe H. of
Londō aforefayde marchaunttayloure borowed of
your fayde oratour. xii. li. fterlyng to be payde to the
fayde John at a certayne daye betwene them agreed, whych daye was expyred, and the fayde fumme
of moneye not payed, wherfore the fayde Andrewe
for that he had not readye money, defyred your fup-
pliaunte to take a certayne whyte brode clothe in
pawne conteynyng. xl. yardes cut in peeces, for the
fayde xii. li. whych cloth was folde and deuyded to
your fayde oratour by a byll of fale, wherein ÿ fayd
A. ftandeth bounde wyth condicion in the fame byll
declared, ÿ yf the fayd clothe were not redemed by a
daye certayne in the fayde byll lymyted, that then ÿ
fame cloth to be to the onlye vfe of youre fayde oratour for contentati on ⁊ hole payment of the fayd. xii
li. Syns the whyche tyme, the fayde A. counfayled
your fayde oratour to put forth the fayde clothe to
one L. M. of London fherman for to be dyed of fe-
uerall coulours for hys moofte profyte by the meanes wherof the fayde John w. was cōtented to take
the fayde brode cloth for the payment of hys fayde
moneye, and afterwarde the fayde cloth was delyuered

nered to the sayde L.M. and wythin.vi.dayes after
the delyuerye of the sayde clothe to the sayde L. one
R. M. Spaynyarde affyrmed a playnte of dette a=
gaynst the sayde A.and accordyng to the custome of
the sayde cytie of London ,hath caused attachement
to be made of the sayde brode cloth,as a dette due by
the sayde A.vnto the sayde R. where the sayde cloth
is your sayde oratours. Notwythstandyng by rea=
son of the sayde attachement your sayde oratour re=
teyned counsayl in the Guyldehal in Londō, where
the matter was,beyng at yssue, whereupon the Iu=
rye was panelled, syns the which tyme for the space
of thre courte dayes, youre sayde oratour dyd gyue
attendaunce there to haue the sayde matter harde, &
the sayde playntyfe and counsayle wolde not suffre
the sayde Iurye to appeare, so longe as youre sayde
supplyaunte dyd applye and pursue hys cause in ef=
fect herin. And for that the sayde R. and hys coūsayl
wolde not procede in the sayde action,your sayde o=
ratour supposed that it shulde nomore be called vpō
by occasyon whereof your sayde oratour beynge a=
bout hys busynesse in the countrye,and in the meane
tyme the sayde L. M. wyth hys counsayle hauynge
knowledge,that youe sayde oratour was oute of the
cytie into the countrye, instauntly laboured the Iu=
rye to appeare in the absence of your sayde oratour,
and by theyr subteltye and crafte , the sayde Iurye
dyd appeare,and passed agaynst your sayde oratour
contrary to al ryght lawe and good cōscience,which
shalbe to the great impoueryshment and vndoynge
of youre sayde oratour for euer , vnlesse youre good
lordeshyps leful fauour & succour be to hym shewed
             Bb.iii.   in

in thys behalfe. In confyderation wherof, myght it therfoze pleafe your good lozdfhyppe to graunt the kynges wzytte of Cerciozari, to be dyrected to the mayze and fhyzyffes of the cytie of London, comaun dyng them and euerye of them by bertue of the fame to certifye befoze your good lozdfhyppe in the kynges mooft honourable court of Chauncery at a certayne daye by your lozdfhyppe to be limytted þ fayd attachement and all the matter cocernyng the fame, and to examyne the fayde matter, and al the circumftaunce thereof, and to ftande to fuche an ozdze and direction therein as fhal ftande with ryght equytie and good cofciece. And your fayd ozatour fhal pzay to God foz the pzeferuation of your good lozdfhyp longe to contynue.

℄A byll of complaynt foz the ryght of landes
where a ftate was made by difceyt, and to
requyze a fubpena bpon the fame.

Ooft húbly fheweth bnto your good lozdfhip your dayly ozatour w.L. of w. in þ coutye of M. That where one w.L. late of S. in þ cou tye of k. by his lyfe tyme was lawfully feafed in his demeane as of fee, of ꝫ in one mefuage ꝫ bii. acres of land, fet, lying ꝫ being in þ towne ꝫ felde of S. afoze fayd to þ yerly balue of. xx.ꙅ. fterlyng. And he fo fea fed of the pzemyffes had iffue, one R.L. his fon, and dyed. After whofe death the fayd R. was diftract ꝫ of no hole memozie, ꝫ fo dyed woout iffue of his body lawfully begotten. Afterwhofe death the fayd mefu age and other the pzemyffes defcended and came bn to one R.L. as bzother and heyze bnto the fayd W. L. whiche R. hath iffue, one Thomas R. hys fonne.
And

And so it is good lorde, that aswell the sayd Robert
the father as also the sayde T.his son hath by theyr
dede of release released all theyr ryght tytle and in∤
terest of and in the sayde messuage and other the p∤
mysses to your sayde oratour and his heyres, as by
theyr sayde dede of release doth appeare. All that not
wstandyng good lorde. Certayne euidences, dedes,
charters, wrytynges and minimentes concernynge
the premysses, be come to the handes and possessyon
of one S.w.who by hauyng of the same euydences
hath conueyed Indentures of a bargayn and sale to
be made of the premysses by the sayde w.T.,beyng a
distract man & of no wyt, vnto the sayde S.whyche
S.by force of the same, and hauyng the euydence in
hys custodye conueyed dyuerse secrete estates, to the
vse of the sayde.S. and hys heyres, by the supporta
tion counsayl and mayntenaunce of one wyllyã N.
and John T. agaynst all lawe, ryght, andgood con
scyence, and by the confederacye and supportation
of the sayde U.and Thomas, the sayde S.w. with
hys extorte power doth wrongfully detayne & kepe
the possessyon in the premysses from your sayde ora∤
tour agaynst al ryght and good iustice. In tendre cõ
soderation whereof, it maye please your lordshyp to
gyue therupõ the kynges wrytte of subpena to be di
rected to the beforenamed S. w.U. and J.T. com∤
maundyng them and euery of them by the same per
sonally to appeare before your lordshyp in the kyn∤
ges courte of Chauncerye at a certayne daye to thẽ
limytted, and vnder a certayne payne there to make
answere to the premysses. And further to stande and
obeye all suche ordre and direction in the premysses

as by your lozdshyppe shalbe thought moost reaso=
nable ,accozdyng to ryght and good Justyce . And
your ozatour shall daylye pzaye foz the pzeseruation
of your good lozdshyppe longe to endure.

℄ A byll of subpena foz a tytle
of landes entayled.

IN moost huble wyse sheweth & cōplayneth vn=
to your good lozdshyppe , your daylye ozatour
R.R. husbandeman, that where one w. R. late
of Shzaley in the coūtie of wozcet husband. graūd
father of your sayde ozatour was lawfully seised in
hys demeane as of fee,by due course of enheritanuce
vnto hym lawfully descended frō his auncestours, &
other lawfull conueyaūce in the lawe, of and in one
mesuage and. cc.acres of lande, meddowes,wood &
pasture wyth theyz appurtenaunces in Shzaley a=
fozesayde.And the sayde w.R so being of the pzemis
ses seysed aboue.lvii.yeres now past. Jt was condi
scended,graunted and agreed betwene the sayde w.
R.and one J.E.late of Hamptoncurlewe in ẙ sayde
countye deceassed,that A.R.then sone and heyze ap=
paraūt of the sayd w.R.befoze a certayne day shulde
mary and take to hys wyfe one A. E. doughter of ẙ
sayde J.E.And that the sayde w.R. in consyderati
on thereof,and foz that the sayde A.shuld be greatly
auaunced and pzeferred in goodes and substaunce,
by that maryage of the sayde A . wolde immedyat=
ly after the sayde maryage hadde and solempnysed,
conueye and make vnto the sayd A.& Agnes,a good
suffycyent & lawfull estate in the lawe, of and in the
sayde

sayde mesuage, landes, tenementes, and other ý pre
mysses. To haue and to holde vnto the sayd Alerãd
and Agnes, and to the heyres males of theyr bodyes
lawfully begotten. And afterwarde the sayde A. ac
cordyng to the sayd agrement, dyd mary and take to
his wyfe ý sayd Agnes E. Immedyatly after which
maryage had and solempnised, the sayde W.R. ac
cordyng to hys sayde promysse ʒ agrement dyd law
fully infeoffe, of and in the sayd mesuage, landes, te
nementes, and other the premysses, the sayd A.R. ʒ
Agnes then his wyfe. To haue and to hold vnto the
same Alerã. and Agnes, and to the heyres males of
theyr two bodyes lawfully begotten, by force wher
of the sayde A. and Agnes were seysed of and in the
pmysses in theyr demeanes as of fee tayle specyal, ʒ
they so beyng therof seysed, the sayde A. and Agnes
had issue male betwene them lawfully begotten one
J.R. and your sayde oratour, and one W.R. and the
sayde W.R. the elder dyed, by and after whose deth
the reuercion in fee symple of the premysses descen
ded vnto the sayde Alerañ. as sonne and heyre vnto
hym. And afterwarde the sayde Alex. and Ag. dyed,
after whose death the sayde mesuage, landes, teneme
tes, and other the premysses desceded and came, and
of ryght ought to discende and come vnto the sayde
J.R. as sonne and heyre male of the body of ý sayde
Alex. and Agnes lawfully begotten, by force wher
of the sayde John R. entred into the sayde messuage
landes, tenementes and other the premysses, and
was therof seised in hys demeane as of fee tayle spe
cyall. And he so beyng therof seysed, the sayd J.R. a
bout.iiii. yeres now past, of the sayde mesuage and
Cc   other

other the premyſſes dyed ſeyſed wythout any yſſue
male of hys bodye lawfully begotten,by force wher
of the ſayde meſuage and other the premyſſes diſcē=
ded and came,and of ryght ought to diſcende & come
vnto your ſayde poore oratour as brother and heyre
male to the ſayde J.R.by vertue of the gyfte afore=
ſayde.So it is my ſinguler good lorde,that as well
the dede of entayle made of and in the premyſſes by
the ſayde W.R. the graundfather vnto the ſayde J.
R.and Agnes, and to the heyres males of theyr bo=
dyes lawfully begotten,as is aforeſayde,as dyuers
other charters,euydences, dedes, wrytynges , and
mynimentes concernyng the premyſſes , prouynge
the ſayde intreſt and tytle of your ſayde oratour , in
and to the premyſſes ben deceytfully cōmen to the hā
des and poſſeſſyon of Joh.w. and Elynor his wyfe,
late wyfe of the ſayde J.R.G.w.gentleman,and T.
S.the elder, and there as they haue conueyed & put
them, and by colour of hauyng of the ſayde euyden=
ces,dedes,wrytynges,and mynimentes in theyr hā
des and poſſeſſyon,the ſame J.w.and E. haue now
of late wrongfully entred into the ſayde meſuage &
other the premyſſes. And the poſſeſſyon therof do ſo
yet wrongfully deteyne and kepe from your ſayd ora
tour,and alſo the rentes,yſſues,and profytes therof
haue wrongfullye receyued , pceyued , and taken to
theyr owne vſe by the ſpace of.iii.yeares paſt,and ſo
yet do,contrarye to all ryght & good conſcience. And
a brit that your ſayde oratour hath often and ſondry
tymes requyred and inſtauntly deſyred the ſayde J.
w.and E.G.w. and T.S. as well to delyuer vnto
your ſayde oratour the ſayde euydences,dedes, wry
tynges,

tynges and minimentes concernyng the premysses,
as also to auoyde the possessyon of the premysses, &
peaceablye and quyetlye to permyt and suffre youre
sayde oratour and hys assygnes to haue and enioye
the same, and to receyue and take the rentes and pro
fytes therof to hys owne vse, accordyng to his sayd
intrest and tytle therein, whyche to do they at all ty‐
mes haue refused and denyed, and yet do, contrarye
to all ryght and good conscience. And forasmoche as
your sayde oratour knoweth not the noumbre, con‐
tentes, ne other certayntyes of the sayde euydences,
deades, wrytynges and mynimentes, nor wherein
they be conteyned. And also for that the sayde J.w.
E.G.w. and T.S. be of greate substaunce & ryches,
and also greatly frended and borne in the sayd coun
tye of warryk. And your sayde oratour beyng but a
poore man, and hauyng but fewe frendes in ẏ sayde
countye, the same your sayde oratour is and shall be
therfore wythout remedy concernyng the premisses
by the due course and ordre of the comen lawe, and
otherwyse, vnlesse your good lordshyppes ayde and
fauour be vnto hym shewed in thys behalfe. In con‐
syderation wherof it maye please your good lorde‐
shyppe (the premysses tenderly consydred) to graunt
vnto your sayde oratour, the kynges most gratious
seuerall wryttes of subpena, to be directed vnto the
sayde J.w.E, G.S. and T.S. comaundynge them
and euery of them by the same, personally to appere
before the kynge in hys moost honourable courte of
Chauncerye at a certayne daye, and vpon a certayne
payne by your good lordshyppe to be lymytted ther
in, and there to make answere to the premysses, and

further to be ordzed therin, as shall accozde w ryght
and good conscience. And your sayde ozatour shall
daylye pzaye. ꝛc.

℟ The answer of J.w.to the byll of com=
playnt of Rycharde R.husbandman.

He sayde defendaút sayth, that the sayd byll
of complaynt is vncertayne and insuffycient
in the lawe to be answered vnto, and ꝑ mat=
ter therin conteyned vntrue, and pzincipally ymagi=
ned and pursued by the vnlawfull pzocurement, be=
ryng and suppoztation of one w.C.esquyer, to thin=
tent to put the sayde deff.to trouble, costes and expē
ces intendyng therby so to vnquyete and impouerish
the sayd deff.as they shoulde be fayne to leaue theyz
ryght tytle and interest of and in the pzemysses, so ꝑ
he the sayde w.C.myght purchace and bye the same
of the sayde complayntiffe, and of late the sayd w.C.
hath made meanes vnto the sayde J.w.nowe deffē.
to bye hys tytle and intrest of and in the pzemysses,
and thzetned hym to haue the same , and that yf he
wolde not let hym haue it wyth hys good wyll, that
then he wolde haue it agaynst hys wyll, whosoeuer
toke hys parte, and yf the contentes of the sayde byll
were true, as they are not, it were then matter deter
minable at the cōmē lawe, and not in this honozable
courte , wherunto the sayde deff.pzayeth to be relea=
sed. And neuerthelesse, the auaútage of the pzemisses
vnto thys deff.at al tymes saued, foz further answer
vnto the sayd byl and declaration of the truthe of the
contentes of the sayde byll, the sayde deff.sayen, and
euery

euery of thē ſayth that lōg tyme befoꝛe ꝑ ſayd A. R.
mētioned in ꝑ ſayde byll of cōplaynt, any thyng had
in the ſayde meſuage, and other the pꝛemyſſes , oꝛ ꝑ
ꝑ ſayd w.R.was therof infeoffed T.R. of P.T.R.
of S.ꞇ T.w.of E.were therof ſeyſed in theyꝛ demea
nes as of fee,ꞇ ſo beynge therof ſeyſed by theyꝛ wꝛy=
tyng indented,redy to be ſhewed,the ſame meſuage
and other the pꝛemyſſes conteyned in the ſayd bylle
of complaynt,amongeſt other thynges gaue,dimyſ=
ſed,delyuered, and by theyꝛ ſayd wꝛytyng indented
confyꝛmed,vnto the ſayde w. R.mencyoned, in the
ſayd byll of cōplaynt,and vnto A.his wyfe.To haue
and to holde the ſayde meſuage and other the pꝛe=
myſſes,vnto the ſayd w.and A.foꝛ terme of theyꝛ ly=
ues,and the lyfe of the longeſt lyuer of them,and af=
ter theyꝛ deceaſſe,the ſayde T.T.and T.wylled and
and declared in ꝑ ſayd wꝛyting indented,that ꝑ ſayd
meſuage and all other the pꝛemyſſes,ſhulde remayn
vnto the ſayde A. mencyoned in the ſayde byll of cō=
playnt,and vnto A.hys wyfe,and vnto the heyꝛes ꞇ
aſſygnes of the ſayde A.foꝛ euer, wythout that,that
the ſayde w,R. dyd enfeoffe of and in the ſayd meſu=
age,landes,tenementes and other the pꝛemiſſes, the
ſayde Alex.and Agnes,to haue to them and to their
heyꝛes males of theyꝛ two bodyes lawfully begot=
ten,oꝛ that the ſayde Alex.ꞇ A.were ſeyſed of and in
the pꝛemiſſes in theyꝛ demeanes as of fee tayle eſpe=
cyall,as in the ſayde byll of complaynt is ſurmyſed,
and wythoute that after the deathe of the ſayde w.
that the remaynder of the pꝛemyſſes in fee ſymple
deſcended vnto the ſayde Alexandꝛe , as ſonne and
heyꝛe vnto him , oꝛ that after the death of the ſayde

Alexand. and A . the sayde mesuage ⁊ other the pꝛemysses descended, and of ryght ought to descende oꝛ
come vnto the sayd J.R.in the tayle especyal,as son
and heyꝛe male of the bodye of the sayde A.⁊ Agnes
lawfully begotten, eyther of any other discent of en
herytaunce therin of a mere fee simple oꝛ other , the
sayde J . by hys entrye into the sayde mesuage and
other the pꝛemysses , after the death of hys father ⁊
mother was then seysed of ⁊ in hys demeane as of
fee tayle especyall oꝛ of any suche estate dyed seysed,
oꝛ that after the death of the sayde J . that the sayde
mesuage and other the pꝛemysses,oꝛ any part oꝛ par
cell therof descended and came, oꝛ of ryght ought to
descende ⁊ come vnto the sayde complaynüt,as bꝛother and heyꝛe male vnto the sayde J. R . by vertue
of any gyfte oꝛ otherwyse, as in the byll of cõplaynt
is vntruly surmised,but the sayd deff.do auerre and
are ⁊ shall be at all tymes redy to pꝛoue, as this honourable courte shall awarde , that the sayd mesuage and all other the pꝛemysses by and immedyatly
after the death of the sayde John R. descended,and
of ryght ought to descend ⁊ come vnto one A.dough
ter and heyꝛe of the sayde J. lawfully begotten on ẙ
bodye of the sayde Elynoꝛ one of thys deff. ẙ whych
A.is yet in playne lyfe, and in the warde and custodye of her sayd mother,and wythout that that anye
dede of tayle made of and in the byll by the sayd w.
R.the graüdefather,oꝛ anye other euydence , dedes,
wꝛytynges oꝛ mynimentes concernyng the pꝛemysses pꝛouynge the sayde entrest and tytle of the sayde
cõplaynaüt,of and in the pꝛemisses, and euery parte
oꝛ parcell therof,be comen into the hãdes ⁊ possessiõ
of

of the fayde J. w. & E. his wyfe, oz eyther of them,
oz to the cuftodye oz poffeffyon of any other by theyz
delyuerye, conueyaunce, oz appoyntmente, but truth
it is that the fayde deff. haue in their cuftody one wzi
tynge indented redy to be fhewed, wherby ý remayn
der of the pzemiffes is conueyed vnto the fayd A. and
Agnes hys wyfe and to the heyzes and affygnes of
the fayde Alex. foz euer, as is afozefayd, and dyuers
other euydence and wzytynges, pzouynge and concernyng the conueyaunce of ý fee fimple of the fayde
meffuage, and other the pzempyffes, vnto the fayde
Alex. and other his aunceffers, the which charters,
euydences and wzytynges, the fayde deff. do ftyl wō
them deteyne and kepe as good and lawfull is foz
them to do, as well foz the profe and pzeferuation of
theyz ryght tytle and intreft vnto the thyzde part of
the fame pzemiffes foz the dowzie of the fayde E. as
foz the pzeferuation of the ryght tytle and intreft of
the fayde A. doughter and heyze of the fayde J. of &
in the fayd meffuage and other the pzempyffes and wō
oute that the fayde deff. haue at anye tyme wzongfully entred into the meffuage and other the pzemiffes oz into any part therof, oz the pzofites therof, do
wzonfullye deteyne and kepe from the fayde com-
playntes, oz the rētes, iffues, & pzofytes therof haue
wzongfully reftrayned, perceyued, and takē to their
owne vfe, as in the fame byll is alfo vntruly furmy-
fed. &c.

     ¶A byll of complaynte to the Chaun-
       cerye foz a dette wythoute a
         fpecyaltye.
             Cc.iiii.   In

IN mooſt humble wyſe ſheweth and complay=
neth vnto your good lozdſhyppe, your dayly o=
ratour and pooze bedman J.G.of H.in the cou
tye of D.þ where the ſayd J.G.by waye ofpzeſt at þ
feaſt of Pēthecoſt, in the.xxiiii. yere of the raygne of
our ſoueraygne loz de the kynge that nowe is , dyd
delyuer vnto one w.L.late of H.in the ſayde countie
of Dozſſ.the ſumme of.xviii.li. of lawfull money of
Englande to be payed vnto him at the feaſt of ſaynt
Andzewe then next enſuyng , befoze whych day the
ſayde w.L.by hys laſt wyll and teſtament conſtitu=
ted and made one E.then hys wyfe , hys executryx
and dyed,and left vnto the ſayde E. then hys execu=
trix of hys owne propze goodes(all hyz dets payed)
the ſumme of an. C.li. of whome your ſayd ozatour
ſondzye and manye tymes hath requyzed paymente
of the ſayde.xviii.li. whiche to content and paye the
ſayde E dyd neuer vtterlye denye , but dyd requyze
reſpyte foz the payment of the ſame, and befoze the
ſayde E.dyd content and paye any peny of the ſayd
xviii.li.the ſayde E. in her death bed by her laſt wyl
and teſtament dyd conſtitute and make one J.S.
her ſonne her executour,and dyed, and leaſt to hym
ſuffycient of the goodes of the ſayd w. foz the cōten=
tation and paymente of the ſame.xviii. li. and after
dyed, ſythen whoſe death the ſayde complayntyſſe
dayly, ſondzye and many tymes requyzed the ſayde
J.S.to cōtent and paye vnto him the ſayde ſumme
of.xviii.f. whyche to do he hath at all tymes refuſed,
and yet doth,contrary to ryght and good conſcience
to the vtter vndoynge of your pooze ozatour foz e=
uer.And foz bycauſe your ozatour hath no eſpecyal=
tye,

tye wherby he shulde charge the executour of the ex
ecutrix of the sayde w.L. he is therfore wythout re
medye by the ordre of the comon law of this realme
and is lyke vtterlye to lese the sayde . xviij.li. vnlesse
your gracyous fauour be to hym shewed in thys be=
halfe. In tendre consyderation wherof, it maye ther=
fore please your good lordshyppe (the premysses có=
sydred) to graunte the kynges wrytte of subpena to
be directed to the sayde J.C. commaundyng hym by
the same personallye to appeare before youre good
lordshyppe in the kynges moost gracyous courte of
Chauncerye.&c.

   ℀ The answere to the same bylle.

He sayde J.S. by protestation, not knowyng
that the sayde complaynaunt dyd delyuer to the
  sayde w.L. in the sayd byll named the summe
of.xviij.li.or any parte therof by waye of prest, as in
the sayde byll is surmytted, he further sayth, that ý
byll of complaynt is vncertayne and insuffycyent in
the lawe to be answered vnto, and moch of the mat=
ter therein conteyned is fayned and ymagyned, for
vexation and trouble of the sayde J.S. the aduaū
tage therof to hym at all tymes saued. The sayde J.
S. for further answere vnto the sayde bylle, sayeth
that longe tyme before the sayde Elyn.L. was cósti
tute and made executrix vnto the sayde w.L. ý sayd
E. was maryed vnto one R.S. father of this defen=
daunt by the space of.xx.yeres and more, which sayd
R.S. by hys last wyll and testament constituted, or=
deyned and made the sayde E . and the sayde J.S.
hys executours and dyed, and leafte to the ordre and
      Do   dispo

dyſpoſition of hys ſayde executours goodes and catalles of his owne proꝓꝛe to the value of two. C.li.
ſterlyng and aboue. All whych the ſayde goodes and
catelles, oꝛ the mooſt parte of the ſame, being and re
maynyng in the handes and cuſtodye of the ſayde E.
ſhe the ſame Elyn. maryed and toke to huſbande the
ſayde w. L. whyche ſayde w. after the maryage had
betwene hym and the ſayd E, dyd myſpende, waſte
and conſume of the ſayde goodes and catalles late
of the ſayd R. S. to þ value of one. C. ⁊ lx. li. ſterling
and aboue. And afterwarde the ſayde Wyllyam L.
by hys laſt wyll and teſtament oꝛdeyned, and made
the ſayde Elynoꝛ executrix therof, and dyed a verye
pooꝛe man, hauyng no maner goodes noꝛ catalles
at the tyme of hys death of hys owne proꝓꝛe, to the
value of twentye ſhyllynges ſterlynge. And afterwarde the ſayde Elynoꝛ by her laſte wylle oꝛdeyned
thys defendaunt executour therof, and dyed, ſythen
whoſe deathe there hath not commen to the handes
of thys defendaunt of the goodes late the ſayde w.
L. to the value of twentye ſhyllynges ſterling, with
out that, that the ſayde w. L. at hys death lefte vnto
the ſayde Elynoꝛ of hys owne proꝓꝛe goodes, to the
ſumme o f an hundꝛed. li . ouer hys dettes payed , oꝛ
yet the ſumme of twentye ſhyllynges ſterlynge , oꝛ
that the ſayde Elynoꝛ after the death of the ſayd w.
L. dyd euer conſent oꝛ agree to paye the ſayde. xviii.
li. vnto the ſayde complaynaunt, oꝛ dyd requyꝛe him
to reſpyte the payment therof, oꝛ that the ſayde El.
at the tyme of her death leafte vnto the ſayde defendaunt ſuffycyent of the goodes of the ſayde w. L. foꝛ
the contentation and payment of the ſayde. xviii. li.

as

as in the ſayde byll of complaynt vntruly is ſurmyt
ted.And wythout that, that anye other thynge com=
pꝛyſed in the ſayde feyned byll of the foꝛſayde J.S.
whych is materiall to be anſwered vnto,and in this
anſwere not confeſſed,auoyded,oꝛ trauerſed,is true
All whych matters the ſayde J.S. is redy to auerre
as thys honourable courte ſhall awarde, and pꝛay=
eth to be diſmyſſed wyth hys reaſonable coſtes and
charges in this behalfe ſuſteyned,ꝛc.

¶An other fourme of a byll foꝛ
a ſubpena.

JN mooſt humble wyſe,theweth and complay=
neth vnto your good loꝛdſhyppe, youre pooꝛe ⁊
dayly oꝛatour. J.A.of R. in the countye of N.
That where one w.H. late of London dꝛaper, was
ſeaſed in hys demeane as of fee, of ⁊ in one meſuage
and.xx.acres of lande,wood and paſture,ſet, lyinge
and being in the towne and feldes of R. and ꝑ ſayde
w.ſo being ſeaſed of the pꝛemiſſes at London afoꝛe=
ſayde,by pꝛoteſtatiō therof dyed ſeaſed.After whoſe
death the pꝛempyſſes deſcended, and of ryght oughte
to deſcende vnto your ſayde oꝛatour, as to the vncle
and nexte heyꝛe of the ſayde w.L.deceſſed,that is to
ſaye bꝛother of w. L. father of the ſayde w.deceſſed.
So it is ryght honourable loꝛde, that ſyns the deth
of the ſayde w.dyuers and ſondꝛye euidences, dedes,
charters,wꝛytynges, and other mynimentes concer
nynge the pꝛemyſſes be commen to the handes and
poſſeſſyon of R.H.ꝛc.who by the coloure of hauinge
of the ſayde euydences , haue vnlawfullye entered

into the premysses, and therof haue taken the profy=
tes to theyr owne vses by the space of. vii . yeres last
past, without hauyng any iuste coloure of tytle so to
do. And albeit that your sayde oratour hath dyuerse
tymes syns the death of the sayde w. requyred the de
lyuerye of all the sayde euydences of the sayde R. H.
and of euery of them, that notwythstandynge they
and euery of them, the same to deliuer, haue alway=
es denyed, and yet do o denye, contrarye to all lawe
equytie and good conscyence. It maye please ther=
fore your good lordshyppe (the premysses considred)
forasmoche as your sayde oratour, for the obteyning
of those euydences, hath no remedy, by course of the
commen lawes of thys realme, for that he knoweth
not the certayne nombre of the sayde euydences, ne
wherin they be conteyned to graunte vnto your ora=
tour, the kynges moost gratious wrytte of subpena
to be directed to the forsayde R. H. &c. commaunding
them and euery of them, by the same personallye to
appeare. &c.

¶ A byll of complaynt, where a quest hath passed in a matter wrongfully alleged.

IN moost humble wyse sheweth and complay=
neth vnto your mooste honourable good lord=
shyppe, your poore suppliaunt and contynuall
oratour P. de U. of the cytye of London broker, that
where as one I. M. of the sayde cytye, marchaunte
straunger, wythin the sayde cytye was possessed of &
in certayne lynnē clothes, to the value of. xxij. li. x. s
sterlyng

ſterlyng, and to your pooꝛe ſuppliaũtes knowledge
then and as yet,as of his owne mere pꝛopꝛe goodes
and cattels,and ſo therof beynge poſſeſſed, the ſame
within the ſayde cytye delyuered to your pooꝛe oꝛa=
tour being a bꝛoker ſafelye to kepe and to ſell ⁊ mar=
chaundyſe, by the diſcretion of your pooꝛe ſuppliaũt
to thuſe of the ſayd A. by foꝛce wherof your oꝛatour
made ſale therof to certayne perſonnes wythin the
ſame citie,and the money,goodes, and marchaũdice
therfoꝛe receyued and takẽ, delyuered vnto the ſayd
A.And ſo it is (ryght honourable loꝛde) that after ⁊
ſyns the ſale therof made, one Jaſp. S. marchaunt
ſtrauger ꝑtendyng a pꝛopertye in thefoꝛſayde lynen
clothes,hath commenced an action vpon hys caſe a=
gaynſte your pooꝛe ſuppliaunt in the Guyldehalle,
ſet and being wythin the foꝛſayd citie befoꝛe ꝑſhiꝛiſ=
ſes therof,and thereupon hath declared, that he the
ſayde J.ſhulde haue loſt thoſe goodes,and that they
came to the handes and poſſeſſyons of youre pooꝛe
ſuppliaunt within the ſayd cytie, by waye of trouer
And further ꝑyour oꝛatour was ſõdꝛy tymes requy=
red to make deliueraunce therof to the ſayde J. and
that refuſed,⁊ the ſame afterwarde ſold,and the mo
neye therfoꝛe receyued conuerted to your oꝛatours
vſe,to whych matter one J.O. your pooꝛe ſupplian
tes attourney raſhlye without aduyſement oꝛ coun=
ſayl therin taken,ſayd that your oꝛatour dyd not ſel
the ſayde clothes noꝛ any parte therof,and vpon the
ſame matter whether anye ſale therof was made by
your ſuppliãt oꝛ not, an iſſue was takẽ,and the Ju=
rye tryed, ſwoꝛne, and charged, founde a ſale made
by youre pooꝛe oꝛatour of the ſayde clothes (as the
                     Dd.iii.   truthe

truthe was) nothyng regardyng in whome the pro=
prtye of the sayd goodes was at the tyme of the sale
therof made, bycause by the plee so vnaduysedly ple
ded,it was confessed in poynt of iudgement,the pro=
pertie therof to be the sayd J.S.and so it is ryght ho
nour able lorde, that the sayd attourney myght haue
taken a i yssue,that your oratour solde no clothes of
the sayde Jaspers , bycause of truthe the sayde clo=
thes were the propre clothes of the sayde A.and not
the clothes of the sayde J. and so the Jurye shoulde
haue tryed in whome the propertie was,and bycause
the propertie was not put in yssue,the Jurye had no
warraunt to enquyre therof. And in case they hadde
bene the clothes of the sayde Jas. as they were not
in dede , your poore oratour ought not by thorder of
the lawe to haue ben charged,bycause they were de=
liuered to your oratour by thehandes of the forsayd
A.to sell,and your oratour dyd accordynglye,and p
money,goodes,& marchaudise therof receyued,dely
uered to the sayde A.and so yf any trespasse or wrog
was done to the sayde Jas. it was done by the sayd
A.and not by your poore oratour, agaynst whome p
sayde A. maye take hys action, for youre poore ora=
tour at the tyme of the sayd actio comenced, neyther
had the sayde goodes in hys possessyon , ne anye o=
ther thynge in lyinge or consyderaunce of the same
goodes.And also there is a custome within the sayd
cytie, that yf an vpholster or broker sell any good w
in the same cytie, to any parso or parsons within the
same citie,vpon the delyuerye of anye parson,for or
at the request of hym, hauyng wytnesse of the dely=
uery therof to hym made, or brynge oute the partye
who

who delyuered them vnto hym, not being hym selfe
particeps criminis, shulde be discharged and not dã=
pnifyed, for ꝑ his offyce doyng in making sale ther=
of. And also by thordre of the commen lawe of thys
realme, a man cõmyng iũmediatly to the possessyon
of goodes not being partie to the fyrst wronge shall
not be charged in an action of trespasse, whyche
matters or any of them, yf they had ben pleded, had
bene a sufficient matter of barre, and bycause they
were not pleded, your poore supplyaunt coulde not
be receyued to gyue them in euidēs to the Jury, and
so your poore oratour is lyke to paye vnto the sayde
J. the value of the sayde clothes, the sayd J. hauing
no propre ryght ne tytle to the same, vnlesse youre
moost honourable good lordshyppes fauour be she=
wed herin. In consyderation wherof, it maye please
your most honourable good lordshyp (the premisses
tenderly consydred) to graunt the kynges moost gra=
cyous wrytte of Cerciorari to be directed to the shi=
riffes of the sayde cytye, cõmaundyng them and eue
ry of them to certifye before your good lordshyp the
hole recorde of the premisses depending before them
or eyther of them, in ꝑ kynges moost gracious court
of chauncerye, at a certayne daye by your good lord=
shyppe to be lymitted, and therin further to procede,
and further to graunt the kynges moost gracyous &
spedy wryttes of subpena to be directed to the sayde
J. cõmaundynge hym personallye to appeare before
your good lordshyppe in the kynges sayde courte of
his chaun. at a certayne daye, and vnder a certayne
payne by your good lordshyp to be lymitted therein
to stand to the premysses, and further to take suche

               Dd.iiii.   direction

direction,ordre and decree therein , as maye stande with equitie, Justyce & goodcōscience,and your poze ozatour shall dayly praye to almyghty God, foz the pzeseruation of your mooste honourable good lozd∕shyps estate longe to endure.

¶A warraunt foz a summe of moneye.

TO our right trusty & welbeloued G.L.our re∕ceyuer in our lozdshyppes of C. and G. oz to anye other oure receyuers there foz the tyme beynge,gretynge . We wyll and charge you that of the pzofytes and reuenues of our lyuelod in your re∕cept at the feast of E next cōminge,&c.without anye longer delaye ye content and paye vnto our welbelo ued w.N.marchaunt.x.li.whych we owe vnto hym foz certayne stuffe to our vse of hym bought & recey∕ued,and foz payment of the sayde sūme ye take foz vs suffycient acquyttaunce,whiche wyth these oure letters shalbe therfoze to you suffycient warraunte and dischatge at your accomptes,then next to be gy∕uen afoze our audytours there foz the tyme beynge, whome we wyll and charge to make you due allo∕waunce in thys behalfe by these oure sayde leters. Gyuen.&c.tali die.&c.

¶A warraunt dozmaunt.

BE it knowen to al men by these pzesentes,that we syz T.S.Erle of D.and lozde S.haue gy∕uen and graunted, and by these pzesentes gyue and

and graunt vnto our welbeloued syz Joh.H.knight
and M.hys wyfe,otherwise called dame M.D. one
stagge and two buckes in somer , and an hynde and
two does in wynter,yerely to be taken in the .ii.par=
kes of our yle of A.oz in the chace belongynge to the
same of our gyfte yerly durynge theyz lyues,and the
lenger lyuer of them. And we lycence and gyue au=
cthozitie and power to the sayd syz John & dame M
and eyther of them duryng theyz lyues, and the len=
ger lyuer of them, and theyz suffycient deputie yerly
in the tymes of season and conuenyent to go into the
sayd parkes oz chace,callyng the keper oz kepers ther
of wyth them , there to hunt and kyll the same dere.
And them to cary awaye at theyz libertie & pleasure
with such conuenyent nombze of personnes as shall
lyke them,foz and about the doing of the same. Any
acte , estatute oz other thynge made to the contrarye
notwythstandyng.And further we wyll that, yf the
sayde syz John and dame M. yerly somtymes wyll
not come them selues, noz eyther of them foz ꝑ same
Then J wyll that my kepers of the same parkes oz
chace foz the tyme being, vpon a byll sygned with ꝑ
hande of the sayde syz John,oz dame M.concerning
the same, shall kylle and delyuer from yere to yere to
the bzynger of the same letters,the sayde somer dere
and wynterdere wythout any restraynt oz gaynsay=
yng by them oz any of them, in any wyse to be made
oz done.In witnes wherof to thys our present wzy=
tynge,we haue put our seale,the.x.of Maye.&c.

⸿A dede vpon landes gotten by
fyne and recouerye.

      Ee Sciant

The boke of sondry

Ciant pcesē.ɛc.ꝙ nos H.D.ɼ T.H.ad instan.
Set spͤualē reꝗsitionē.w.H.et A.bzozis eiͧ,dimi
simͧ,tradidimͧ,liberauimus et hac psenti car
ta nostra confirmauimus,pzefat.w.H.et A.illū me
suag.ɛc.in E in com̄.B.ɛc.Que nos pzefati H.ɼ T.p
ꝗtnē in Cuꝝ.dn̄i regis apud westm̄.a die pasche in.iti.
septimanas anno regni Henrici octa. regis Anglie,
Fracie,Hibern̄.ɼ fidei defensozis.ɛc.coza J.E.R.E.
L.P.et J.M.Justic.et aliis dn̄i regis fidelibus tūc
ibidē pn̄tibus inter nos pfat.H,et T.ꝗrent.et pzefa.
w.H.et A,bzozem eius defozc.inde leuat.habuimus
nobis pzefat.H.et T.et heredͨ mei pzedic.H.imperpe.
pzout per recozdū inde plenius liquet. Habendͨ et te
nendͨ mesuagiū pzedic.ɛc.cū pertin̄.pfat.w.et A. he
redͨ et assignatis suis ad bsum eozumdem w.ɼ A.he
redͨ et assign̄.suozum imperpetuum.Ac insuper.cum
littera atturn̄.ɛc. Jn cuius rei.ɛc.

An other.

Ciāt.ɛc.ꝙd nos T.L.miles R.w.ɛc.dimisimͧ
ɛc.C.T.w.B.ɛc.maneriū de S.ac mesua.ɛc.
Que habuimͧ nobis ɼ heredͨ.dict.R.w.p finē
iter nos ꝗr.ɼ w.militē,ɼ B.bzozē eiͧ defozc.i cur.dn̄i
regis termin̄. pasche ac regni dn̄i reg. nūc.ɛc.cozam
R.B.milit.ɼ sociis suis iustic.dicti dn̄i reg.de cō.Bā
co pzout per finem plene liquet ꝙꝗdē finis fuit ad
bsū mei dict.T.L.et heredͨ meozū.Habendͨ ɼ tenendͨ
pzedict.maneriū ac oia et singula cetera pzemissa cū
ptin̄.pfat.T.T.ɼ w.B.ɛc.heredͨ etassign̄.suis ad bsū
mei dicti T.L. ɼ heredͨ meozū ɼ adinde pimpledͨ bl
timā bolūtatē mei dict.T.L.fact.seu fiens de capita
libͧ dn̄iis.ɛc.Ac insup cū littera attur. Jn cuiͧ rei. ɛc
A dede

¶ A dede of ſettyng ouer of a warde.

Omnibus chꝛiſtifidelibus ad quos pꝛeſẽs ſcri
ptũ peruenerit. Margareta G.generoſa ſalutem in domino ſempiternam. Sciatis me
pꝛefat.Margaretam pꝛo certa pecunie ſum-
ma mihi pꝛe manibus ſolut.dediſſe,conceſſiſſe, et hoc
pꝛeſenti ſcripto meo confirmaſſe dilecto mihi Ed-
wardo E.ciui et aurifabꝛo ciuitatis Lonõ , cuſtodiã
omnium terr.et tenementoꝛũ ,redditũ , et reuerſiõ.
cum pertinenciis que nup̃ fuerunt T.P.nuper de L.
defuncti.Et que per ſiue poſt moꝛtẽ ipſius T.ad ma
nus H.ducis.J.comitis.L.et N. deuenerũt ſeu deue
nire debuer.ratiõe minoꝛis etatis. A.P. filie et hereõ pꝛedict.T.Ac cuſtoõ et maritagiũ ipſius A. abſ-
ꝗ diſparagatione.Ac etiã omnia ilł.terr.⁊ tenemẽta
que deſcender. et venire diſpoſcũtur pꝛedict.Eliano-
re vt conſanguinee et hereõ Anne W . Que quidem
cuſtoõ.omnium pꝛedict terr . et tenementoꝛũ , ac cuſtoõ et maritag.pꝛedic. A . abſꝗ diſparagatione nuper habui mihi ex dono conceſſione et ſcripti confir-
mac.pꝛefat.ducis.Ac totum ius, titulum, intereſſe et
demanõ mea que vnquam habui, habeo, ſeu quouiſmodo in futurum habere potero de et in eiſdem. Ha-
benõ et tenenõ cuſtoõ pꝛedict.pꝛefat.E. et aſſignatis
ſuis a die confectionis pꝛefectionis pꝛeſencium vſꝗ
ad plenam et legittimam etatem pꝛedict hereõ vna
cum maritagio eiuſdem hereõ abſꝗ diſparagatione,
vt pꝛedictũ eſt, ſimul cũ omnibus exit.pꝛoficuis ⁊ re
uentionibus inde medio tẽpoꝛe ꝓuenieñ.ſiue creſcẽ.
abſꝗ aliquo mihi inde reddenõ ſeu compotũ facienõ
In cuius rei.⁊c.

Ee.ij.   Here

¶Here folowe the fourme of let=
ters testimonyalles.

¶A letter of testimonye foꝛ an obligation
confessed in a Courte.

VNiuersis et singulis christifidelibus ad quos
pꝛesêtes littere peruenerit H.H.maioꝛ ⁊ alder=
mañ.ciuitatis London, salutê in dño sempi=
ternã.Quia de cõmissi.nobis officij debito veritatis
testimonio tenemur subuenire⁊ ea ꝗ coꝛã nobis acta
sunt pꝛout iudicis incumbit officio fidelit testificari.
Hinc est qd vniuersitati vꝛe tenoꝛe pꝛesentiũ innote
scimus per pꝛesentes qd die confectionis earundem
accessit ad pꝛesentiam nostrã dilect⁹ conciuis noster
G.R. pannarius et coꝛã nobis exhibuit quoddã scri
ptũ relaxat.cera rubea impꝛessa sigillat.in hec verba.
Nouerint.⁊c.qd quidã scriptũ vt pꝛefat.G.R.coꝛam
nobis asseruit et affirmauit supꝛadict.w.S. in Cur.
dñi reg.in loco nꝛo iudiciali videlicet in camera·G.ci
uitatis pꝛedic.in pꝛesentia dilecti nobis J.H adtunc
vnius attur.siue pꝛocurat.in eadê cur.sigillauit ac ei
dem T. liberauit ꝗ vero J.H. die cõfectiõis pꝛesent.
ad instantiã dict.G.R. coꝛam nobis vocatus vincu=
loꝛ iuramenti astrictus deposuit et affirmauit qd
ipse scriptũ illud manu pꝛopꝛia in pꝛedic. loco nostro
iudiciali scripsit ⁊ qd idê scriptum in pꝛesentia sua si
gillat.⁊ liberat.fuit foꝛma supꝛamemoꝛata. In quoꝛ
oĩm ⁊ singuloꝛũ pꝛemissoꝛũ fidê et testimoniũ. Si=
gil.officij nostri maioꝛatus ciuitatis pꝛedic. pꝛesentí
bus duximus apponend. Scriptum. xii . die Maii.
Anno domini.M.CCCCC.xl.⁊c.

Aij

¶ An other teſtimoniall in Engliſh
foz the approuyng of a teſtament.

TO all them to whom thys preſent letters ſhal
come. E. S. mayze, and the Aldermen of the ci
tie of London, ſenden gretynge in oure Lozde
God euerlaſtyng. Fozaſmoch as by the dutye of our
offyce, apperteyneth ſuche thynges as befoze vs be
ſhewed, wytneſſed ⁊ affyzmed, to teſtify and recozde
yf we therto be requyzed. Therfoze it is that we cer⸗
tifye vnto you by theſe our preſent letters, that ẏ day
of makyng of the ſame we ſawe and behelde a teſta⸗
ment oz laſt wyll (as we were enfourmed of one E.
wyddowe) wzitten in paper, and ſealed in theſe woz
des. This is the laſt wylle.⁊c. Furthermoze knowe
ye that the ſayde daye of makynge of this preſentes,
came pſonally befozevs J.R. marchaunt of the Sta
ple of Calayes, which befoze vs vpon the holy Euan
gelyſtes of God ſwozne, ſayde, depoſed, and affyz⸗
med, that the ſayd teſtament oz laſt wyll was wzyt⸗
ten wyth the propze hande of the ſame E. M. And
alſo that he herde the ſame E. in her lyfe ſaye diuers
tymes that S . F. late Alderman of the ſayde cytye
of London, T. H. gentleman, ⁊ R. T. mercer, were in
feoffed in all her landes ⁊ tenementes andſhe ſayde,
that the ſayde R. T. ſhulde haue, and wyth them do
lyke as he wolde do of hys owne landes and teneme̅
tes by hym purchaſed . Jn wytneſſe wherof to theſe
preſe̅tes the ſeale of our offyce of mayzaltie of ẏſayd
cytie we haue done to be put. wzytten at London the
x. daye of Febzuarye, the yere of the raygne of our ſo
ueraygne lozde, kynge Henry the. viij. .⁊c.
Ee.iij.

The boke of sondry
A good preſinent of a Teſtamente.

IN the name of God. Amen. The. xxi. daye
of the moneth of Maye, the yeare of oure
Lorde God. M. D. xc. J. R. N. mercer citizin of the cytie of Lond, being of whole
mynde, and in good & perfyte remembraunce, laude
and prayſe be vnto almyghty God, make & ordeyne
this my pſent teſtament, concernyng herein my laſt
wyll in maner and fourme folowyng, that is to ſay.
Fyrſte J commende my ſoule vnto almyghty god
my maker and redemer, and my body to be buryed in
the pariſh churche or churchyarde of ſaynt N. in the
cytie of London. And J bequeth vnto the hye altare
vi. ſ. viij. d. Jtem toward the reparations of ẙ ſame
churche. xiij. ſ. iiij. d. Jtē J wyll that all ſuche dettes
and dutyes as J owe of ryght or of conſcience to a-
ny perſon or perſonnes be well and trulye contented
and payed by myne executours hereafternamed, or
els ordeyned for ſo to be payd wythout any delay or
cōtradiction. And after my dettes payed, and my funerall expences perfourmed, J wyll that al my goodes, catalles, and dettes, ſhall be deuyded into thre e-
quall partes, wherof J wyll that A. my wyfe ſhall
haue one equall parte to her owne propre vſe, in maner of her purparte and reaſonable parte to her of al
my ſayde goodes, cattalles and dettes, after the lau-
dable cuſtome of the cytie of London belongynge.
And the ſeconde equall parte of all my ſayde goodes
catalles and dettes, J bequethe vnto E. and M. my
doughters, and to the chyld now being in ẙ wombe
of my ſayde wyfe, equallye to be deuyded amongeſt
them,

them, and to be delyuered vnto them, whē they shal
accomplysh and come to theyr lawfull ages of. xxi.
yeres, or els be maryed. &c. And yf it fortune anye of
my sayde chyldren to deceasse before they accomplish
theyr sayde ages, and before that tyme be not mary=
ed, that then I bequeth her parte or hys parte, of thē
so deceassyng to the other of them then suruiuing, to
be delyuered vnto them, when they shal accomplysh
theyr sayde ages, or els be maryed. And yf it fortune
all my sayde chyldren to deceasse (as god it defende)
before they accomplysh theyr sayde ages, and before
that tyme be not maryed, then I bequeth as well all
and synguler the sayde parte and porcion of my sayd
chyldren in my forsayde goodes, cattals, & dettes, as
also my legacye to them hereafter bequethed to and
amongest the chyldren lawfullye begotten of the bo=
dy of R.M. of S. in the countye of Kent, to be payed
and delyuered to them at lyke ages, and in lyke ma=
ner, as is appoynted vnto myne owne chyldren, and
euerye chylde lykewyse to be others heyre thereof.
And yf it shall fortune all the children of the sayd R.
M. of his body lawfully begotten, to decease(which
God defende) before they come to their lawful ages,
and before that tyme be not maryed, then I wil that
all theyr sayde partes and porcyons of my sayd goo=
des, cattalles, and dettes, shall wholy be employed
and bestowed in amendyng and repayryng of hygh
noyous wayes, nygh aboute the cytye of London,
and to the maryage of poore maydens, by the discre=
tion of myne executours and ouerseer, yf they be thā
lyuyng, or elles by the discretions of the lorde mayr
and hys brethren the Aldermen of the cytye of Lōd.
                         Ee.iiij.   And

And the thyꝛde equall parte of all my sayde goodes,
catalles and dettes I reserue vnto myne executours
therwyth to perfourme my legacyes and bequestes,
hereafter specifyed, that is to wyte. Fyꝛst I bequeth
to my mother in lawe, mastresse A.C. a iewell of the
balue of.xx.li. Item I bequeth .xxx.li. to be distribu
ted shoꝛtly after my decease to and amongest ꝑ pooꝛe
householders inhabytyng within the sayde paryshe
of saynt N. by the discretion of myne executours and
ouerseer. Item I bequeth vnto the pooꝛe pꝛysoners
in all the pꝛisons and gayles of London and S.x li
sterlyng to be equallye deuyded amongeste them, by
myne executours. Itē I bequeth to master Roger
L.x.li.and a gowne. Item I bequeth to Peter Fos.
my seruaunt.x.pounde , to thintent that he shall in=
struct myne executours faithfully and truly in al my
rekenynges and busynesse. Item I bequeth to A.B.
a blacke gowne. Item I bequeth vnto the masters,
wardeynes and felowshyp of the mercers.vi.pound
foꝛ a recreacyon oꝛ a dyner amōgest them that shal=
be in theyꝛ lyuery at my buryall. Itē I bequeth vn=
to euery of my seruauntes that shall be in my house
and seruyce at the tyme of my deceasse, a gowne. Itē
I bequeth vnto the sayde A.my wyfe.lxxxx. li.of my
sayde poꝛcyon, to thintent and vpon condition, that
she in her wyddowhode by her dede suffycyent in ꝑ
lawe, shall clerely remyt and release all her ryght ti=
tle and interest that she then shall haue oꝛ oughte to
clayme oꝛ haue , by reason of her maryage vnto me,
to, of, and in all and synguler my landes and tenemē=
tes and other theyꝛ appurtenaunces, set, lying, and
being wythin the countye of Essex, and elles where
wythin

wythin the realme of England. And in caſe my ſayd
wyfe then refuſe ſo to do, and not ſo releaſe, that thã
as nowe and now as then, I wyll that my ſayd lega
cye ſo made vnto her of the ſayde. lxxxx.poũd ſhalbe
voyde and of none effect. Item I wyll that my ſayd
wyfe ſhal inhabyte, and haue myne houſe wherin I
nowe dwell, in the ſayd paryſh of ſaynct N.duryng
her wydowhode, and as ſoone and when as ſhe ſhal
be aſſured oʒ maryed to anye other man, that then I
wyl that the leaſſe and termes of yeres of and in the
ſame, ſhalbe ſolde to the mooſt pʒice and furtheraũce
that can be to the pʒofyte of my ſayde chyldʒen.
The reſidue of all my goodes, catalles, and dettes,
after my dettes payed, my funerall expẽces perfour
med, and theſe my legacyes conteyned in this my pʒe
ſent teſtament fulfylled, I wholy gyue and bequeth
to my ſayd chyldʒen equally to be deuyded amongeſt
them, and to be delyuered vnto them accoʒdynge as
I haue aboue wylled and declared, that theyʒ ſayde
owne poʒcyons ſhall be. Pʒouyded alwayes, and it
is my very wyll, mynde, and entent, that ſhoʒtly af‑
ter my deceaſſe, all and ſynguler my wares, ſtuffe of
houſholde, plate, and all other my goodes whatſoe‑
uer they be, ſhalbe pʒyſed by two indifferent perſons
to be named and ſwoʒne by the loʒde mayer of Lon
don, and hys bʒethʒen foʒ the tyme beyng. And all &
ſynguler the poʒcyons therof apperteynynge to my
ſayde chyldʒen, as well theyʒ ſeconde parte, as my
ſayde legacye ſo to them made and bequethed of my
parte immedyatly after the ſayde appʒyſynge, to be
oʒdʒed accoʒdynge to the cuſtome of the oʒphanage
of the cytye of London, by the loʒde mayʒe and hys
ff   bʒethʒe.

bꝛethꝛen. Item I wyl that the yong men being free
of the felowshyp of mercers of London, shall haue
the occupyinge of all my sayde chyldꝛens poꝛcyons
and legacyes, duryng theyꝛ noneages, they puttyng
in suffycyent suretyes therfoꝛe, accoꝛdyng to the sayd
custome of the cytie of London. And I wyll, and my
mynde and entent is, that master H. L. and master
R. M. oꝛ theyꝛ assygnes, shall haue the kepynge, go-
uernaunce, and bꝛyngyng vp of my sayd chyldꝛen, durynge theyꝛ noneages. And of this my pꝛesent testament, I make and oꝛdeyne the sayd Alys my wyfe,
and the sayd master H. and R. myne executours. And
I bequeth to eyther of them foꝛ theyꝛ labour in that
behalfe. xx. li. and a blacke gowne. And of the execution of the same, I make and oꝛdeyne the sayde master Lewes O. ouerseer. And I btterlye reuoke and
adnulle all and euery other foꝛmer testamentes, wyl
les, legacyes, bequestes, executours, and ouerseer, by
me in any wyse befoꝛe thys tyme made, named, wyl
led and bequethed. These wytnesses, A. B. C. D. E.
F. G. &c.

¶ The maner to make a supplication bpõ bꝛea-
kynge of a pꝛomysse and suche lyke.

IN moost humble wyse sheweth vnto your
good mastershyp, your pooꝛe oꝛatour w.
U. of &c. ẏ where one R. M. &c. faithfully
pꝛomysed to delyuer to your sayd oꝛatour
in maryage wyth one A. S. hys doughter, nowe the
wyfe of youre sayde beadman, all maner housholde-
stuffe necessarye foꝛ housholde afoꝛe sufficyent wytnesse redy to testify ẏ same to be delyuered immedyatly after ẏ sayd mariage, wherupon your sayd oꝛatour

tour maryed w the ſayd A.ſythes which tyme right
honourable ſyz your ſayd ozatour hath requyzed the
ſame ſtuffe which ẏ ſaid w.hath alwayes pzomiſed
neuertheleſſe foz the ſpace of. xv. yeres paſt hath de-
ferred wyth fayned pzomyſes the delyuerye therof,
to the great vnquyet and hynderaunce of your ſayde
ozatour, whych now is compelled to requyze ẏ charytable helpe and ayde of youre good maſterſhyppe
herein. Jn conſyderation wherof (yf it wolde pleaſe
your accuſtomable goodneſſe , alwayes to pouertye
extended) to do call befoze you the ſame R.M. and
hym to cauſe,recompence,and content your ſayd oza
tour,aſwell foz the ſayde houſeholde ſtuffe, oz to delyuer the ſame , as alſo foz hys loſſe of greate tyme
and hynderaunce thereaboute expended, youre ſayd
ozatour ſhuld, accozdyng to his mooſt bounden dutye.&c.

¶An other vpon diſceyte by a partener.

JN mooſt humble wyſe complaynyng, ſheweth
vnto your good lozdſhyp, your daylye ozatour.
&c. That where as vpon the ymaginacyon of
honeſtye and good oppynion,that R. C. father vnto
your ſayde ozatour deceaſſed, had in one T. T. &c. ẏ
ſayd R.about eaſter laſt paſt,dyd ioyne in bargayne
w the ſayd T. T.foz ẏ delyuerie of ſomoche wares,
(wherof the moytye was the ſayde Rychardes) as
amounted to the ſumme of.&c.vnto one J.S.of the
kynges maieſties houſholde Eſquyer,foz the which
ſumme of.&c. the ſayde S.ſtode bounde by ſtatute
of the ſtaple,vnto the ſayd R.C.and T.T. payable
at the feaſte of.&c. then nexte.&c. whyche was in the
yere of our ſoueraygne lozde kynge Henrye the. &c.
                 Ff.ii.   And

And to thentente that the same R. beynge a man of
suche honest simplicitie, as dyd neyther suspecte nor
yet mysooubt the good consciece of the sayd T. who
alwayes towardes hym had counterfayted suche
puritye of conscyence, and so honeste behauyoure,
myght the better by the helpe of the same T. come
by hys dette at the tyme to be due, yf he so longe ly=
ued, or els (yf he dyed) that the sayd T. myght be as
a staye and sure meanes to hys executours, for the
getting in of the same. He the same R. trusted ꝑ sayd
T. wyth the custodye of the sayde statute. Soone af
ter the makynge of whyche bargayne, and somwhat
tofore the sayde feaste of, &c. the sayde R. deceassed,
and made your oratour hys executour, therby char=
gyng hym as well wyth the gatheryng in of al such
summes of moneye as were due to the sayde testator
as also wyth the payment of all suche dettes as the
sayde R. dyd owe. And so it is moost gratious lord,
that although youre sayde besechour hath dyuers &
sondrye tymes syns the deceasse of hys sayde father
requyred the sayde T. to haue the moytie of the sayd
&c. due to hym by equytye and conscience, as execu=
tour bnto hys sayde testatour. The sayde T (nowe
declaryng hym what he is) hauyng no regarde ney=
ther to conscyence, commune honestye, nor yet to the
trust he was put in, myndyng yf he can (wyth what
iniurye he careth not) btterlye to debarre your sayd
oratour from the hauyng therof, and he hym selfe a=
gaynst al reason and conscience, to haue the sayd. &c.
for nothyng, hath not onely wyth many sleyght and
subtyll delayes, lyngered and fooded your sayd ora=
tour of longe tyme from hauynge the same, but also
                                                        now

now laſtly hath playnlye anſwered and affirmed, ŷ
your ſayde oꝛatour ſhall haue no parte noꝛ peny ther
of, whych yf it ſhulde thus paſſe, ſhuld be both great
encouragyng to ſuche coꝛrupte conſciéced perſonnes
ſtyll to perſeuer in ſuche theyꝛ lewde demeanour, ⁊
in the meane time, turne to the great impoueryſhing
of your ſayd pooꝛe oꝛ atour. Wherfoꝛe may it pleaſe
your honourable loꝛdſhyp of your accuſtomed equi-
tye, to enioyne the ſayde T. that he repaye vnto your
ſayde oꝛatour the ſayde. ꝛc. moytye of the ſayde. ꝛc. yf
he haue receyued it of the ſayde S. oꝛ yf he haue not
that he be no lette to your ſayde oꝛatour, to do therin
what he can foꝛ the obteynyng and gettyng in of the
ſame. And thus ſhall your ſayde oꝛatour haue cauſe
cótynually to pꝛay foꝛ the pꝛoſp erous eſtate of your
good loꝛdſhyp longe to endure.

⸿A byll of complaynt made foꝛ recoue-
rynge of euydence made by
compulſyon.

IN mooſt humble wyſe complaynyng, ſheweth
vnto your good loꝛdſhyp, your daylye oꝛatryx
J.B. That where as in the yere. ꝛc. it chaunced
the huſbande of your ſayde oꝛatrix togyther wyth-
one. ꝛc. ioyntly and ſeuerally to be bounden in a reco
gniſaunce of the ſumme of. ꝛc. knowledged befoꝛe
your good loꝛdſhyppe in the kynges maieſties court
of Chauncerye, foꝛ the payment e of. ꝛc. payable at a
certayne day now paſt, vnto one. ꝛc. foꝛ which ſúm e
not being payed at the daye due, the ſayde. ꝛc. hath
ſued execution agaynſt your ſayd pooꝛe oꝛatryces huſ

bande,wherupon he was by the fhiryffe of.&c. arre=
fted about.&c.paft,and by all the fayde fpace hath re
mayned in the kynges maiefties pzyfon of marfhal=
fee,to hys great payne of body,impoztable charges,
and in a maner vndoyng,both of hym,your pooze o=
ratrix and theyz fmal chyldzen. which piteous eftate
of hys(wyth hym felfe lamentyng)after he had wel
confydered,he then confulted woith him felfe foz his
beft remedy in that behalfe, and therwythal callyng
to hys mynde,that he had here in.&c.a kynfman and
cofyn called.&c. being of.&c. vnto whome your fayde
ozatrices hufband,foz the vicinitie of blood and abi=
litie of fubftaunce,was bolde to make hys mone foz
helpe in thys hys aduerfitie, then vnto anye other.
But(farre contrary hys expectation,and agaynft al
humanitie) whence youre fayde ozatrices pooze huf=
bande loked mooft after fuccour , thence he receyued
not only leeft helpe,but alfo mooft hurt.Foz the fayd
&c.well perceyuyng thaduerfe eftate that your oza=
trices pooze hufband was and is in, which was the
gredyneffe of the marchaunt foz his money,therneft
thought and care of your pooze ozatrix and her poze
childzen,and the great defyze that her fayd pooze huf
band had(as any man wolde)of lybertie & difcharge
of trouble , wolde by no meanes pzomyfe hys helpe
vnto her fayde pooze hufband herin,vnleffe he wold
be content to bargayne ano fell al hys landes, amou
tyng to the yerelye rent of.&c.vnto hym the fayde.&c.
foz an annuytye of.xx.li.fterlyng to hym duryng hys
lyfe,and foz the fumme of.&c. wherof.&c. to be payed
in hande. Wherunto your fayde pooze ozatrices huf
bande,though the conftraynt of hys fayde cafe was
compel=

compelled to agree & to enseale suche wrytynges as
the sayde.&c.not longe after had brought wyth hym
concernyng the sayd bargayne, nothynge mysdoub⸗
tyng of the sayd.&c.being his cosyn,but that he shuld
haue sealed to none other couenauntes, but onely to
suche as conscience wolde stande with,at which tyme
the same.&c. neyther payed nor proffered any penye
of the sayde.&c.accordyng to hys couenaunt.Which
delaye of payment,both agaynst his promisse & coue
naunt,after her sayd poore husbande hadde studyed
vpõ,& therwithall red ouer the couenautes cõprised
in ẙ sayd indentures ofthis bargayn, which in dede
(moost honourable lorde)were so partially deuysed
for the behofe of the sayde. &c. and agayne so sore a⸗
gaynst your sayde poore oratrices husbande, as (yf
the bargayne had taken effecte) had ben to the vtter
vndoinge ofhym and her wyth all theyrs for euer.
Your sayd poore oratrices husband takyng holde on
that poynt that the sayd.&c.payed not the forsayd.&c
Dyd at theyr next metyng, renounce and say,that he
wolde not stande to the sayd couenauntes & bargain
wherunto the sayd.&c. partly knowledgynge in that
he had not payed nor proffered this &c. sayde before
sufficient witnesse here redy to be sworne, he was cõ
tent,howbeit he sayde that your sayd oratrices pore
husbande shulde pay for the makyng of the wrytyn⸗
ges.For the payment wherof her sayd husbande,as
then hauyng no great store of moneye,was fayne to
gyue hym a golde rynge in pledge to pay the scrybe
for wryting of ẙ same.Al this notwithstanding(moost
honourable lorde)& that your sayde poore oratrices
husbande hath often and sondry tymes syns by many

wayes and meanes requyred the sayde wrytynges,
concernynge the sayde bargayne of the sayde. &c. he
agaynste all naturall loue and humanitie, nothyng
moze coueytynge then the extreme destruction of
her and her sayde pooze husbande, and well perceyuyng how farre he is now vnable to helpe hym selfe
hath vtterly denyed to redze the same, and yet doth,
contrarye to all conscience, equytye, lawe, oz ryght.
In consyderation wherof, may it lyk e your honourable lozdshyp of your accustomed pytie , to call the
sayd. &c. befoze you togyther w the husbāde of your
sayde pooze ozatrix, and there to wyl hym to redely-
uer the sayde wrytynges agayne to her sayd husbād
yf it shal so seme vnto your honour, oz elles there to
shew sufficient matter why he shulde kepe the same.
And youre sayde ozatrix wyth her pooze husbande,
and theyz pooze chyldzen shall pzay. &c.

¶ A byll of a tytle of copye holde
landes.

Humbly complaynynge, sheweth vnto youre
good lozdshyp, your dayly ozatour w. S. o-
therwyse named w. T. of L. cosen and heyze
of J. S. otherwyse called J. T. whyle he liued of. &c
That where as your sayde ozatour at your lozdship
pes last beyng at. &c. dydde exhibyte vnto you a certayne byll of cōplaynt, mētioned therin that the fozsayde J. S. otherwyse called J. T. in hys lyfe tyme
was seysed of and in certayne customary lādes and
tenementes, that is to saye, of and in. &c . holden by
copye of courte roll, of the maner of. &c. at the wyl of
the

the lozd of the ſayd manour, accozdyng to ꝑ cuſtome
the ſame manour, of which one T.L.then was, and
yet is lozde. And that the ſame I.S.ſo being ſeaſed
of the pzemiſſes afterwardes of lyke eſtate dyed ther
of by pzoteſtation ſeaſed, after whoſe death ꝑ ſayde
&c.with thappurtenaunces and the ryght tytle, uſe,
poſſeſſyon and enherytauce therof deſcended & came
and of very ryght ought to deſcende and come vnto
your ſayde ozatour as coſyn & next heyze of the ſayd
I.S.that is to ſaye as yongeſt ſonne of I. yongeſt
ſonne & heyze of the ſame I.S. accozdyng to the au
cyent cuſtome of the ſayde manour. And that youre
ſayde ozatour had oft and ſondzy tymes deſyzed and
pzayed the ſayde,&c.that w lawfull warnynge vnto
the tenauntes of the ſayde lozdſhyp, a court myghte
be holden at the ſayde manour, by whoſe enquerye
the tytle of your ſayde ozatour, myght be pzeſented &
founde in the pzemyſſes, accozdyng as both Iuſtice
ryght and good conſcience doth requyze.How be it,
(mooſt honourable lozde) that notwythſtandynge,
fozaſmoche as the ſayde.&c. hath kept the pzemyſſes
in hys owne hande theſe manye yeares paſt, and the
pzofytes and yſſues therof comynge, hath by ꝑ ſame
ſpace to hys owne pzopze vſe receyued and taken, &
yet doth. Your ſayde pooze ozatour coulde neuer get
the ſame &c.to holde a courte there, myndyng therby
vtter diſherytyng vnto your ſayd pooze ozatour, of
and in the pzemiſſes. Untyl ſuch tyme as your ſayde
mooſt honourable lozdſhyppe, moued wyth your ac
cuſtomed loue to Iuſtice, and pytie towardes pouer
ty, vouchſafed to graut vnto him your benigne leters
directed vnto the ſayde &c.wyllinge hym therby with

         Gg   law.

lawfull warnyng gyuen vnto ꝑ tenauntes of ꝑ sayd
loꝛdſhyp to ſūmō ⁊ kepe a court at the sayd manour,
foꝛ the tryall of the ryght of your sayd oꝛatour in the
ꝑmiſſes.Upō the recept of which letters the sayd ⁊c.
ſūmoned and kept a court at his sayde manour of.⁊c.
wherat vpō ꝑ opē ⁊ playn declaraciō of your sayd o-
ratours title,togyther, w the examinaciō of dyuerſe
wytneſſes,bꝛought in by your sayd oꝛatour, foꝛ the
due pꝛofe of the sayd tytle in ꝑ ꝑmiſſes , and further
vpō the ſhewynge of moche ſubſtanciall ⁊ auncyent
euidence,maynteyning the same,the homage therw
charged ⁊ ſwoꝛne,dyd pſent ⁊ fynde at the sayde. ⁊c.
befoꝛe J.S.ſtewarde of the same court, that ꝑ foꝛesayd J.S. was poſſeſſour and helde the ꝑmiſſes by
copye of Courtroll,accoꝛdyng to ꝑcuſtome of ꝑ sayd
manour,⁊ that alſo your sayd oꝛatour was coſyn ⁊
heyꝛe to the same J.S. accoꝛdyng to ꝑ cuſtome of ꝑ
sayd manour,that is to saye,son of J.yonger son of,
⁊c.as by the copy of ꝑ same courte rolles redye to be
ſhewed moꝛe playnly maye appeare vnto your loꝛdſhyp. After whych pꝛeſentment at the same court, it
was agreed betwixt the sayd ſtewarde in the name
of the sayd.⁊c.and your sayd oꝛatour, that yf ꝑ sayd
⁊c.wolde not declare and ſhewe vnto your sayd oꝛatour,oꝛ to hys learned counſell at London wythin
one terme then next enſuyng,a better tytle and intereſt to the foꝛsayd ꝑmiſſes,then your sayd oꝛatoure
had then ⁊ there already pꝛoued, that thā your sayd
oꝛatour ſhulde haue and enioye the ꝑmiſſes, to him
and to hys heyꝛes,accoꝛdyng to ryght, equytie, and
conſcience,and accoꝛdyng to the cuſtome of the sayd
manour. But so it is(mooſte honourable loꝛde)that
                                                        although

although the ſayd.&c.(as he can not)ſo hath he not
by the ſayde ſpace proued anye maner of tytle o2 co=
lour of tytle,to the p2empſſes,but onely to ſuch and
lyke fraudulent delayes, he entendeth to wery your
ſayde poo2e o2atour from the obteynyng of the p2e=
miſſes,and yf he can,to diſheryte hym from ꝑ ſame.
Wherfo2e may it pleaſe your good lo2dſhip of your
accuſtomable goodneſſe alwayes to pouertye exten=
ded,to graūt vnto your ſayd o2atour ꝑ kynges mooſt
gratious w2ytte of ſubpena to be directed to ꝑ ſayde
&c.commaundyng hym by the ſame,not onely to ap=
peare perſonnally befo2e your good lo2dſhyp in the
hygh courte of Chauncerye at a certayne daye, and
vnder a certayne payne by your good lo2dſhyp ther
in to be lymytted,but alſo to permyt and ſuffre your
ſayde o2atour peaceablye to haue holde o2 occupye,
poſſeſſe and enioye the p2emyſſes afo2ſayde,and the
p2ofytes and yſſues of the ſame,vntyl ſuche tyme as
the ſame &c. hath duly app2oued better tytle to the
p2emiſſes then he hath hytherto done.And your ſayd
poo2e o2atour ſhall.&c.

    ¶ I warrant fo2 a bucke.

WE wyll and charge you,that vnto John Sp.ci=
tizyn of the cytye of Lō. o2 to the b2ynger here=
    of ye delyuer o2 cauſe to be delyuered one bucke
of ſeaſon to be taken of our gyfte wythin our parke
of S.any reſtraynte o2 other commaundement here
tofo2e made to the contrarye,notwythſtandynge.
And theſe letters ſhall be vnto you ſuffycyent war=
raunte and diſcharge in that behalfe. Gyuen vnder
our ſignet,at.&c.

        Gg.ii.   The

The boke of sondrye

¶ The maner how to make
a transumpte.

JOhn Uiscountie Lisle Baron of M. &
S. knyght of the noble ordre of the gar
ter, lorde Basset and Tyasse, one of the
kynges mooste honourable counsayle,
hygh Admyrall of Englande, Ireland
Wales, the towne and marches of Calays, Nor
mandye, Gascoigne and Guyon, and captayne gene
rall of the kynges maiestyes Nauye royall. To all
parsonnes to whome these letters shall come, heare,
se, or reade, gretyng in our Lorde God euerlastyng.
knowe ye, that we (at the request of B. F. factour &
procuratour to the marchauntes here vndernamed)
haue thys daye in our counsayle of the hye Court of
thadmyraltye, done to be dylygentlye sene, red, exa
myned, & perused certayne letters patentes of salue
conducte and pasporte, sealed with the great Seale
of the kynge our soueraygne lorde, whych after due
examinacyon, haue bene founde hole, perfect, sounde,
and integree aswell in the seale as in the wrytynge
without any maner of rasure, cancellacyō, suspicion
or interlynyacyon. The tenures of whych letters pa
tentes oryginall, worde by worde hereafter ensueth
Henrye by the grace of God, Kynge of Englande,
Fraunce, and Irelande, defensoure of the fayth, and
in earthe of the church of Englande and also of Ire
lande the supreme heed. To all and synguler our ad
myralles, byceadmyralles, capitaynes, and al other
our offycers, mynisters, and subiectes, these our let
ters

ters hearyng o₂ seing,gretynge.Know ye,that at þ
contemplacyon of the ryght excellent p₂incesse,the re
gent of themperours lowe countryes, of oure grace
especyall haue graunted and gyuen lycence, and by
these p₂esentes do graunt and gyue licence vnto our
welbeloued J.B.⁊ L.G.and they₂ felowshyp, mar
chauntes Florentynes resident in Andwerp,in B₂a
baunt,they₂ factours and attourneys,and to euerye
of them , that they at all tymes durynge theffecte of
thys our graunt and pmission,acco₂dyng to the true
meanyng of the same,may passe the sees,and by our
hauens,po₂tes,crekes,and passages,wᵗ all maner of
shyppes o₂ vessels,of what countrye,burden,fo₂me,
and qualitie soeuer they be , furnyshed with ancres,
gables, vyttayles, and all other necessaryes , and to
b₂ynge out of the partyes of Fraunce the nomb₂e of
vi.C.tunes of Gascoigne o₂ French wynes,and tho
lous wood into Flaunders,o₂ into any other po₂t of
themperours sayde lowe countrie,at they₂ liberties
And the sayde wyne and wood so b₂ought by them,
into the partyes afo₂esayde , and there vnladen and
discharged.That the vesselles and shyppes, masters
and marchaūtes,pilottes and maryners of the same
and euery of them , of whatsoeuer Ch₂ysten nacyon
they be,maye surely and safely returne into fraunce
afo₂esayde o₂ els where,withoute any molestation,
trouble,o₂ greuaunce, to be done by you , o₂ anye of
yours. So that the same masters, shyppes ⁊ mary
ners, vnder shadowe and p₂etence of this our licence
do not no₂ cause to be done any thynge p̄iudicyall o₂
hurtfull vnto vs,our realmes,o₂ subiectes,o₂ to any
other our frendes, being with vs in leage ⁊ amytie,

Gg.iij.   no₂

nor that any goodes of our enemyes be by them cō=
ueyed and conceled by colour herof,or any moze quā
titie of wyne and woad then is befoze expzessed and
graunted by vs.Wherfoze we wyll ,⁊ commaunde
you,and euery one of you , that ye permyt and snffre
the sayde.John B. and Laurence G .theyz factours
and conductours of the fozsayde wynes and woad,
theyz seruauntes and maryners ,aswell commyuge
out of Fraunce into Flaunders , as returuyng thēce
into Fraunce, to enioye and vse peaceably and frely,
theffecte of thys our licence. And that ye do not in=
uade,appzehend, oz reteyne the sayd shyppes oz ves=
selles,in anye maner of pozte oz passage of thys oure
Realme oz anye other our domynions, as ye tendze
our pleasure,and wyll answere vnto vs foz the con=
trary at your paryl.Any letter of marke,cōtremarke
commissyon oz aucthozitie to you oz any of you con=
trary hereunto gyuen, oz any other thynge, cause oz
matter whatsoeuer they be notwithstandynge.

That expzesse mencyon of the certentye of the pze=
mysses,oz any other gyftes oz grauntes by vs oz a=
ny of our pzogenitours to the fozsayd John B. and
Laurence G. tofoze thys tyme made in these pzesen=
tes are not made any statute oz Act;ozdynacyon,pzo
uysyon oz restraynte therof to the contrary ozdeyned
oz pzouyded , oz elles anye other thynge oz matters
whatsoeuer they be in any wyse notwythstandyng.
In wytnesse whereof we haue caused these our let=
ters Patentes to be made.Wytnesse our self at west
mynstre the seconde daye of Maye,in the.xxxv . yere
of our raygne . Per bzeue de pziuat. sigillo et de da=
ta pzedicta auctozitate parliamenti Mat.

Upon

Upon whyche letters patentes we hygh Admyrall
of Englande aforesayde, haue graunted and gyuen
vnto the sayd marchantes at theyr requeſt theſe our
letters of tranſumpt in this due fourme to be made,
adiudgingand by our auctority decreing lyke fayth
fyrme credyte, and affyaunce to be gyuen in all places, and by all perſonnes to thys copy of tranſumpt
of the ſame letters patentes of Salueconduct,as to
the orygynalles yf they were really ſhewed and exhi
byted.Wherfore we on the behalfe of hys maieſtye,
wyll and commaunde all capytaynes,men of warre
and all other Iuſticers, officers and ſubiectes of the
kynges maieſty, to whom theſe preſentes ſhal come
and of our parte we do requyre all other perſonnes,
that neyther they nor anye of them , by any pretence
or colour,do or ſuffre to be done vnto the ſayde marchauntes, or vnto theyr factours,attourneys,depu-
tyes, ſeruauntes, mayſters of theyr ſhyppes , pur-
cers and maryners , by reaſon of theſe preſent war-
res,any maner of arreſt, interuption, hynderaunce,
trouble or let,contrary or agaynſt theffect,purporte,
mynde and intent of the ſayde letters in anye wyſe,
but to permyt and ſuffre them peaceably and effectu
ally to vſe and enioye the ſame letters accordyngly,
of þ which theſe our letters of trãſũpt be made vpõ þ
vewe and ſyght of þ ſame in the ſayd hygh Court of
thadmyraltye of Englande vnder the great ſeale of
our offyce of hygh admyraltye. Whych in wytneſſe
of truthe, we haue to thys tranſumpt put and aſſy-
gned wyth the ſubſcryption of the hande of our No-
tarye publyque, and Regeſter vnder named.
                Gg.iiii.   Gyuen

The boke of fondzy

Gyuen at London the fourth daye of Maye, in the yeare of our Lozde God. M.D. xliij. and the. xxxv. yere of the raygne of our fayde mooſt excellent foue raygne lozde Henrye the eyght, by the grace of God, kynge of Englande, Fraunce and Irelande, and in earth ſupzeme heed. ⁊c.

¶ After this fourme maye ye make all maner of trã ſumptes, chaungyng the thynges, accozdynge to your matter.

✣ Impzeſſum Lõdini in edib' Edwardi Whytchurche. Cum pziuilegio ad impzimendum ſolum: per ſeptennium.
✣

¶ Theſe bookes be to ſell at the weſt doze of Paules, by Wyllyam Tylotſon.